MICHAEL NEWMAN

# Humanitarian Intervention

*Confronting the Contradictions*

Columbia University Press
New York

Columbia University Press
*Publishers Since 1893*
New York   Chichester, West Sussex

Library of Congress Cataloging-in-Publication Data

Newman, Michael, 1946–
  Humanitarian intervention : confronting the contradictions / Michael Newman.
     p. cm.
  ISBN 978-0-231-15424-6 (alk. paper)
  1. Humanitarian intervention—Developing countries.  2. Peacekeeping forces—Developing
countries.  I. Title.

  JZ6369.N49 2009
  341.5'84—dc22

                              2009002832

♾

Columbia University Press books are printed on permanent and durable acid-free paper.
This book is printed on paper with recycled content.
Printed in India

c 10 9 8 7 6 5 4 3 2 1

References to Internet Web sites (URLs) were accurate at the time of writing. Neither
the author nor Columbia University Press is responsible for URLs that may have expired
or changed since the manuscript was prepared.

# Contents

*Acknowledgements*                                                          viii
*List of Abbreviations*                                                        x
*List of Boxes*                                                             xiii

**Introduction**                                                              1

**1. The Cold War Era—Non-Intervention or a
   Humanitarian Exception**                                                   7
*Non-Intervention and the Post-War Settlement*                                8
*International Law: Constraints on Sovereignty?*                             11
*Defending Non-Intervention*                                                 17
   a) Non-Intervention and the Inside Face of Sovereignty      17
   b) Non-Intervention from an International
      Perspective: The Outside Face of Sovereignty   25
*Intervention and Non-Intervention in Practice*                              28

**2. The Post-Cold War Transformation**                                      38
*Attitudes towards Democracy, Human Rights and Sovereignty*                  39
*International Institutions and Peace-Building*                              42
*Democratisation and the Development of an
   International Human Rights Regime*                                        44
*Humanitarian Intervention*                                                  49
  Part 1 Cases                                                      49
  Part 2 Arguments                                                  69
   a) Ethics and New Norms                                     69

b) International Social Conflict 71
c) Progressive Social Values 73
*Conclusion* 77

3. **Human Rights, Humanitarianism and Intervention** 80
*Human Rights, Regime Change and Humanitarian Intervention* 84
Regime Change 84
Human Rights Violations or Humanitarian Violations? 87
*Humanitarianism* 93
The Traditional View: Humanitarianism as the Antithesis
of Politics and Violence 94
The Perennial Dilemmas of Humanitarian Organizations 98
Rethinking Humanitarianism 104
*Conclusion* 109

4. **Inhumanity and Liberalism** 111
*Neo-liberalism and Violent Conflict* 112
Ethnic Conflict and Market Dominant Minorities 116
Global Governance and New Wars 118
Transitions and Violence 119
*Policy Prescriptions: The Liberal Peace* 121
Angola 124
Rwanda 126
*Conclusion* 137

5. **After Intervention** 138
*International Administration or Liberal Imperialism?* 140
*International Governmental Regimes: Three Case Studies* 145
Bosnia-Herzegovina 145
Kosovo 155
East Timor/Timor-Leste 163
*Assessments and Lessons* 176

6. **The Responsibility to Protect** 181
*Re-Thinking Humanitarian Intervention: Conceptual Issues* 182
Development and Human Security 183
The Responsibility to Protect 188
*Just Wars* 192

CONTENTS

*Right Intention*                                                    196
*Right Authority*                                                    198

*A New Commitment or New Words?*                                     201
*Conclusion*                                                         211

**Afterword:  Facing the Future—Humanitarianism and Politics**       **213**

*Bibliography*                                                       219

# Acknowledgements

This book has had a long period of gestation, though I was hardly conscious of this for much of the time. It really started during the early 1990s, as Yugoslavia disintegrated and I found it difficult to define my own position in the intense debates over intervention that were taking place. This became still more problematic at the end of the decade when, like so many, I believed that some kind of external support for the Albanian population in Kosovo was vital, but that the NATO bombing of Serbia was totally unjustifiable. Finally, I decided to write on the topic in the aftermath of the war against Iraq—when, in my view, the military action had nothing to do with any of the principles that had been proclaimed in support of 'saving strangers' in the early post-Cold War era. I am therefore aware that the contradictions that the book seeks to confront have been in my own mind as well as in the international situation.

Many people have helped me in this work, including those who have not been aware of their contribution. For colleagues, students and friends have strong views on the issue of humanitarian intervention, and our discussions and sometimes heated arguments helped me to appreciate the complexity and multi-dimensional nature of the subject. Others have contributed in more tangible ways and this certainly includes colleagues at London Metropolitan University. Bob McKeever facilitated my sabbatical leave for a semester, while Marko Bojcun, Frank Brouwer, Dave Edye, Gus Fagan and Stefano Fella shared aspects of my work while I was away, and I am grateful to them all. But, above all, I owe a debt of gratitude to Peter Gowan, who has inspired so many at the university. He has constantly influenced my thinking by challenging it so profoundly while always being supportive. Our debates on humanitarian intervention have been crucial in helping to formulate my own views and it is to Peter that I dedicate this book.

# ACKNOWLEDGEMENTS

I did most of the writing in Perugia, having first been introduced to Umbria by another friend and colleague, Valerio Lintner, nearly twenty-five years ago. I want to thank him for all his help in making arrangements in Italy throughout this period. There was, of course, no obvious connection between Perugia and humanitarian intervention and someone even suggested that it would be difficult to write about situations of mass atrocities in so beautiful a location. But it was not, in fact, irrelevant to become conscious of the dark and often brutal history behind the wonderful exterior of the city, perhaps suggesting the need for a longer-term perspective on current events. In any case, I want to thank Eva Baldella, Leonardo Panciotti, Clara De Ferrari and their families for their hospitality in Perugia.

This is the third time Hurst and Co. have published my work and I very much appreciate Michael Dwyer's rapid decision to take this one on and his role in the publication process. Marjorie Mayo, Bill Bowring and two anonymous referees read an earlier draft of the whole manuscript and I am very grateful for their comments and criticisms, which led to some important revisions and, I hope, improvements, in the final draft. My daughter, Kate, not only read and commented on several chapters, but has also educated me on development issues over the past few years, and the book has benefited greatly from her advice. I also want to thank my brother, Jeff Newman, and my sister-in-law, Hannah Edmonds, for their help with the proofreading. As always, Ines not only had to put up with me and support me while I was working on the project, but she also read and commented critically on a whole draft making severable valuable suggestions. But at least this time, there was Perugia as a compensation!

# List of Abbreviations

| | |
|---|---|
| AU | African Union |
| BiH | Bosnia and Herzegovina |
| CDR | Coalition pour la Défense de la République (Rwanda) |
| CIA | Central Intelligence Agency |
| CNRT | National Council of Timorese Resistance |
| DRC | Democratic Republic of Congo |
| ECOMOG | Economic Community of West African States Monitoring Group |
| ECOWAS | Economic Community of West African States |
| END | European Nuclear Disarmament |
| EU | European Union |
| EULEX | European Union Rule of Law Mission in Kosovo |
| FALINTIL | Armed Forces for the National Liberation of Timor Leste |
| F-FDTL | Timorese Defence Force |
| FRETILIN | Revolutionary Front of Independent East Timor |
| GDP | Gross Domestic Product |
| G20 | Group of Twenty |
| HCA (hCa) | Helsinki Citizens' Assembly |
| ICC | International Criminal Court |
| ICISS | International Commission on Sovereignty and State Intervention |
| ICRC | International Committee of the Red Cross |
| ICTR | International Criminal Tribunal for Rwanda |
| ICTY | International Criminal Tribunal for Yugoslavia |
| IHL | International Humanitarian Law |
| IMF | International Monetary Fund |

LIST OF ABBREVIATIONS

| | |
|---|---|
| INGO | International Nongovernmental Organization |
| INTERFET | International Force for East Timor |
| KFOR | Kosovo Force |
| KGB | Committee for State Security (Soviet Union) |
| KLA | Kosovo Liberation Army |
| L20 | Leaders 20 |
| MPLA | Movimento Popular de Libertação de Angola |
| MRND | Mouvement Révolutionnaire National pour le Développement (Rwanda) |
| MSF | Médecins sans Frontières |
| NATO | North Atlantic Treaty Organization |
| NED | National Endowment for Democracy |
| NGO | Nongovernmental Organization |
| PIC | Peace Implementation Council (Bosnia) |
| PNTL | National Police Force of Timor-Leste (PNTL) |
| OAS | Organisation of American States |
| OAU | Organisation of African Unity |
| ODIHR | Office for Democratic Institutions and Human Rights |
| OECD | Organisation for Economic Co-operation and Development |
| OSCE | Organisation for Security and Co-operation in Europe |
| R2PCS | Responsibility to Protect-Engaging Civil Society |
| RPF | Rwandan Patriotic Front |
| RS | Serb Republic |
| RTLMC | Radio-Télévision Libre des Mille Collines (Rwanda) |
| RUF | Revolutionary United Front (Sierra Leone) |
| SRSG | Special Representative of the Secretary-General |
| UK | United Kingdom |
| UN | United Nations |
| UNAMID | United Nations-African Union Mission in Darfur |
| UNAMIR | United Nations Assistance Mission for Rwanda |
| UNDP | United Nations Development Programme |
| UNEF | United Nations Emergency Force |
| UNEP | United Nations Environment Programme |
| UNHCR | United Nations High Commissioner for Refugees |
| UNICEF | United Nations Children's Fund |
| UNMISET | United Nations Mission of Support in East Timor |
| UNMIT | Integrated Mission in Timor-Leste |

| | |
|---|---|
| UNITA | União Nacional para a Independência Total de Angola |
| UNITAF | United Task Force (Somalia) |
| UNMIK | United Nations Mission in Kosovo |
| UNMIT | United Nations Integrated Mission in Timor-Leste |
| UNOSOM | United Nations Operations in Somalia |
| UNPROFOR | United Nations Protection Force (former Yugoslavia) |
| UNTAET | United Nations Transitional Administration in East Timor |
| US | United States |
| WFM-IGP | World Federalist Movement-Institute for Global Policy |

# List of Boxes

1. Iraq, 1991 52
2. Somalia, 1991–93 53
3. The Yugoslav Context and the War in Bosnia 60
4. Kosovo, 1998–99 65
5. Key Principles of the International Red Cross and Red Crescent 96
6. 1986 UN Declaration on the Right to Development 184
7. The Responsibility to Protect: Principles for Military Intervention 194

*To Peter Gowan*

# Introduction

In the last decade of the twentieth century a very significant new development affected both the theory and practice of international intervention in domestic conflicts and crises. Beginning with the establishment of 'safe havens' after the US-led war against Iraq in 1991, and accompanying complex international involvements in Somalia and Bosnia-Herzegovina over the next four years, the doctrine of 'humanitarian intervention' suddenly acquired prominence. This was a doctrine declaring that, in cases where a state was carrying out or sanctioning massive human rights violations, the 'international community' had a right, or even a duty, to intervene in support of the victims. This constituted a major departure from the norms of the Cold War era that had maintained, at least in theory, the inviolability of the sovereign state, protected by the principle of non-intervention.

These changes led to an increasingly intense debate. While some believed that they signified a new international conviction that the prevention of suffering superseded the importance of state sovereignty, others interpreted the transformation as an attempt by the most powerful Western states to create new norms to justify their expansion. NATO's intervention in Kosovo in 1999 constituted a turning point. This was the most controversial case so far, both because it was carried out without authorization by the United Nations and because many found the nature of the military action difficult to reconcile with humanitarian principles. Kosovo finally shattered the fragile international agreement that had appeared to exist over the previous interventions. Subsequently, Kofi Annan, as Secretary-General of the UN, attempted to build a new consensus to reconcile the doctrine of sovereignty with the protection of human rights, but when an important International Commission on Intervention and State Sovereignty sought to achieve this in 2001 (ICISS

1

2001), the international agenda had already moved on. By then the attacks on the Twin Towers had taken place and George W. Bush had announced his global war on terrorism, which now became the dominant international theme. While humanitarian intervention had, in principle, elevated ethical considerations over the routine amorality of international politics, the war on terror seemed to constitute a dramatic regression to an earlier era, with *raison d'état* triumphing over human rights.

For some of the most vehement critics of the US, there was little difference between humanitarian intervention and the attack on Iraq in 2003. If the expansion of an American 'empire' is regarded as a continuous strategy, both humanitarian principles and the war on terror may be viewed as alternative ways of legitimizing the same general aim. However, for those who had believed that the new emphasis on humanitarianism and human rights signified a positive development, the situation in the early twenty-first century contained some troubling questions. Many wondered whether their earlier support for humanitarian intervention had been naïve or even based on a wilful refusal to face the facts of the new world order. This was particularly problematic for those on the left and centre-left, who had demanded more robust military action to protect the Bosnian Muslim population against Serbian paramilitary forces and now feared that this might have paved the way for a disastrous war against Saddam Hussein. Yet many of them still believed that there should be international intervention, including the ultimate possibility of military action, to prevent an oppressive dictator from carrying out mass atrocities behind the protective shield of state sovereignty. This left a very large number of people uncertain as to how to reconcile their opposition to recent Anglo-American policy with their belief that 'something must be done' to protect populations at risk. In other words, they now had beliefs that appeared contradictory.

This book is aimed particularly at this broad section of left-wing and left-liberal opinion, and it is based on the belief that the contradictions are inherent in the contemporary world situation. It therefore rejects two more obvious positions, recently classified by one author as the 'muscular humanitarians' and the 'anti-imperialist absolutists' (Kurasawa, 2006). The first endorses military intervention throughout the world in the name of a global crusade for democracy and human rights, while the second rejects, on principle, each and every use of military force by powerful Western states. But while these two positions are polar opposites in most respects, they often share one conviction that distinguishes both from that which underlies this book. For neither is normally anxious to draw a distinction between humanitarian intervention and regime change: muscular humanitarians celebrate the extension of 'freedom', while 'anti-imperialist absolutists' are so hostile to any possible expansion of Western influence that they sometimes lose sight of the victims of atrocities. Unlike both of these positions, this book is written in the conviction that there is a relevant difference between using military power for human protection purposes and doing so in order to topple regimes that are out of favour in Washington. The main stages in the argument are set out below, but it is first necessary to clarify the key concept.

Terminology is particularly problematic on this topic. This is partly because the phrase 'humanitarian intervention' has been interpreted in a number of ways. The media and politicians sometimes use it to refer to any form of aid or assistance carried out for humanitarian purposes. This might appear quite reasonable for, in everyday life, we might think of intervention as taking a variety of forms, perhaps based on an analogy from medical intervention. However, in international relations and international law, the term has been used in a far more restricted sense to refer to:

the threat or use of force across state borders by a state (or group of states) aimed at preventing or ending widespread and grave violations of the fundamental human rights of individuals other than its own citizens, without the permission of the state within whose territory force is applied (Holzgrefe, 2003, p. 18).

Actions of this kind violate the norm of non-intervention because coercive force is carried out without the consent of the state in question. In general, this distinguishes humanitarian intervention from humanitarian assistance, although there could be circumstances in which a state's denial of such aid raised the question of whether it should be delivered without consent. The ICISS anticipated this possibility in situations of 'overwhelming natural or environmental catastrophes, where the state concerned is either unwilling or unable to cope, or call for assistance, and significant loss of life is occurring or threatened' (ICISS, 2001, para. 4.20, p. 33).

This appeared a rather unlikely scenario until the attitude of the regime in Burma/Myanmar in the aftermath of the cyclone in May 2008 led to active discussion about the delivery of humanitarian assistance even if this was opposed by the generals ruling the country. This would lead to a further extension of humanitarian intervention, making it still more controversial.

There is some debate as to whether or not intervention must be through *military* means. Some believe that the use of economic sanctions designed to bring about the requisite change should be included within the definition, but this book will restrict it to the use, or threatened use, of armed force. The term has also sometimes been used to include military intervention by external forces to rescue their own citizens when they are threatened by violence in another country. As in the definition quoted above, I will exclude such usage. If it were accepted, it would mean that the intervention in Rwanda in April 1994 to evacuate Europeans during the genocide could be regarded as a case of humanitarian intervention. In fact, this is rightly widely regarded as a shameful episode that rather blatantly demonstrated a belief that the lives of white Europeans were more valuable than those of black Africans.

Yet the problems with the term are not solely about clarity of usage, but also arise from its emotive connotations. If the words 'humanitarian' and 'intervention' are conjoined, there is an implicit suggestion that an intervention has been carried out for humanitarian reasons. Many have therefore opposed the terminology because they have not believed that humanitarian motives have accounted for particular interventions or, more fundamentally, because military action is seen as the antithesis of humanitarianism (see chapter 3). This usage also excludes humanitarian assistance, development aid, and mediation in conflicts and conflict prevention activities. Although I believe that effective actions of this kind are the most valuable forms of external involvement, the book will adhere to conventional usage until chapter 6. At this stage I adopt the terminology of 'the responsibility to protect', as recommended by the International Commission on Intervention and State Sovereignty (ICISS) in 2001. This phrase was subsequently also taken up by the United Nations, following the World Summit Declaration in September 2005. I believe that it has some advantages, partly because it encompasses a far wider range of possible actions and policies than military intervention. However, it is confusing to use it in relation to the past, which is why the more conventional terminology is used for most of the book.

The structure of the argument is as follows. Chapter 1 examines the legal and normative international order during the Cold War period, which generally followed the principles of state sovereignty and non-intervention. The chapter discusses arguments that were supportive of this system but, while acknowledging their merit, it refutes absolutist arguments against intervention. However, this is certainly not because it seeks to elevate the importance of military means—quite the reverse. The normative position underlying the book is a strong commitment to peace and a belief that forcible intervention is likely to do more harm than good in any but the most exceptional circumstances. However, it is, I believe, necessary to establish a justification for the use of force as a theoretical possibility. Once this is acknowledged, arguments about the appropriate policy in any specific situation may be conducted in terms of *relative*, rather than *absolute* considerations.

Chapter 2 then discusses the shifts that took place after 1989, explaining the attractiveness to much left-wing and left-liberal opinion of such notions as strengthened international human rights regimes, the alleged obsolescence of the nation-state, and new forms of peace-keeping. In this context, it explores the growth of support for humanitarian intervention, examining this in relation both to selected international crises of the era and to some significant arguments and interpretations. While much of the analysis was cogent and persuasive, I suggest that it often failed to appreciate the realities of power and some of the drivers of the new interventionism.

Chapter 3 adopts a more critical perspective. Noting the way in which the case for intervention was stretched to serve the agenda of the US government, it argues that the criteria under which there could even be a *conceivable* case for humanitarian intervention need to be highly restrictive, so as to preclude military intervention for the purposes of regime change. More controversially, it also suggests that the understanding of humanitarianism itself needs to be broadened. Traditionally, this has been interpreted as an apolitical realm solely concerned with the relief of suffering in emergency situations. However, this has excluded consideration of the wider *causes* of such suffering. A major contention of the book is that the boundaries between politics and humanitarianism are less clear than is often assumed, and the concept of humanitarianism should incorporate recognition of the need for development assistance. Furthermore, I argue that this wider concept implies a critical evaluation of the impact of current Western policies upon many developing and transitional countries.

This claim is then reinforced in chapter 4, which demonstrates the destabilizing effects of pressures to adopt neoliberal economic regimes and rapid democratization. It suggests that these can contribute to the generation of conflicts to which humanitarian intervention may then be proclaimed as a necessary response. It also shows that recent liberal approaches to peace-making can lead to an intensification of conflicts, with the case of Rwanda highlighted as the most horrific episode of this kind. This critical analysis is taken further in chapter 5, which examines international governmental regimes *after* the interventions in Bosnia, Kosovo and East Timor; it suggests that these often appeared to subordinate both humanitarian considerations and the establishment of conditions necessary for a sustainable peace to the imposition of a particular model. All this implies the need for a new conceptual framework as a basis for policies that embrace a wider conception of humanitarianism.

Chapter 6 provides this, drawing particularly on the notions of human security and 'the responsibility to protect'. It argues that these indicate the kinds of policies necessary to reduce violent conflict in developing and transitional countries, while also helping to define the very exceptional circumstances in which military intervention could be legitimate. However, I also suggest that the international responsibility is currently being interpreted too narrowly and without sufficient emphasis on the need for a fundamental change in international political economy. For concentration on the atrocities that might conceivably require a military response enables the rich North to continue to evade its responsibility for contributing to the situation in which such crimes may occur. Finally, the conclusion evaluates the contemporary situation and considers the prospects for the implementation of a more viable and progressive approach in future. Here I also argue that an enlarged conception of humanitarianism can provide a basis for human protection by addressing issues of poverty and inequality, but that this is no substitute for politics and the traditional demands of the left for justice, equality and emancipation.

The major purpose of the book is to rethink humanitarian intervention, both in the light of experience and theoretically. Hence it is rather different from the vast polemical literature that now exists on both sides of the debate. It also differs from the ever-increasing number of specialist studies on aspects of the topic in such fields as international relations, international law, peace and conflict studies, contemporary history, political philosophy, international political economy and development studies. It draws on the existing literature in many of these fields rather than contributing original research into specific cases of humanitarian intervention. In this way I hope to provide some new links across disciplines and perspectives that will stimulate both political and academic debate and engage the general reader. At the same time the book aims to clarify some of the inherent contradictions in a complex subject.

# 1

# The Cold War Era—Non-Intervention or a Humanitarian Exception?

The coalition that defeated Nazi Germany established the post-war system on the basis of the sovereign state. This meant that the operating principle of the international order followed the assumptions initially established in seventeenth-century Europe: that each state was responsible for its own domestic affairs and was entitled to expect other states to respect its autonomy in this realm. This chapter argues against interpreting this as an absolute principle, by supporting the idea that there are some circumstances in which military intervention, without the consent of the target state, is justifiable as the sole means to protect a population from massive violations. However, the purpose of this argument is certainly not to uphold militarism or even to suggest that such interventions are normally an effective response to atrocities. In fact it would be possible to accept the proposition of this chapter and still to oppose the overwhelming majority, or even all, of the interventions that have been carried out. For the objective is to establish a theoretical proposition in favour of humanitarian intervention as a possibility, so that it cannot be precluded *on principle*. This means that all alternative positions in any particular case need to be advocated on their merits rather than on absolute grounds.

Although the Cold War era undermined the legal and normative order established after the Second World War in many respects, in relation to the issue of humanitarian intervention, the years from 1945 until 1989 may be considered as one period. The chapter therefore begins with a brief explanation of relevant aspects of the international order in those years. It then considers some of the arguments in favour of the principle of non-intervention, acknowledging their strength, but suggesting that they cannot be accepted in their entirety. This is followed by a discussion of some cases during the Cold War era that demonstrated that the existing norms could have negative consequences when populations were exposed to state violence.

## Non-intervention and the post-war settlement

When the post-war international system was constructed in 1945, the dominating consideration was the preservation of peace. Thus the most important element of the Charter of the United Nations was the removal of the right to declare war from the prerogatives of the state. This was effected by ensuring that only the Security Council had the right to determine the existence of any threat to peace, and to decide what measures should be taken in these circumstances (Chapter VII, Articles 39–42). The only exception to the need for Security Council authorization was in Article 51, allowing for the inherent right of individual or collective self-defence in the event of an armed attack against a Member State. However, even this was regarded as a temporary measure, for self-defence was permissible only *until* the Security Council had decided what measures were necessary to maintain international peace and security. These could, of course, include authorization for continuation of the military action that a victim (or victims) of aggression was already undertaking.

In principle, this removal of the unilateral right to make war constituted a transformation of the inter-state system. In practice, of course, this was not to be the case, and the period between 1945 and 1989 would be one of unprecedented violence, with the UN unable to operate effectively. In some cases, most notably the Korean War, it was persuaded (or, perhaps, manipulated) to support a military action, which was, in fact, a US-led coalition; in others (most notably the Vietnam War), there was never a formal declaration of war.[1] Nevertheless, the system was built upon the recognition of states as the central element of the international order. Intimately related to this were the twin principles of sovereignty and non-intervention.

---

[1] Under the so-called Gulf of Tonkin resolution of August 1964 Lyndon Johnson claimed that there had been an unprovoked attack by North Vietnamese forces and he was authorised by Congress to take 'all necessary steps' to protect the forces of the United States and its allies. This enabled the US to escalate the war without any formal declaration.

Sovereignty is a multi-dimensional concept that is highly ambiguous and has been a topic for theoretical and practical disagreement since it first arose in sixteenth-century Europe (Newman, 1996, pp. 4–15). Yet if the *substance* of sovereignty is difficult to define, this has probably reinforced its appeal as a political idea: whether genuinely democratic or a rationale for centralised dictatorships, whether for liberation against external domination or for aggression against other peoples, the claim of possession of sovereignty has been immensely powerful in justifying state policy. The counterpart of sovereignty has been non-intervention. Article 2 of the UN Charter has particular relevance in this respect, with paragraphs (1), (3) and (4) inscribing the principle of sovereign equality, stipulating that all disputes should be settled peacefully, and proscribing the threat or use of force against the territorial integrity or political independence of any state.[2] Certainly Article 2 (7) made it clear that the Security Council could permit actions within the normal domestic jurisdiction of a state after already authorizing enforcement measures under Chapter VII. But this was not envisaged as a limitation of the non-intervention principle, since it was intended to refer to a situation in which a state had carried out external aggression and its defeat then depended upon military action within its territory. The final element in this principle of non-intervention was the stipulation that in any situation that could potentially threaten the peace, international involvement within a sovereign state was possible only with the consent of the parties to the dispute. The relevant section of the UN Charter was Chapter VI, on the Pacific Settlement of Disputes, Article 33 to Article 38.

Despite this centrality of sovereignty and non-intervention in the post-war international order, it is not difficult to identify the differences between legality and reality. In the early post-war era European empires still dominated much of the world, with control over millions of people exercised by the metropolitan centres of power. The claim that sovereignty applied equally to all states was therefore maintained only by the denial of the right of statehood to the majority of nations. Because the illegality of intervention only applied to *states*, imperial powers could, and did, intervene with impunity against the

---

[2] Article 2(1) The organization is based on the principle of the sovereign equality of all its Members. (3) All Members shall settle their international disputes by peaceful means in such a manner that international peace and security, and justice, are not endangered. (4) All Members shall refrain in their international relations from the threat or use of force against the territorial integrity or political independence of any state, or any other manner inconsistent with the purposes of the United Nations.

subject peoples within their empires. This changed to some extent with decolonization in the 1950s and 1960s, but both the Soviet Union and the US frequently intervened within their respective spheres of influence. It is also evident that the legal definition of 'intervention' is highly restrictive. As already noted in the introduction, 'intervention' is taken to mean *coercive* intervention (normally military) without the consent of the state in question. Other actions, such as economic pressure through trade and aid regimes or inducing a weaker state to allow the stationing of troops or military bases on its territory, do *not* constitute intervention in international law. For it is not intervention in a legal sense if the weaker state has consented to the economic or military policy in question, even if such 'consent' has been secured through a mixture of bribes and threats. Thus formal legal equality has coexisted with massive inequality and the continued domination of the strong over the weak. Yet far from *undermining* support for the norm of intervention, such inequality reinforced it, as the history of decolonization demonstrates.

Having secured freedom from imperial control, the leaders of newly independent states were determined not to allow any restrictions upon their hold on political power. As they normally occupied a very circumscribed role in the international economic and financial system designed by the Western powers, and were often still subject to informal domination by ex-colonial masters, the possession of full sovereign statehood was seen to be crucial. Newly independent states therefore played an important role in reaffirming the doctrine of non-interference, for example by a UN General Assembly Declaration in 1970 affirming that every state had 'an *inalienable* right to choose its political, economic, social and cultural system, without interference in any form by another State' (Chesterman, 2002, p. 107). Nor was this simply a protection against the rich West for, following its establishment in 1963, the Organization of African Unity (OAU), for example, was adamant that the territorial boundaries bequeathed by the colonial powers should be maintained and that each state should respect the internal sovereignty of all other members. This was seen as necessary to maintain peace in a continent where arbitrary boundaries, dividing ethnic communities, could otherwise have fuelled continual conflicts. And more generally states, underpinned by the overwhelming majority of political movements, were anxious to uphold the system of sovereignty and non-intervention.

Finally, the importance of the norms of sovereignty and non-intervention is also indicated by the extent to which even the superpowers attempted to legitimise their behaviour in relation to them. This meant that intervention was either covert—through such organs as the CIA and the KGB—or backed by the claim that it had been *requested* by the relevant state authority. It might have been common knowledge that the US intervened in Guatemala in 1954 to preserve the dominance of interests favourable to the American-owned United Fruit Company, but Washington still followed the formality of claiming that the overthrow of the government was a Guatemalan action. It was obvious to the whole world that the government of Czechoslovakia did not voluntarily request the intervention in 1968, but the Soviet Union made sure that approval for it was announced in Prague. Even when the superpowers were in flagrant contravention of the *spirit* of non-intervention, they thus sought to uphold it in formal terms.[3]

Sovereignty and non-intervention were therefore established legally within the UN Charter and provided the norms for the international system between 1945 and the end of the Cold War. Nor did the Charter make any explicit exception to allow coercive intervention for humanitarian reasons. Certainly, it did not attempt to define the situations in which the Security Council could declare that there was a threat to international peace and security and authorise enforcement action. In principle, therefore, there was nothing to prevent the Council from permitting collective humanitarian intervention, but such actions were certainly not envisaged in 1945.

## International law: constraints on sovereignty?

Yet it would be misleading to suggest that state sovereignty and non-intervention were the *sole* features of the international legal and normative system established in 1945. After all, the defeat of Fascism, and the subsequent war crimes trials of Nazi and Japanese leaders, seemed to contain the message that states were *not* inviolable. If political leaders could be found guilty of 'crimes against humanity', this suggested that sovereignty was not a complete protection against international accountability. Such issues were not entirely overlooked in the legal basis of the post-war international system.

The Preamble to the Charter talked of 'We the Peoples of the United Nations', rather than simply referring to states or governments, and immediately after declaring the need to 'save succeeding generations from the scourge

---

[3] On the other hand, the subsequent invention of the so-called Brezhnev Doctrine to justify the intervention in Czechoslovakia had no legal status. This was the claim that states in the socialist bloc had limited sovereignty in the sense that external intervention was justified when socialism as a whole was being threatened by the actions of one state.

of war', it pledged a reaffirmation of 'faith in fundamental human rights, in the dignity and worth of the human person, in the equal rights of men and women'. This led, in December 1948, to the Universal Declaration of Human Rights, proclaimed by the General Assembly as

[A] common standard of achievement for all peoples and all nations, to the end that every individual and every organ of society, keeping this Declaration constantly in mind, shall strive by teaching and education to promote respect for these rights and freedoms and by progressive measures, national and international, to secure their universal and effective recognition and observance, both among the peoples of Member States themselves and among the peoples of territories under their jurisdiction.

A rather long list, including civil, political, cultural and social and economic rights, was then proclaimed, and these rights were subsequently codified and monitored by a whole host of different specialised bodies. However, while the Declaration of Human Rights and several subsequent Conventions indicated acceptance of some *normative* principles, their impact in practice was very limited.

First, the fact that the founding members of the UN were prepared to agree that human rights existed and needed to be protected did not mean that they were acknowledging limits on state sovereignty as the fundamental principle of the international system. For states themselves were the bodies that were supposed to protect those rights and, if they did not do so, international bodies had very limited enforcement powers. The sole exception to this was in (Western) Europe, where in 1950 (with effect from 1953) a group of liberal democratic states that already agreed on fundamental principles transferred some significant powers to safeguard civil and political rights through the European Convention on Human Rights.[4] (The protection of social rights was much weaker, even after the signing of the European Social Charter in 1961, with effect from 1965). Elsewhere there was no comparable transfer of powers. Secondly, throughout the period there was no agreement about the most important rights, with liberal capitalist states emphasizing civil and political rights, while the Communist and developing countries emphasised socio-economic ones. During this era discussions about human rights in the UN as a whole and in the specialist committees commonly amounted to little more than mutual recrimination and propaganda. On the other hand, there was clearly a *potential* tension between the doctrines of state sovereignty and human rights. If people translated their aspirations into demands for *rights*

---

[4] The formal title was the Convention for the Protection of Human Rights and Fundamental Freedoms.

they were hardly likely to accept the legitimacy of states that denied them those rights. This meant that the very discourse of rights was potentially destabilizing for the system of state sovereignty, even if this was not acknowledged in the laws and norms of the era. This potential conflict between the two principles was intensified in the 1970s when the United States began to emphasise international human rights in its foreign policy, albeit in a highly selective way. The Soviet Union thus accepted the Helsinki Accord of 1975, including a definition of human rights that went some way towards the Western version, in return for the apparent acceptance of its control over its East European satellites. However, at this stage there was little indication that any political or legal commitments to international human rights constituted a serious threat to the non-intervention principle.

A second relevant body of law was derived from the 1948 Genocide Convention. This was the direct result of the Nazi extermination policies and followed an original declaration by the General Assembly of the United Nations in its Resolution 96 (I) dated 11 December 1946. This stated that genocide was a crime under international law, contrary to the spirit and aims of the United Nations and condemned by the civilised world. Two years later this led to the adoption of a Convention (with effect from 1951), the most important articles of which were as follows:

Article I: The Contracting Parties confirm that genocide, whether committed in time of peace or in time of war, is a crime under international law which they undertake to prevent and to punish.

Article II: In the present Convention, genocide means any of the following acts committed with intent to destroy, in whole or in part, a national, ethnical, racial or religious group, as such:

(a) Killing members of the group;
(b) Causing serious bodily or mental harm to members of the group;
(c) Deliberately inflicting on the group conditions of life calculated to bring about its physical destruction in whole or in part;
(d) Imposing measures intended to prevent births within the group;
(e) Forcibly transferring children of the group to another group.

Two points about the definition caused controversy, both at the time and subsequently. First, it explicitly excluded *political* groups—primarily as a result of Soviet opposition. Secondly, it did not cover the phenomenon subsequently known as 'ethnic cleansing'—acts of terror intended to drive a national minority from its homeland, rather than actual extermination. Nevertheless, in theory the Genocide Convention was a major development, with obvious relevance to the issue of humanitarian intervention. However, there was also an important ambiguity about its legal status.

When the Genocide Convention was initially discussed, many hoped that genocide would be recognised as a crime of universal jurisdiction, meaning that it would be subject to prosecution wherever a suspect was found. However, this was not accepted, so that perpetrators were liable to prosecution only by the courts of the territory where the crime took place or by an international criminal court (Inazumi, 2005, pp. 59–62). Since the latter court was established only in 1998 (with effect from 2002), this meant that during the Cold War genocide was normally regarded as punishable only by a court within the territory on which it had taken place, although Israeli courts ruled that it was subject to universal jurisdiction with the trial of Adolf Eichmann. A requirement for domestic jurisdiction obviously made it quite unlikely that such trials would be instituted unless there was a change of regime, with the new rulers wanting to charge the previous government with the crime. In many respects, therefore, the Genocide Convention seemed simultaneously to deny the sanctity of state sovereignty and to confirm it. However, there was a further ambiguity because it was specified that, in addition to genocide itself, the following were also regarded as offences under the Convention: conspiracy to commit genocide, direct and public incitement to commit, attempting to commit, and complicity in genocide. This put an emphasis on trying to *prevent* the crime and appeared to impose a duty on states to intervene in some way if there was evidence that genocide was likely. The extent of this obligation was unclear but, as was widely noted in relation to Rwanda in 1994, the deliberate avoidance of the term by the major powers implied that they believed they might have such a duty had they acknowledged that genocide was taking place (Schabas 2005, pp. 142–3). However, during the Cold War period the Convention was only invoked once—in relation to the massacres of Palestinians by Christian militia under Israeli protection in the camps of Sabra and Chatila in Lebanon in 1982. Needless to say, the Israeli authorities did not accept the claim. There were many other, still more severe, atrocities in which it could have been invoked, above all those committed by the Pol Pot regime in Cambodia in the 1970s (see below), but no such charge was made. And, while many countries signed the Genocide Convention relatively quickly, they were not anxious to make it legally binding by ratifying it: for example, the UK only did so in 1970, while the USA delayed until 1988.

The other potentially relevant constraints on state sovereignty were derived from other branches of international law. International Humanitarian Law

(IHL) is derived from a longstanding tradition which, for example, made a distinction between combatants and civilians. However, the more specifically humanitarian aspects of the modern doctrine are normally held to originate in Henry Dunant's observation of the appalling suffering of soldiers after the Battle of Solferino in 1859, leading to the establishment of the Red Cross. IHL is specifically intended to solve humanitarian problems arising from armed conflicts by protecting people affected by them, and by limiting the rights of parties to a conflict to use whatever means they wish. The first major source was the 1864 Geneva Convention for the Amelioration of the Condition of the Wounded in Armies in the Field, but IHL was subsequently developed through numerous treaties and declarations, with the four Geneva Conventions of 1949 and the two Additional Protocols of 1977 becoming its primary sources. The first three Geneva Conventions deal exclusively with the position of combatants and prisoners of war, but the fourth convention provides protection for the civilian population in times of war. Influenced by decolonization, and the struggle against apartheid, Protocol 1 subsequently extended such protection to the victims in wars against racist regimes, and wars for self-determination and against alien oppression. Protocol II extended the protection to victims of internal conflicts in which an armed opposition controlled enough territory to enable it to carry out sustained military operations.

IHL prohibits a wide range of acts of violence against people in the hands of a wartime enemy, including murder, torture, rape, inhuman treatment, collective punishments, the taking of hostages, and the denial of right to a fair trial. It insists that parties to an armed conflict must distinguish between civilians and combatants and between military and civilian objects, and it also proscribes attacks against military objectives if they would cause disproportionate harm to civilians or civilian objects. In principle, IHL binds all parties to an armed conflict, including state and non-state armed actors, and states have duties of compliance. They are therefore supposed to adopt national legislation implementing their treaty obligations, and they have a duty to search for people suspected of committing or ordering grave breaches of IHL and either bring them to trial themselves or hand them over to another state for trial. Furthermore, states have a *collective* responsibility to ensure respect for the Conventions, and under Additional Protocol 1 they also undertake to act in co-operation with the UN in situations of serious violations of the Protocol or Convention. Finally, and in line with its role in the origins of IHL, the International Red Cross and Red Crescent movement (ICRC) is specifically

15

named, and provisions of IHL mandate it or allow it to carry out tasks aimed at protecting and assisting victims of war, encouraging states to implement their obligations, and promoting and developing the law, and it also has a right of initiative in these respects. There was also an expansion of international humanitarian law, beyond the Geneva Conventions, during the Cold War years, with codification of humanitarian principles in specific areas, such as the Convention on the Status of Refugees (1951) and the Guiding Principles for the Treatment of Internally Displaced Persons (1989).

In theory, then, IHL was quite extensive in terms of its range and its enforcement procedures. In practice, of course, it was limited by the general weaknesses of enforcement in international law—the difficulties in securing sanctions against states, particularly the most powerful. Furthermore, IHL is specifically limited to protecting people in conditions of *war*. It does not, therefore, cover the situation of those persecuted in peacetime.

The other relevant branch of international law covered 'crimes against humanity'. The term originated in the preamble to the 1907 Hague Convention, but it was the International Military Tribunal at Nuremberg after the Second World War which incorporated crimes against humanity into international law for the first time, defining them in Article 6 (c) as:

murder, extermination, enslavement, deportation, and other inhumane acts committed against any civilian population, before or during the war; or persecutions on political, racial or religious grounds in execution of or in connection with any crime within the jurisdiction of the Tribunal, whether or not in violation of the domestic law of the country where perpetrated (quoted in Robinson, 1999, pp. 44–5).

This formulation was incorporated with some amendments in the Tokyo International Criminal Tribunal (1946) and in Allied Control Council law. But for the rest of the Cold War period there was no agreed definition, although particular crimes against humanity, such as genocide, apartheid and enforced disappearance, were identified (Robinson, 1999, p. 45). Nevertheless, there was a widespread assumption that crimes against humanity differed from crimes under IHL in that they could be committed in times of peace as well as war. They were also deemed to be part of *jus cogens*: that is, the international legal norms that override all other rules of international law, including treaties.

Finally, the concept of universal jurisdiction applied to crimes that were seen to be so gross that prosecution ought to be possible irrespective of the place of the crime or the citizenship of the defendant. During the 1990s, it was widely accepted that this applied to torture, genocide, crimes against humanity and serious violations of the Geneva Conventions relating to victims of war (Forsyth 2006, p. 113). In principle, therefore, state sovereignty had not offered protection for those committing such atrocities during the Cold War era, although, as already noted, the Genocide Convention had not included a provision for universal jurisdiction. In practice, however, universal jurisdiction was a dead letter because most states were not prepared to accept it.

There are very considerable overlaps between International Human Rights Law, the Genocide Convention, International Humanitarian Law, and Crimes against Humanity. In theory, as will be suggested in chapter 3, a *prima facie* case for humanitarian intervention could be based on gross violations of certain categories of international law. In practice, no such procedures were activated during the Cold War. The use of legal terminology may have implied an analogy with domestic legal systems, in which there were clear enforcement mechanisms. But the reality of the international order was constructed on the (unequal) power of states and the non-intervention principle. The body of international law that applied to peoples rather than states, or stipulated the ways in which states should treat human beings, may have had some normative impact, but during the Cold War period it hardly affected sovereignty as the basis of the inter-state system.

## Defending non-intervention

Until the late 1980s the conventional wisdom, shared by the left, was in support of the principle of non-intervention. Although it is, in my view, necessary to supersede this principle in certain cases of the most extreme atrocities, I also acknowledge the importance of the arguments in favour of state sovereignty. This section discusses some of the most significant of these, dividing them into two broad categories. The first set of arguments in favour of the non-intervention norm proceeds primarily from a consideration of an *internal* situation (the inside face of sovereignty) while others are embedded largely in an *international* perspective (the outside face of sovereignty). Although such arguments are inter-related and overlapping, I will discuss them in turn.

a) *Non-intervention and the inside face of sovereignty.* The sovereignty principle began its development in sixteenth century Europe as part of the struggle by monarchs to secure domestic control from both internal and external challengers. The nature of the internal regime was therefore not the primary concern, for sovereignty was mainly a doctrine for states embodied in the person of their rulers. The Treaty of Westphalia in 1648, which constituted a formal recognition of the non-intervention norm in the international realm, was similarly 'blind' to the internal characteristics of the system that was to be protected from external encroachment. In essence, non-intervention therefore originally had nothing to say about the political merits of the domestic order that the doctrine served to protect. But liberals and the left supported the non-intervention principle after the Second World War because it had become connected with the idea of self-determination.

In historical terms, this came about once sovereignty was partially transferred from states to 'the people' and 'the nation'. This evolution was intimately connected with political movements, to which the left has been sympathetic: democratization through the notion of *popular* sovereignty, and emancipation from imperial powers through struggles for *national* sovereignty. But while left-wing support for non-intervention might seem straightforward in relation to such cases as the Sandinista regime in Nicaragua battling against US subversion in the 1980s, a problem clearly arises when a regime threatened with intervention is carrying out massive atrocities against its own population. If a universal principle of non-intervention is to be defended, it would also need to apply to cases of this kind. One source for such an argument was originally developed in a short essay by John Stuart Mill (1806–73) in his 'A Few Words on Non-Intervention' (1859).

Mill was writing as a nineteenth-century liberal, sharing the imperialist prejudices of the era, and he therefore claimed that his principles of non-intervention applied only to 'civilised nations' and not 'barbarians'. However, if this is ignored and his principles are applied universally, they clearly expressed an influential and important idea. For Mill drew a distinction between the notion of *self-determination* and that of *political freedom*. As a liberal, he clearly favoured the development of freedom (as he defined it), but he implied that states should be treated as self-determining, even if there was no internal freedom. For the test of whether a people had become fit for popular institutions was whether they were 'willing to brave labour and danger for their liberation' (Mill, 1963, p. 381). Freedom could not be achieved from the outside, and if external forces used force to establish liberal institutions these would not survive because the people would not have developed the qualities on which such institutions depend. However, freedom would be achieved once they attained these qualities, because no repressive government could then survive if the population had sufficient determination to bring about change. He therefore argued that the principle of non-intervention should be upheld even in situations when the population was struggling against its own government to secure freedom, and there is no humanitarian exception in Mill's argument, which was, in effect, a categorical defence of non-intervention.[5] Its basis lay in the belief that intervention was more likely to be carried out by those who were supporting despots *against* the people than by the advocates of freedom. If therefore a powerful state declared its renunciation of the use of force against those in revolt against another state, it would become the 'idol of the friends of freedom' (Mill, 1963, p. 384). For the declaration itself would ensure the 'almost immediate emancipation of every people which desires liberty sufficiently to be capable of maintaining it' (Mill, 1963, p. 384). The idea is understandable in the context of nineteenth century liberal optimism, but it was a harsh argument, as it could be read in such a way as to justify non-intervention even if a brutal regime was slaughtering its opponents.

An argument about non-intervention, which was written in the Cold War era and influenced by Mill, was that of the political philosopher Michael Walzer, in *Just and Unjust Wars*. He wrote this work as an open opponent of the American war in Vietnam, and his attempt to differentiate this from 'a just war' is an undercurrent throughout the book.[6] Walzer was thus writing from a left-liberal perspective, and took up Mill's notion that there is some kind of 'fit' between a government and its people:

The rights of states rest on the consent of their members. But this is a consent of a special sort......Over a long period of time, shared experiences and cooperative activity of many different kinds shape a common life. "Contract" is a metaphor for a process of association and mutuality, the ongoing character of which the state claims to protect against external encroachment. The protection extends not only to the lives and liberties of individuals but also to their shared life and liberty, the independent community they have made, for which individuals are sometimes sacrificed (Walzer, 1977, p. 54).

This suggested a kind of organic unity between the state and the people, and Walzer argued against external intervention because of this notion of a 'fit' between the two. In another essay, he reinforced this point with a 'thought experiment'. He asked whether it would be justifiable (if possible) for an

---

[5] Mill did accept the possibility of intervention by liberal forces when there had already been external intervention to uphold absolutism, but this was because the conflict had thus become international. This was not a humanitarian argument.

[6] However, the emphasis in some of Walzer's more recent writing is very different, particularly in his partial defence of US military action in Iraq in 2003 (Walzer, 2005, pp. 143–68).

enlightened external government (Sweden) to transform an authoritarian, patriarchical system (Algeria) into a democratic egalitarian one by use of a chemical that caused no harm to anyone except to induce amnesia. He was categorical in his answer:

They should not use it because the historical religion and politics of the Algerian people are values for the Algerian people...which one valuation cannot override. It may seem paradoxical to hold that the Algerian people have a right to a state within which their rights are violated. But that is....the only kind of state that they are likely to call their own (Walzer, 1980, p. 226).

Walzer has been justifiably criticised, as has communitarian liberalism more generally, for appearing to suggest that there are particularistic bonds that provide a shared ethical and political life within a given community. Cosmopolitan liberals have rejected this because it runs counter to the idea that there is a common humanity in which each individual's life is the key consideration (Lu, 2006, pp. 72–80; pp. 95–109; Thompson, 1992, pp. 1–23). Moreover, since the notion of a 'fit' is said to apply to non-democratic states, it might be asked how Walzer sought to judge the evidence as to whether the population really accepted a regime or was doing so through subtle forms of repression (Semb, 1992, pp. 35–6). These are, I believe, well-founded criticisms, but by concentrating on the weakness of Walzer's position when taken to its logical extreme they miss the crucially important point that he was making. For the nub of this argument was surely that there is, and must be, a close relationship between the people living in a particular location and the political institutions through which they govern themselves and are governed. This suggests that the idea of distinctive 'political cultures', related in complex ways to customs, beliefs and histories, must be taken very seriously. Interpreted in this way, Walzer provides a weighty argument against the assumption that liberal (or socialist) ideas are self-evidently of universal validity—still more against the notion that they can be externally imposed.

Yet it must be noted, again, that Walzer's argument is against external regime change, rather than humanitarian intervention. Certainly, he was keen to establish tight constraints on any derogations from the non-intervention norm and was well aware of the danger that states would seek to mask interventions based on ulterior motives by making humanitarian claims. But, rather than categorically defending the norm of non-intervention, Walzer was actually *supporting* the case for intervention for humanitarian purposes in certain circumstances. Borrowing the language from an early seminal text on international law, he was thus categorical that 'Humanitarian intervention is justified when it is a response (with reasonable expectations of success) to acts "that shock the moral conscience of mankind" (Walzer, 1980a, p. 107).[7]

In this context, he had no doubt that the Indian intervention in East Pakistan/Bangladesh was justified because of the atrocities carried out by Pakistan (see discussion of this episode below, pp. 30–1). He also argued in favour of *accepting* such interventions as a moral principle, rather than adhering to an absolute legal position of non-intervention, and he was certainly not a categorical defender of the non-intervention norm.[8]

A more specifically left-wing argument in favour of the non-intervention norm (straddling domestic and international arguments) has been based on the conviction that the *real* purpose of any such intervention will be to promote the interests and ideologies of those who carry out the action. Such views have been reinforced by the nature of the interventions in the post Cold War era, but they also arise from both theoretical insights and empirical experience. Furthermore, they clearly have much justification. Consider, for example, the history of Cuba since the revolution in 1959.

By March 1960 the United States began to plan the overthrow of Castro's regime, and in April the following year it intervened militarily with the abortive Bay of Pigs invasion. Subsequently, it abandoned military measures, but engaged in subversion (including numerous assassination plots against Castro) and subjected it to an increasingly tight economic embargo to bring about regime change. Under the Helms-Burton Act of 1996 it has also specified the conditions under which it would accept that there was such a transition. These include the restoration of private property rights, progress towards a market economy, a pluralist political system and the abolition of the Department of State Security in the Cuban Ministry of the Interior. The Act even specified that Raúl Castro must not succeed Fidel (Gott, 2005, pp. 329–32).

While Cuba is a one-party state that does not hold democratic elections, very few governments share the perspective of the US administration (effectively lobbied by the Cuban exiles in Florida) that this means that it is

[7] The original formulation was: '[W]hen a state commits cruelties against and persecution of its nationals in such a way as to deny their fundamental human rights and to shock the conscience of mankind, the matter ceases to be of sole concern to that state and even intervention in the interest of humanity might be legally permissible' (Oppenheim, 1966, originally 1905), quoted in Chesterman, 2002, p. 2).

[8] By the time the third edition of the book was published soon after the Kosovo war, there had been a major shift in Walzer's thinking and the emphasis was now upon *defending* humanitarian intervention, rather than stressing its exceptional nature (Walzer, 2000, pp. xi–xvi).

legitimate for the United States to try to overthrow it. Most do not accept that the violations of human rights that have occurred in Cuba since 1959 have been sufficient to warrant the forms of intervention that the US has carried out. Nor would they agree that there is any compelling evidence that the Cuban people do not regard the regime as their own government. It is, in fact, quite obvious that successive US governments have been committed to *regime change* even when they have sought to invoke humanitarian justifications for intervention.

Fears that *any* weakening of the non-intervention norm would simply make it easier for the US, and other capitalist states, to use humanitarian arguments to overthrow regimes that blocked their interests were therefore significant in left-wing support for the non-intervention norm. As already noted, this left-wing view was often coupled with the belief that the nation-state also provided the most viable framework in which any transition to socialism could come about. Certainly, this was an operating assumption of social democracy during the Keynesian era, and it was shared by the majority of the communist movement. But there was little attempt to provide an *explicit* argument in favour of the non-intervention norm, beyond the defence of particular states threatened with the prospect of external coercion and a general argument against imperialist intervention. However, Ralph Miliband (1924–94) attempted to develop a more specific socialist argument.

Miliband, an independent Marxist thinker, was quite explicit in his view that the best chance of achieving socialism was within a *national* context, and he always emphasised the extent to which the international arena needed to be viewed in terms of international class alignments (Newman, 2002). Like the majority of Marxists, therefore, he had little doubt that, whatever pretexts were given, Western military interventions were primarily designed to defeat movements that might threaten capitalist interests. It was therefore almost axiomatic that interventions of this kind should be opposed and that, at the very least, moral and material support should be given to a national or left-wing movement that was seeking to resist imperialist domination. However, in 1980, following the Vietnamese invasion of Cambodia (precipitating a Chinese attack on Vietnam) and the Soviet intervention in Afghanistan, Miliband also sought to develop a non-intervention principle that would govern the relationships between *socialist* states (Miliband 1980).

He derived this from a two-dimensional analysis. On the one hand, he retained a class perspective, which held that the capitalist and socialist systems had different drives that affected their international relations. He therefore distinguished between interventions that were clearly counter-revolutionary and those that were, at least in theory, broadly 'progressive'. However, he also insisted that the principle of national self-determination meant that an external socialist power could not impose a regime on another country through force of arms. Basing his view primarily, but not solely, on Soviet interventions in Eastern Europe and latterly Afghanistan, he argued forcefully that such attempts would never secure popular support in the target state, and could not be justified by arguing, for example, that the establishment of a friendly regime would enhance security, or that socialism would be built over time. In one respect, this was a Marxist version of Mill's argument, for he was also arguing that a socialist democracy could never emerge on the basis of foreign intervention.

There was no serious consideration of a humanitarian exception in Miliband's outlook, although the Vietnamese overthrow of the brutal Khmer Rouge regime had been an important factor in leading him to write the article, and he also mentioned the overthrow of Idi Amin's murderous dictatorship (these cases will be discussed below, pp. 31–6). In fact, both episodes demonstrated why humanitarian intervention needed to be treated quite differently from interventions that were carried out either for traditional state policy reasons or for regime change. At one point he did pose the question of whether military intervention might be justified in the case of particularly tyrannical and murderous regimes. He continued:

The argument is obviously attractive: one cannot but breathe a sigh of relief when an exceptionally vicious tyranny is overthrown. But attractive though the argument is, it is also dangerous. For who is to decide, and on what criteria, that a regime has become sufficiently tyrannical to justify overthrow by military intervention? There is no good answer to this sort of question; and acceptance of the legitimacy of military intervention on the ground of the exceptionally tyrannical nature of a regime opens the way to even more military adventurism, predatoriness, conquest and subjugation than is already rife in the world today (Miliband, 1980, pp. 16–17).

In his view the rejection of military intervention did not preclude other forms of pressure, including sanctions, a boycott or even a blockade. And he accepted that the fight against Nazi Germany had been justified because it was not only a tyranny, but also bent on war and the subjugation of Europe. But, 'In socialist terms the overthrow of a regime from outside, by military intervention, and without any measure of popular involvement, must always be an exceedingly doubtful enterprise, of the very last resort.' (Miliband, 1980, p. 17) This provided no answer as to the circumstances, if any existed apart from those in Nazi Germany, which would justify intervention. Certainly, he saw neither Cambodia nor Uganda as suitable cases.

The problem was that Miliband, like much of the left in this era, was unable or unwilling to think about these issues. It seems that either the insistence on a class perspective precluded the possibility of considering the position of 'ordinary people' in situations where atrocities were being committed, or else discussion of humanitarian justifications was ruled out for fear that it would open the flood-gates. Post-Cold War practices have certainly demonstrated the justification for such fears. But, rather than effectively ignoring the topic or insisting that humanitarian crises can always be resolved without military means, the appropriate conclusion is surely to insist that any derogations from the non-intervention norm need to be very tightly defined.

A further argument for maintaining non-intervention, with which I have considerable sympathy, also spans the domestic and international realms: this is a claim, derived from the tradition of non-violence, that coercive interventions almost inevitably have non-humanitarian outcomes.[9] There are, of course, different emphases within this tradition, from an outright refusal to entertain the use of force in *any* situation to an overwhelming preference for its avoidance unless there is strong evidence that no other means will be effective. Both ends of this spectrum can agree that if coercive intervention becomes accepted as a general solution to conflict, there is a danger of institutionalizing of military responses permeating political, social and economic structures (Atack, 2002, p. 290). Any emphasis on *military* responses to humanitarian crises could therefore squeeze out non-violent and non-military approaches for dealing with conflict, leading to cycles of confrontation and violence. This raises still more fundamental issues about the nature of power. The conventional wisdom holds that military resources, and the willingness to use them, are the ultimate form of power. But Jonathan Schell has argued very effectively that there have been numerous situations in which non-violent protest has overthrown repressive forces that appeared to wield enormous power (Schell, 2005). Hannah Arendt's theory of violence as the antithesis of power has also been cited in relation to humanitarian intervention (Young, 2003, pp. 264–90). The general argument from the non-violent tradition is thus that the use of military force may be a substitute for actions and

---

[9] The tradition of non-violence was not normally invoked specifically against humanitarian intervention in the Cold War period, because such interventions were comparatively rare. But it merits a brief discussion, since this was certainly an active school of thought at the time, and has been evident in the debate about intervention in the post-1989 period.

approaches that might secure the kinds of co-operation able, conceivably, to make armed force redundant. Furthermore, the resort to military means is always liable to reinforce the dominance of those who control these resources, while reliance upon other ways to resolve crises, such as mediation and economic support, could shift power in alternative directions.

I am in full agreement with this viewpoint, which is why this book will argue that military intervention can be justified only in very restricted circumstances. However, I cannot accept the total pacifist position as suggested by Gandhi when he argued that non-violent resistance would be the best way of defeating Hitler;[10] it seems equally unlikely that this approach would rescue the victims of some other particularly brutal regimes. For this reason it seems more plausible to suggest that the overwhelming emphasis should be upon peaceful solutions, but that military action for humanitarian reasons cannot be ruled out in all circumstances.

b) *Non-intervention from an international perspective: the outside face of sovereignty.* The international arguments for non-intervention have been persuasive, and may be summarised quite easily. The first, which is highly influential, proceeds from the basis of international law. Since the UN Charter has been the most important international legal document since 1945, and since it simultaneously established recognition of state sovereignty as the foundation of the system and the precondition for maintaining peace and security, most international lawyers hold that respect for these principles is required.[11] Although Simon Chesterman's book *Just War or Just Peace?* was a post-Cold War work, first published in 2001, it provides a very important statement of this viewpoint, based on an exploration of the historical evolution of the legal position since the sixteenth century. Noting that there had been interventions for all kinds of reasons since 1945, he asked 'whether, in the case of allegedly humanitarian interventions, it is better for this to be principled or unprincipled', and he argued unreservedly for the latter position: '[I]t is *more* dangerous to hand states a 'right' ... than simply to assert the cardinal principle of the prohibition of the use of force and let states seek a political justification for a particular action if they find themselves in breach of that norm.' (Chesterman, 2002, p. 231)

[10] Harijan, 6 October 1938 in *The Collected Works of Mahatma Gandhi*, Vol. 67, Ahmedabad, Navajivan Trust, 1976, pp. 404–6; and Harijan, 20 November 1938 in *The Collected Works of Mahatma Gandhi*, Vol. 68, Ahmedabad, Navajivan Trust, 1977, pp. 137–41.

[11] The minority position will be considered in chapter 3.

Chesterman claimed that providing additional justifications for intervention would probably increase the number of interventions undertaken in bad faith. It would be more satisfactory to take the view that any intervention, allegedly on humanitarian grounds, was illegal, but that in certain extreme circumstances such a delict might be tolerated. In judicial terms this might translate into a finding of illegality, but imposition of only a nominal penalty. Any alternative, which facilitated interventions that had nothing to do with humanitarianism, would undermine the whole basis of law as the foundation for international order.

This is a forceful argument, but it meant that a *justified* case of humanitarian intervention would be treated as an illegal act. Arguably this is not an important problem for a major state that has sufficient power to defy sanctions of any kind, which are in any case unlikely to be imposed, simply because it is a major state. But during the Cold War justified interventions were carried out by smaller states (see below, pp. 31–6) and this could conceivably happen again. The argument that maintaining the legal position of non-intervention is more important than providing any principled justification for a restricted category of humanitarian interventions could *deter* smaller states from carrying out actions that might be ethically praiseworthy. This legal argument is therefore placing principles of international order above the interests of those suffering from the kind of brutality that might otherwise warrant a humanitarian intervention. The need to restrict interventions as far as possible, and also to prevent major states from manipulating the international order, is clear. But it does not follow that this kind of legal absolutism is the best way of achieving these objectives.

Many arguments, based in International Relations theory, have also defended non-intervention for a variety of reasons. The first might be considered principles of international order, described as a 'pattern or structure of human relations such as to sustain the elementary or primary goals of coexistence among states' (Bull, 1971, p. 270, quoted in Semb, 1992, p. 70). In itself, strict adherence to the non-intervention principle may suggest a conservative stance of *Realpolitik*, based upon complete indifference to atrocities *within* states so long as peaceful coexistence was maintained. However, it did not necessarily imply this. It was also compatible with a view that avoidance of inter-state warfare was ultimately still more likely to reduce human suffering than increasing the probability of more wars by eroding the non-intervention norm. John Vincent, a progressive liberal international relations theorist, also suggested an explicitly humanitarian justification for non-intervention. While firmly defending this principle, he combined the argument about the preservation of a peaceful international order with the claim that this was also the best way to secure justice in the world as a whole: preservation of this order provided the kind of security in which states, which he regarded as the sole effective agencies for welfare and rights, could maximise the benefits for their populations (Vincent, 1974, p. 346). This position thus straddled defences of sovereignty from both the inside and the outside.

The second level of concern was not so much about international order *per se* as about the position of the states within it. It was, in fact, the point noted earlier: once there was any movement away from theoretical acceptance of the sovereign equality of states, was it not almost inevitable that the powerful would find pretexts for intervention, while weaker states—above all those that had recently achieved their independence—would be the victims? In other words, the norm of non-intervention protected the weak and constrained the powerful.

Overall, then, the International Relations argument against the humanitarian intervention doctrine, shared by much left-liberal and left-wing opinion, was that

[I]t is a doctrine used by the great against the small, that it smacks of imperialism, that it disguises ignoble motives (or conversely, that it expects too high a standard of behaviour), that it might encourage counter-intervention, and that it is in general heedless of consequences (Vincent, 1986, p. 45).

These were formidable arguments, and many of them have been reinforced by the experience of intervention in the post-Cold War era. However, none of them was decisive. It was no doubt true that small states were more likely to be the victims and there should preferably be equality and consistency, but 'the fewer genocidal governments the better, no matter whether the states they represent are big or small' (Semb, 1992, p. 64). Similarly, not all humanitarian interventions would imperil the international order and, even if it were accepted that the security of states was a precondition of justice, in cases of wholesale massacre within a state the international order would embody injustice if this was not stopped (Semb, 1992, p. 75). As Vincent himself acknowledged, there was no guarantee that states would promote justice even if they were protected from international intervention, and he accepted that in certain circumstances, 'in which local governments were implicated by failing to meet their responsibilities...there might fall to the international community a duty of humanitarian intervention' (Vincent, 1986, pp. 126–7).

Yet even if none of the arguments against humanitarian intervention is decisive, their cumulative effect is still very significant. Taken as a whole, they demonstrate that the case for breaching the non-intervention norm needs to be drawn highly restrictively so that it could apply in a very limited number of cases. However, the restrictiveness of the norm during the Cold War period had some negative effects, as the following section will show.

## Intervention and non-intervention in practice

There was no case during the Cold War years in which the Security Council authorised intervention on humanitarian grounds. Yet there were certainly occasions when justifications for transgressing the principle of state sovereignty might have been made on the grounds of international humanitarian law, or crimes against humanity, or genocide or massive human rights violations. For example, the case of Burundi illustrated the way in which the non-intervention norm was maintained for reasons of *Realpolitik* and to shield states that were carrying out atrocities.

Both Burundi and Rwanda secured independence in 1962 from Belgium, which had carried out a particularly blatant form of divide and rule between the Hutus and Tutsis, using the latter as their instruments for colonial domination (see chapter 4). In both countries the Tutsi were the minority, but in Burundi they managed to maintain control after independence. In 1965 a mutiny by Hutu army and police officers led to reprisals, and after a coup the following year there were purges and executions of Hutus. In 1972 the regime was threatened by a renewed Hutu uprising leading to the deaths of hundreds of Tutsis. This led to state-directed reprisals, apparently in a co-ordinated plan, targeting prominent Hutu political leaders and also those who were wealthy and educated. Between 100,000 and 200,000 Hutus were massacred and the killings continued into 1973 (Meredith, 1985, p. 217, Kuper 1982, pp. 62–3). Clearly, there were possible grounds for some kind of humanitarian intervention here, and this was not a key site of Cold War confrontation, although a State Department memorandum still sought to prevent any US action on the grounds that this could be exploited to the advantage of the Soviet Union or China.[12] Nor was the reason for a failure to act ignorance of what was

---

[12] Memorandum for Henry Kissinger, 10 October 1972 http://www.state.gov/r/pa/ho/frus/nixon/e5/54745.htm in Foreign Relations of the United States, Vol. E-5 *Documents on Africa, 1969–76.*

happening for, less than three weeks after the killings began, the Belgian Prime Minister informed the Cabinet that genocide was taking place in Burundi (Kuper, 1982, p. 163). The reasons for non-intervention (except through diplomatic representations and humanitarian assistance) were quite different. France supported the Burundi government (as did China and North Korea), and although the UN Sub-Commission on Prevention of Discrimination and Protection of Minorities forwarded a complaint against Burundi to the Commission of Human Rights, no significant action was taken.

This was not simply because of indifference in the Security Council, for the Organization of African Unity (OAU) also played a role. The Secretary-General of the organization, accompanied by the Tanzanian Prime Minister and the President of Somalia, visited Burundi three weeks after the killings began and announced solidarity with the President of Burundi, and a formal resolution the next month effectively confirmed this. For, as already noted, the OAU was vigilant against any new signs of neo-colonialism and African leaders had established a firm principle of non-intervention in state sovereignty. With the emphasis on the struggle against apartheid and the white minority regime in Rhodesia, there was no appetite to become involved in the internal affairs of Burundi, and the UN Security Council had neither the unity nor the will to try to persuade the OAU to shift its stance or take any effective action itself (Kuper, 1982, pp. 164–5).

This example of non-intervention was one of many such episodes, and it is instructive in two respects. First, it demonstrates the ways in which political considerations combined with the legal position and norm of state sovereignty to prevent the consideration of enforcement action. Secondly, and hypothetically, it seems likely that the doctrine of humanitarian intervention could have been established more easily in this case than many others. The Soviet-US confrontation was much less intense here than in many other parts of the world, and although any attempt to authorise an intervention would still have been divisive, the reality was that there was no real wish to establish a humanitarian exception to the non-intervention norm.

Unilateral humanitarian intervention (that is, intervention not authorised by the Security Council) was always bound to be most problematic. Under the Charter, unilateral action could be justified only in self-defence or when the Security Council authorised individual states or regional bodies to act on its behalf. This left the question as to whether the Security Council might tacitly accept a humanitarian justification by permitting unilateral action on the bogus grounds of self-defence in circumstances when a major reason for such intervention was in fact humanitarian. There were three interventions in the

1970s, which might be considered humanitarian, which have been analyzed in this context (Wheeler, 2000).

The first concerned the Indian action in the creation of Bangladesh in 1971. Since independence West Pakistan had dominated and exploited the Bengalis in East Pakistan, with the disparity in per capita income between the West and East increasing by a factor of six between 1947 and 1969. In the elections in October 1970, after a long period of military dictatorship, the Awami League gained a massive majority of the seats in the East on a programme of very extensive autonomy. This soon evolved into a call for independence and in March 1971 the military forces of the government in West Pakistan responded by carrying out brutal atrocities on such a scale that the International Commission of Jurists argued that there was 'a strong prima facie case that the crime of genocide was committed against the group comprising the Hindu population of East Bengal' (quoted in Kuper, 1982, p. 79). Estimates of the numbers killed vary between one million and three million, and the UN Relief Committee in February 1972 believed that over 1.5 million houses had been destroyed and that there were some 10 million refugees in India. It was widely agreed that the Pakistani army had sought to eliminate resistance in the East by massacres, terror and deliberate atrocities. This was only stopped by unilateral Indian action.

By late November 1971 an Indo-Pakistan conflict appeared imminent and, after Pakistan launched a pre-emptive air-strike on Indian airfields in early December, there was a full-scale war in which Pakistan was defeated within twelve days and Bangladesh was established as a separate state. Before the Indian intervention there had only been inconclusive discussion in the UN, although there was full awareness of the situation. This was not the fault of the Secretary-General who, in July 1971, drew attention to the situation and the potential threat to peace and international security that it posed (Kuper, 1982, p. 173). Certainly humanitarian assistance was sent, but there was no consideration of enforcement action against Pakistan, and it was only with the Indian invasion that urgent discussion took place in the Security Council. Although India did mention humanitarian considerations in its justifications for its action, its *primary* arguments were about self-defence and the refugee crisis (Wheeler, 2000, pp. 55–65, p. 74; Chesterman, 2002, pp. 73–5). And although the Council acquiesced in the Indian action, it did not accept any humanitarian justification. At most it was prepared to accept that there was a threat to peace and security, but it still criticised the Indian attack. India's role in the establishment of Bangladesh was seen as the negation of Pakistan's state sovereignty, although it was also accepted that West Pakistan should have addressed the grievances in the East.

Apart from the apparently general wish to uphold the doctrine of state sovereignty—even when there was a strong case for arguing that there were massive human right violations, crimes against humanity and genocide—the sub-text was the Cold War and partisan divisions between the Great Powers. Humanitarian considerations were therefore subordinate to *Realpolitik*. Thus China and the USA supported Pakistan, while the Soviet Union was aligned with India. But despite its support for India, the Soviet Union was not prepared to mention humanitarian reasons as a justification for the action. Upholding state sovereignty (except, of course, *in practice* in its own satellites) was so important that the Soviet Union was not willing to provide any legitimacy to a humanitarian intervention, even in the case of an action that it supported.

The second case was the most horrific in the whole Cold War period—that of Cambodia/Kampuchea. Cambodia was a victim of the Vietnam war, with the Vietcong using the country as a route from North to South Vietnam. This precipitated massive bombing by the US, which caused great suffering and death, and destroyed infrastructure and agriculture. Following this, in 1975, the Khmers Rouges under Pol Pot took power in Cambodia, implementing an ideology that combined elements of nationalism with an eccentric and extreme form of revolutionary Marxism. Apart from executing large numbers of those involved—or allegedly involved—in the previous regime, the Khmers Rouges sought to 're-educate' urban populations by compulsorily moving them to the countryside. Those who were regarded as intellectuals or part of the elite were singled out for particularly vicious treatment, but ordinary people from humble backgrounds were also executed for the most minor violations of discipline. The countryside could not support this mass movement of population and hundreds of thousands of people also died from starvation. It is impossible to determine how many perished during the four-year regime, but it may have been as many as two million out of a total population of seven million (Neher, 2003, p. 172).

While it was difficult to secure entirely accurate information on the situation, fairly reliable reports soon became available. Finally, in March 1978 the Commission on Human Rights of the United Nations invited a response from the Khmers Rouges regime to reports on Human Rights violations, and in January 1979 the Sub-Commission on Prevention of Discrimination and Protection of Minorities prepared an overall analysis. This was based on submissions from the governments of Canada, Norway, the UK, the USA and Australia, with additional evidence and reports from Amnesty International and the International Commission of Jurists. In September 1978, the Soviet press also took up the issue in a very forthright way, with the *New Times* openly labelling the crimes a 'Policy of Genocide' by the Kampuchean government (Kuper, 1982, pp. 155–8). The use of this term by the Soviet Union was perhaps surprising, as it had been intent on excluding *political* crimes of this kind from the concept, but many others would agree that a genocide was indeed taking place. Yet the pressure on the Khmers Rouges government had developed slowly, and had not led to any result, when the whole issue became intertwined with long-term regional conflicts.

Vietnam had historic rivalries with Cambodia and Thailand, as well as China. Chinese-Soviet relations were also extremely poor at the time, and the newly united Vietnam was now a close ally of the Soviet Union, while the Khmer Rouge regime was a protégé of China. Clearly both China and Thailand would oppose any action by Vietnam against Cambodia. However, Vietnam was far stronger than Cambodia, and also had grievances, arising from the Khmers Rouges' treatment of Cambodia's Vietnamese minority, and because of Cambodian incursions into Vietnamese territory as part of the long-term border dispute. In January 1979 Vietnam launched full-scale military action against Cambodia, conquering the whole country, deposing the Khmers Rouges, and installing a pro-Vietnamese government. This precipitated a Chinese attack on Vietnam and a month-long war between the two countries, but that did not lead to any withdrawal of Vietnam from Cambodia. And although there were some Vietnamese atrocities in Cambodia, at least initially, the overthrow of the Pol Pot regime was generally welcomed by the population, since this prevented the Khmers Rouges from continuing with their massacres and forced 're-education' programmes.

There is therefore a very strong case for regarding this as a justified unilateral humanitarian intervention—even though the Vietnamese never suggested that this was the reason for their action (Wheeler, 2000, pp. 102–10). Instead they made an entirely unconvincing claim that the Khmer Rouge regime was overthrown by domestic forces in protest against its policies, and that the Vietnamese had simply lent their support when invited to do so. This followed from the fact that neither the Vietnamese government nor their Soviet backers wanted to legitimise the notion of humanitarian intervention, because of the precedent that it might set elsewhere. This led to one of the most cynical episodes in Western policy during the Cold War.

As noted above, Western governments had been mounting a case against the Khmers Rouges before the Vietnamese invasion. In fact, many of them had been deeply critical of the slow pace at which the UN was moving. Thus the UK delegate had commented on the reports of human rights involving thousands of deaths, and systematic brutality at the whim of the authorities, with the slaughter in many cases of entire families. He continued, 'All those atrocities had aroused the conscience of the world, but the Commission [UN Commission on Human Rights] had disregarded them for political reasons' (E./CN.4/SR, Quoted in Kuper, 1982, p. 171).

This was part of a Western argument that the Commission on Human Rights was keen to expose atrocities in right-wing countries, such as South Africa and Chile, but reluctant to address human rights violations in left-wing regimes. However, as soon as Vietnam carried out the invasion, Western Cold War *Realpolitik* predominated over all other considerations. Vietnam was a Soviet protégé and the Soviet Union was the major 'threat'. Since the change in US policy at the beginning of the decade, China was no longer seen in this way. Thus the West now totally reversed its stance on the Cambodian situation. Instead of recognizing the government installed there by the Vietnamese, the US and the UK now joined China in continuing to recognise the deposed Khmer Rouge regime as the legitimate government of Cambodia. Instead of acquiescing in the overthrow of Pol Pot as beneficial to the people of Cambodia, the West implemented sanctions against Vietnam, which continued until the end of the Cold War. And in the Security Council meeting following the Vietnamese intervention, the French representative explicitly placed the preservation of the non-intervention norm above all humanitarian considerations:

...the idea that the existence of a detestable regime justifies foreign intervention and legitimises its forcible overthrow is extremely dangerous [since] in the long run it would endanger the very existence of an international order by making the survival of every regime dependent on its neighbour's judgement (Statement by Jacques Leprette, 11 January 1979, quoted by Semb, 1992, p. 71).

The Western states and China demonstrated their belief that it was more important to counter the Soviet Union and its allies than to save the victims of one of the most brutal regimes in the twentieth century.

The third case, which raises some different issues, was that of the Tanzanian intervention in Uganda in April 1979. When Idi Amin had seized power in a military coup in January 1971 there had been considerable tacit support for his action in the West, particularly within the British government. However,

33

he began to murder officers loyal to the previous regime almost immediately and in mid-1971 the mass killings started, with action against particular ethnic groups, real or supposed political opponents, and religious groups, and massacres of entire villages (Kuper, 1982, pp. 166–7; Meredith 1985, pp. 200–2). In August 1972 his honeymoon with Britain also ended with a decision to expel 75,000 Ugandan Indians with 90 days' notice, but this populist measure was probably designed to divert attention from the still more brutal atrocities that were continuing. By the time that he was deposed after eight years of rule, it is thus estimated that Amin's army and other forces of repression had killed approximately 300,000 people (Wheeler, 2000, p. 111).

Once again, the question of what *action* might be taken against the regime was overlaid by broader political considerations. The International Commission of Jurists submitted five complaints of human rights violations to the Secretary-General of the UN between 1974 and 1976, and in January 1977 Amnesty International also submitted a complaint. The Secretary-General went so far as to ask Amin to conduct an investigation, but even this lacklustre proposal was more resolute than anything adopted by the UN Commission on Human Rights. For the Commission was deadlocked as a result of international divisions. Attempts in March 1977 to call for an inquiry into the human rights situation were therefore blocked by a Cuban resolution, supported by a majority of African, East European, Middle Eastern and Asian countries (Kuper, 1982, p. 168). This was presumably based on the common premise that pressure on the Amin regime was a form of neo-imperialist intervention against an African state. However, five Nordic states attempted to circumvent this and jointly sponsored a UN General Assembly resolution of concern about the human rights situation in Uganda in December 1977. This expressed the hope that the Organization of African Unity (OAU) would take up the issue so as to bring about the cessation of the violations. Such OAU action was indeed the key to any international progress on the issue, but non-intervention was still the default position in the OAU. However, Julius Nyerere of Tanzania challenged this, at least in part.

Nyerere had been close to Milton Obote, the deposed Ugandan leader, and this, with some basic doubts on his part about the non-intervention policy, led the Tanzanian government to raise general principles about the OAU charter in 1975 (Welch, 1981, p. 405, quoted in Wheeler, 2000, p. 113). By October 1978 the relations between the two governments had deteriorated sharply and Ugandan forces crossed the frontier. Nyerere became impatient with OAU mediation attempts and sought to change its founding charter so that states that were guilty of massive human rights violations were no longer offered protection. In December, he noted:

'a strange tendency in Africa...a tendency which, if we do not consider it carefully, will badly damage respect for our continent....Amin is a killer. Since he took over the leadership of Uganda....he has killed many more people than Smith [the leader of the white minority regime in Rhodesia] has done. He has killed many more people than Vorster has done in South Africa. But there is a strange habit in Africa: an African leader, so long as he is an African, can kill Africans just as he pleases, and you cannot say anything. If Amin was White, we would have passed many resolutions against him. But he is Black, and Blackness is a licence to kill Africans. And therefore there is complete silence; no one speaks about what he does.' (*Africa Contemporary Record*, 11 (1978–79), B394, quoted in Wheeler, 2000, pp. 115–6)

Yet Nyerere was not actually calling for humanitarian intervention. His hope was that the Ugandan people would themselves overthrow the Amin regime, although Tanzania was now providing covert support to opposition forces. However, the uprising did not occur and in April 1979 Tanzanian troops invaded and overthrew the government. Although the Tanzanian forces remained for some months and could be accused of propping up a new government, Nyerere probably would not have authorised the invasion had Uganda not attacked Tanzania first. Certainly he used the argument of self-defence, rather than humanitarian intervention, to justify the invasion. This was no doubt both because he was aware that the OAU would be far more likely to support this justification than any other, and because he generally held this view himself (Wheeler, 2000, pp. 130–4). In general the OAU tacitly accepted this, but Tanzania was still criticised by President Numeiry, the outgoing OAU Chairman, at a Heads of State meeting in July 1979, and also by the Nigerian Head of State, General Olusegun Obasanjo. Numeiry argued that Nyerere should have accepted OAU mediation rather than taking unilateral action, while Obasanjo specifically condemned the notion of humanitarian intervention, arguing that pressure and moral exhortation were the only legitimate actions when a member state was guilty of human rights violations (Wheeler, 2000, pp. 127–8).

The reaction of Western governments was also significant. No-one was inclined to shed a tear over the downfall of Amin, but nor did they specifically endorse the Tanzanian action either. The general view was that precedents for unilateral intervention should not be established and that Nyerere had neither sought Security Council authorization nor taken immediate action in self-defence. But there was a stark contrast between the acquiescence in this case and the condemnation of the Vietnamese intervention in Cambodia a few months earlier. On this occasion, the Cold War conflict with the Soviet Union was much less relevant. And there was perhaps a second, un-stated factor that may have been significant: the question of whether the West really *cared* what happened in sub-Saharan Africa when one government deposed another.

None of the three interventions above—India in relation to East Pakistan/Bangladesh, Vietnam in relation to Cambodia/Kampuchea, or Tanzania in relation to Uganda—could be said to have been solely humanitarian in motivation, and this may not even have been a factor in the Vietnamese action in Cambodia. Yet each intervention was against a regime that was carrying out atrocities on a massive scale, and these were curtailed as a result of the intervention. There were therefore good reasons for suggesting that humanitarian *consequences* followed from the actions. Furthermore, there are no very compelling reasons for believing that the atrocities would have ended quickly, or ended at all, without those interventions. It seems more probable that the slow and ineffective discussions that had taken place in relation to Burundi would have been repeated. It would be an exaggeration to suggest that the non-intervention norm was itself responsible for the atrocities or even for the failure to act, for there were also many other reasons, including cynical *Realpolitik* and the Cold War. But the sovereignty argument certainly provided a convenient alibi for refusing to act, and registering disapproval of those that intervened.

Episodes of this kind led Leo Kuper to argue:

....the sovereign territorial state claims, as an integral part of its sovereignty, the right to commit genocide, or engage in genocidal massacres against peoples under its rule, and... the United Nations, for all practical purposes, defends this right. To be sure, no state *explicitly* claims the right to commit genocide—this would not be morally acceptable even in international circles—but the right is exercised under other more acceptable rubrics, notably the duty to maintain law and order, or the seemingly sacred mission to preserve the territorial integrity of the state (Kuper, 1982 p. 161).

This was an important rejoinder to those who were defending non-intervention as an inviolable principle.

\* \* \*

In the early twenty-first century, there has been concern that the doctrine of humanitarian intervention simply provided a basis for the expansion of the dominant Western powers, and many on the left have rejected the whole principle. This chapter has drawn attention to the quite different problems of the Cold War era when there was no acceptance, either in theory or in practice, of the principle of humanitarian intervention as a derogation from the non-intervention norm. If the partial rehabilitation of Pol Pot by China and the West was perhaps the most extreme case, with the subordination of genocide to *Realpolitik*, there were many other occasions when major states placed wider strategic considerations well above any concern for human life. Any full evaluation of humanitarian intervention must therefore surely accept that a *failure* to recognise its necessity in exceptional circumstances may result in atrocities and injustice. However, the end of the Cold War would lead to a major shift in doctrine and practice, creating a completely new situation. This is the subject of the next chapter.

# 2

# The Post-Cold War Transformation

During the 1990s, a transformation took place in relation to humanitarian intervention. Between the Second World War and 1989 the dominant normative assumption had been in line with the mainstream interpretation of international law—that coercive intervention was incompatible with state sovereignty and therefore illegitimate. This was to change during the 1990s as a series of interventions took place, with a considerable degree of international support. However, the apparent shift in opinion was short-lived. In 1999 the Kosovo crisis and NATO's massive bombing campaign, without UN authorization, against Serbia (which with Montenegro had retained the name of the former Yugoslavia) created a major international crisis; any incipient consensus on shifting the boundaries of the non-intervention principle seemed to be eroded. By the end of the decade the overwhelming international pre-eminence of the United States remained unchallenged, but the normative position was therefore much less clear.

A major cause of the transformation at the beginning of the decade was clearly the collapse of the Soviet bloc between 1989 and 1991. During the Cold War there had been little possibility for a doctrine of humanitarian intervention to emerge: mutual rivalries and ideological conflicts were too great and coexistence had been built upon sovereignty and non-intervention. The end of US-Soviet hostilities then provided a 'space' for the development of new international norms, and it seems clear that the increase in intervention was related to the (temporary) emergence of a unipolar system based on the United States as the sole superpower. This change in the distribution of international power also suggests the inadequacy of viewing the interventions simply as improvised reactions to particular crises. For those reactions were embedded in wider policies and strategies, which also accounted for differential responses to the various conflicts. However, the concern here is not only with the events themselves, but also with the ways in which they were *perceived* and *interpreted*, particularly by left-liberal and left opinion. And these did not arise simply from a view of humanitarian intervention, as an isolated phenomenon, but as part of a much broader outlook, which was also undergoing transformation at the end of the Cold War.

This chapter is therefore structured as follows. Section 1 considers the attitudes of left-liberal and left-wing opinion at the end of the Cold War in relation to such inter-related concepts as democracy, human rights and the sovereign state. The convergence between these ideas and apparent international developments is demonstrated in Section 2, which focuses on international organizations and peace-keeping, and Section 3, which outlines the new commitments to democratization and human rights. Section 4 turns to humanitarian intervention, with the first part looking at some major episodes and the second part examining three theoretical approaches developed by contemporary thinkers in relation to the new developments. As later chapters will demonstrate, I believe that there were some major weaknesses in both the practice and the underlying assumptions of humanitarian intervention during this period, because of its close association with Western policy priorities. However, the purpose of this chapter is to examine the emergence of humanitarian intervention both in practice and in the realm of ideas and interpretations.

## Attitudes towards democracy, human rights and sovereignty

It is not difficult to understand why liberal opinion was broadly optimistic at the beginning of 1990s. Most liberals had been opposed to communism and therefore had little reason to regret the disappearance of the Soviet bloc. Attached to liberal-democracy, and convinced that freedom, rights, and justice could flourish to their fullest extent within such a system, they would naturally tend to welcome the new prominence of such ideas at the end of the Cold War. However, this was less obvious in relation to more specifically left-wing opinion.

Throughout much of the twentieth century, there were tensions between socialist ideas and the theory and practices of liberalism. In particular, the Marxist revolutionary tradition was generally highly critical of liberal-democracy as an expression of capitalist class rule. While defenders of the system celebrated pluralism as the embodiment of democratic life, the Marxist critique was that liberal democratic forms masked a *concentration* of real power, and that the political and civil rights were both limited and expressed an atomistic and individualist notion of society. Although Marxism tended to avoid predictions about the institutional forms that a post-capitalist society would develop, the general assumption was that these would facilitate expression of social solidarity rather than individual interests. However, during the Cold War era the social democratic movement had increasingly accepted liberal-democracy as a permanent political form. To the extent that it continued to view itself as representing the working class, it saw its role as enhancing the power and position of that class within the framework of capitalist society; and until the 1970s or early 1980s its economic thinking was based largely upon Keynesian demand management.

By the end of the Cold War, the left as a whole was undergoing an ideological crisis, particularly as a result of evidence of repression in Communist countries, the rise of new social movements within capitalism, and the fragmentation of the traditional working class (Newman, 2005). Certainly, there was opposition to contemporary developments in liberal-democracy, particularly in the Reagan-Thatcher era, with its elevation of neo-liberalism as the new orthodoxy. But this was no longer reflected in support for the alternative political and economic project that had been implicit in most forms of classical Marxism. There was now an emphasis on democracy being expressed at a variety of levels and in several forms. Furthermore, there was a renewed interest in such conceptions as civil society, citizenship and rights as crucial components in *any* system. There was active debate about the constituent elements of such concepts—for example, how they could be broadened to encompass social and environmental rights and sexual equality, and whether they were inherently liberal and Western or universal—but many of the disagreements were within a broadly shared theoretical framework. Finally, there was also a move away from the notion of the centrally planned economy, with debate about 'how much market' and how public goods could be provided, rather than a rejection of the whole notion of the role of markets in the allocation of goods and the determination of prices. Meanwhile, social democracy was undergoing its own theoretical crisis, as the conditions for Keynesian demand management were eroded, and weakening perceptions of class undermined political support for parties and trade unionism. The redefinition of social democracy would not take the same form in all countries, but even before the end of the Cold War it was clearly moving further from traditional definitions of socialism.

Such developments in both economic and political thinking made the boundaries between liberal and much left-wing thought more 'fuzzy' than previously. In particular, there was a broad movement of opinion in support of *democracy* and *human rights* as crucially important values, even if both remained contested concepts. Secondly, there was a decline in the use of class as the primary category to explain historical processes or to determine policies and attitudes. There was also much convergence in the belief that sovereignty was being reconstituted.

At the end of the Cold War it was evident that the sovereign state was being pushed off its pedestal; in both academic (Camilleri and Falk, 1992; Walker and Mendlovitz, 1990) and journalistic literature (Ohmai, 1995), and in political and social movements, a new consensus appeared to be emerging that the state was being 'hollowed out', with a fragmentation of power and allegiance. This, it was argued, resulted from such developments as economic internationalization, the communications revolution with the rapid international transmission of ideas, environmental processes, and the increased movement of peoples. Normative conclusions were also drawn from the analysis or embedded within it, with the claim that the defence of state sovereignty had been negative because it legitimised the pursuit of self-interest, competition and *Realpolitik* or even led to ethnic exclusiveness and external aggression. Many concluded that, instead, new political, social and economic formations should be emphasised that cut across state power. If the sovereign state embodied the notion that power was concentrated in one supreme entity, which represented a single society externally, it was now argued that power needed to be dispersed and represented on a variety of levels. This also meant that new significance was attached to the notions of international rights, international legal frameworks, transnational citizenship, and global movements (Held, 1993, Meehan, 1993). Few were advocating total abandonment of the state, rather these were seen as *complementary* developments, which were displacing the sovereign state as a unique focal point of allegiance and activity. Implicit in all this was a cosmopolitan outlook, whether or not this was formally theorised. All this also had implications for the notion of non-intervention.

During the Cold War era non-intervention was the concomitant of sovereignty. But this was tied up with the notion that the sovereign state was a kind of private realm in which outside interference was prohibited. As Catherine

Lu has argued (Lu, 2006, pp. 68–9, 85), there is an analogy here with the way in which the family was also traditionally viewed. Child abuse and violence against women are now seen as criminal activities whether they take place inside or outside the family; this means that the notion of a family as a private realm has been replaced with social and legal regulation to establish the boundaries of permissible behaviour. Similarly, the notion that international concern for atrocities, wherever they are committed, constitutes *interference* assumes that the affairs of the sovereign state are a private sphere. If it is acknowledged that there is legitimate involvement in protecting the lives and rights of people across the world, this concern might be termed 'international responsibility' rather than interference. Certainly, a cosmopolitan framework would take the latter view, for it begins with an ethical theory built upon the well-being of the individual.

By the 1980s and 1990s, this perspective (rather than, for example, one of international class alignment) was increasingly influential on the left and lib-eral-left. However, since coercive intervention involves violence, this was certainly not the preferred form in which the new notions of international responsibility would be expressed. More typically, liberal and left-wing opinion was attracted by international developments, which appeared to embody some of these ideas. Two elements were particularly notable: the apparent strengthening of international institutions, particularly the United Nations, in relation to peace-keeping, and the general shift towards democratization as a policy goal by major institutions, with the simultaneous development of a strengthened international human rights regime.

## International institutions and peace-building

Throughout the Cold War, the UN was relatively impotent in relation to peace and security, subordinate to the wishes of the superpowers. Occasionally it appeared to move beyond the limitations of the Charter, which were extended, in practice if not in legal theory, by Secretary-General Dag Hammarskjöld, in the aftermath of the Suez War. The UNEF mission to separate Israeli and Egyptian forces was based on the consent of the parties (under Chapter VI, as specified in the Charter), but the UN was proactive, inducing the parties to accept an armed peace-keeping mission rather than simply facilitating an ongoing peace-making process by lending its support (Findlay 2002, pp. 20–50). However, the strategy behind this approach was to prevent regional conflicts from becoming drawn into the main superpower confrontation. When the peace-keeping attempt in the Congo in the early 1960s became enmeshed in Cold War divisions it was unable to act effectively (Findlay, 2002, pp. 51–89). And although there were several other missions in the era, budgetary pressures and a low threshold of tolerance by the superpowers for any independent action curtailed the UN's peacekeeping potential.

Even before the collapse of Communism in Eastern Europe, Gorbachev's attempt at a rapprochement with the West initiated a process of change. In September 1987 he wrote an article in *Pravda* and *Izvestia* seeking wider use of peacekeeping forces and calling on the Permanent Five Members of the Security Council to become 'guarantors' of international security (Chesterman, 2002, pp. 120–1). Over the next two years peacekeeping forces were deployed in several areas, with a role in intra-state conflicts in Namibia, Angola, and Central America. The shift in superpower relations also brought about, finally, a decisive change in the Cambodian situation. Several rounds of negotiation ultimately led the five Permanent Members of the Security Council to draft a framework for a comprehensive settlement, which was accepted by all the Cambodian parties in September 1990, and formally adopted at a peace conference in Paris in October 1991. This was to lead to the largest peace-keeping operation that had ever been mounted by the UN. But, of wider significance, such missions constituted a major transformation in the *nature* of peace-keeping, which involved deep penetration into the domestic politics of the state in an attempt to create a post-conflict structure that would operate on broadly liberal-democratic principles (Paris, 2004; Bellamy, Williams and Griffin, 2004).

Finally, in 1992 Boutros Boutros-Ghali, the Secretary General, published the most ambitious document on peace-keeping ever produced by the UN, *An Agenda for Peace* (Boutros-Ghali, 1992). This envisaged a transformation to 'peace-building' in which the objective was no longer simply to manage conflict, but to transform violent conflicts by helping to rebuild societies through creating viable institutions, facilitating reconciliation, and reconstructing economies. This went far beyond the Cold War approach, holding up a model of peace-keeping which involved both civil and military aspects. These aspirations for the UN to become an effective peace-building institution were in harmony with the emerging liberal and left-wing consensus of the early post-Cold War era. The idea of the body with the greatest international legitimacy also embodying a conception of international responsibility for the creation of peace, both within and between states, was highly attractive.

While liberal and left-wing hopes would always tend to focus on the UN, as the repository of international legitimacy, this was often coupled with support for regional bodies. In this respect, the EU had particular importance because many believed that it had the potential to be transformed into a model of post-national citizenship, and a guarantor of democracy, rights and welfare in Europe. Furthermore, there appeared to be a chance at the beginning of the 1990s that the EU would establish a new model of security, based on the notion of 'civilian power', and that this would help transform relationships across Europe as a whole. The tendency to concentrate (perhaps excessively) upon Europe in the early post-Cold War years was not entirely the result of Eurocentrism; it also reflected the fact that integration was more advanced in this region than any other. But there was also a wider move towards regional integration in parts of Asia. None of these regional bodies went as far as the EU in establishing limited forms of supranationalism, or in stepping tentatively towards notions of post-national citizenship, but there were cogent reasons for believing that these developments might also facilitate the establishment of peace and co-operative relationships.

## Democratisation and the development of an international human rights regime

The new consensus on the left in favour of human rights and democracy was matched, at least *in theory*, by a commitment to these values by all the major international institutions in the latter stages of the Cold War and the early post-Cold War period.[1]

The UN was perhaps the most significant in this respect. After the Universal Declaration of Human Rights in 1948, it had been very difficult for the UN to make statements about the principles of political organization because of the Cold War division. However, the shifts in peacekeeping practices were accompanied by doctrinal statements and policy developments. In December 1991 the General Assembly passed a resolution declaring that 'periodic and genuine elections' were a 'crucial factor in the effective enjoyment...of a wide range of other human rights'. A similar emphasis was imported into the UN Development Programme (UNDP) from the early 1990s, with the claim that 'good governance' was important in poverty eradication and development.

Another highly significant shift was evident in the Organization for Security and Co-operation in Europe (the OSCE). This body (originally known as

---

[1] For a very useful summary of the new policy commitments by the various institutions, see Paris (2004), pp. 22–35.

the Conference on Security and Co-operation in Europe), which had been created in the 1970s as part of the Helsinki process reflecting the East-West détente of the era, had operated on the principle that the participating states would 'respect each other's right freely to choose and develop its political, social, economic and cultural systems as well as its right to determine its laws and regulations'. In June 1990 this was transmuted into a resolution that 'the development of societies based on pluralistic democracy and the rule of law are prerequisites for progress in setting up the lasting order of peace, security, justice and cooperation that they seek to establish in Europe'. The resolution included a list of governmental structures and processes that the OSCE would now promote, and a new Office for Democratic Institutions and Human Rights (ODIHR) was established. This drafted rules and regulations for democratic elections, particularly in the former Soviet bloc, and supported both civil society organizations and more formal election processes in transition countries. While the formal commitment was to democracy, the underlying assumptions were implicitly based on the liberal model.

It is less surprising that the commitment to democratization was evident in all the primary institutions that had been dominated by the West during the Cold War. Thus in 1989 the EU incorporated democracy and human rights conditions into the Lomé Convention with developing countries, and they were also conditions for accession to the Union itself (a requirement formalised and consolidated in the 1997 Treaty of Amsterdam). Similarly, the Organization of American States (OAS) now also became converted to democracy. Previously, this had been one of the organizations through which Washington had upheld 'friendly regimes' (whatever their political system) in the hemisphere, but from 1991 onwards there was a steady evolution in the formal commitment to democracy, culminating in the signing of the Inter-American Democratic Charter in September 2001. This reaffirmed the goal of promoting democracy in the Americas and specifically provided for suspension of the membership of any state in which there was an unconstitutional interruption of democracy. NATO took a similar line and the 1994 Partnership for Peace programme (establishing a framework for co-operation, mainly with former Warsaw Pact states) stipulated both that any state wishing to join must commit itself to the preservation of democratic societies and that democracy was a condition for full membership.

Finally, a broadly similar evolution was evident in international nongovernmental organizations (INGOs). In the early 1980s, a US government initiative led to the establishment of the National Endowment for Democracy (NED), which channelled funds to four other US-based NGOs, and in 1992 Britain followed suit with the Westminster Foundation for Democracy. This trend was equally apparent in other advanced capitalist countries and was reinforced by George Soros' Open Society Institute. As Paris notes, other INGOs were critical of aspects of this trend, but very few now advocated policies that totally contradicted it, such as development through a centrally planned economy with single party government. While many advocated more radical policies, emphasizing empowerment and participation for example, they still adhered to a broadly Western conception of (liberal)-democracy as the key to both development and peace (Paris, 2004, pp. 32–5).

During the same period there was rapid development in the related area of international human rights. As noted in chapter 1, during the Cold War period the notion of an international human rights regime implicit in the Universal Declaration of 1948 had been constrained (if not stillborn) because of its subordination to state sovereignty and the East-West conflict. In the 1990s this appeared to be changing. The number of states ratifying the International Covenant on Economic, Social and Cultural Rights and the International Covenant on Civil and Political Rights grew from around 90 to nearly 150 during the decade. And in 1993 over 170 countries participated in the World Conference on Human Rights in Vienna. This was the first such meeting for 25 years, and after these discussions the UN General Assembly voted to establish the post of a UN High Commissioner for Human Rights to co-ordinate the UN's work in this field and to promote universal respect for Human Rights (Brown and Ainley, 2005, p. 209). INGOs (and national NGOs) were an important influence upon this development. With a very rapid growth in numbers registered at the UN (Willetts, 1996, pp. 31–59; Brown and Ainley, 2005, pp. 209–10) and a changed conception of their role (see chapter 3), the combined effect of NGOs' activities was also to increase the pressure for a strengthening of the legal framework for the prosecution of individual perpetrators of war crimes. There was thus substantial NGO involvement in the Coalition for an International Criminal Court.

The agenda for this was subsequently shaped by the 'ethnic cleansing' in Bosnia-Herzegovina and the genocide in Rwanda (see below) and the *ad hoc* tribunals that were established by the Security Council to deal with them— the International Criminal Tribunal for Yugoslavia (ICTY) in 1993 and the International Criminal Tribunal for Rwanda (ICTR) the next year. Both these tribunals were deeply flawed (Forsyth, 2006, pp. 96–106), but they established some legal precedents that were carried into the International Criminal Court

(ICC). Until the 1990s, the notion of a 'war crime' had been that of a crime carried out in an inter-state war. However, the ICTY was also empowered to prosecute people for crimes against humanity within an *intra-state* war, while the ICTR did not even refer to war. This implied that such crimes could also take place in peace-time and within a state. The trial of Jean Kambanda, formerly Prime Minister of Rwanda, for genocide also established precedents for government leaders to be held responsible for atrocities committed while in office.[2]

All this influenced the campaign for an ICC, which was established in a conference in Rome in 1998. After the founding statute was ratified by 60 states, it came into effect in July 2002, with powers to prosecute acts of genocide, crimes against humanity, and war crimes.[3] It followed the ICTY and ICTR in holding that prosecutable crimes against humanity or acts of genocide covered offences both in intra-state wars and in times of peace, and no exceptions were made for people holding particular positions within a state. Cases could be referred to the Court by states that had ratified the ICC statute, the Security Council, or the Prosecutor. In addition non-signatory states, NGOs and individuals could also petition the Prosecutor to begin an investigation.

An allied development in international human rights protection was in the field of 'universal jurisdiction'. In this respect, the decision of the British House of Lords in 1999 to allow the extradition of General Pinochet to Spain for trial on charges of state-sponsored murder and torture of Spanish nationals while he had been head of state in Chile was very significant. Although he was subsequently released by the Home Secretary (on grounds of ill health), the House of Lords decision did establish a precedent that a former Head of State could be extradited for such crimes. In other words, there were limits to the protection offered by state sovereignty (Sands, 2006, pp. 23–45).[4]

[2] Kambanda had been arrested in July 1997 and was convicted of crimes against humanity and sentenced to life imprisonment by the ICTR on 4 September 1998. He later appealed, but the Appeal Court maintained its original judgement and sentence.
[3] It would also be able to prosecute the crime of aggression, but only if a definition of this could be agreed, which was never likely, particularly after the intervention in Kosovo.
[4] However, the limitation in the House of Lords ruling was that sovereign immunity would have applied had Pinochet still been Head of State. More recently, the extradition and trial of Charles Taylor, former head of state in Liberia, to Sierra Leone reinforced this trend. From 2003 the US exerted pressure and inducements on Nigeria to surrender Taylor, although he had been exiled there under a peace agreement, so that he could stand

Despite these developments in establishing a stronger international human rights regime, it was not, of course, entirely clear that the trend was in this direction, for some key states always had deep reservations. Thus China and the United States refused to accept the Rome Statute establishing the ICC in 1998 and, of the five permanent members of the Security Council, only France and the UK have ratified it. The United States has also opposed universal jurisdiction, instead advocating a strengthening of domestic legal systems to prosecute for human rights violations under national laws. Nevertheless, during the 1990s there were good reasons for believing that there was a trend towards the establishment of a stronger international legal regime.

During the period 1995 to 2000 the US Government supported the establishment of the ICC, but always argued that it should be controlled by the Security Council or that US officials and nationals should be exempted from prosecution. On the final day of the Clinton administration the US government signed the treaty, but claimed that it had fundamental flaws and would not be sent to the Senate. Throughout this period there were good reasons for believing that Clinton was pandering to Republican opposition to constraints on US autonomy and that a new Democratic administration might eventually sign up, perhaps after extracting further concessions. However, Bush immediately renounced the statute and adopted a policy of total opposition to the ICC, and was soon putting great pressure on all those who signed it to agree to the exemptions sought by the US (Sands, 2006, pp. 54–68). And after 9/11 human rights were subordinated to the 'war on terror'. Russia and China had never wanted a strong international human rights regime in any case and, without the adherence of the US, they had no incentive to support such developments. Russia did sign the ICC treaty in 2000, but has not ratified it, while China has remained adamantly opposed to the Court. It is therefore no longer plausible to suggest that there is a trend in this direction. However, during the 1990s it appeared that there was.

In the 1990s there was thus a convergence between liberal and left-wing themes and many of the (apparent) international policy developments that

---

trial for possible crimes against humanity and war crimes in the Special Court for Sierra Leone. Following an official request by the new President of Liberia in March 2006, Nigeria agreed to hand him over and he was subsequently arrested and taken to Sierra Leone. After the British government pledged to imprison him if he were found guilty, in June 2006, the UN Security Council agreed to send him to The Hague for trial. This began in June 2007, but was then postponed in order to give Taylor's defence team time to prepare; it was resumed in January 2008.

could be observed. This did not mean that the left was uncritical of all that was happening. It opposed neo-liberal economic policies and was conscious of the negative effects of such policies on both developed and developing countries. Many also criticised the model of democracy that was being promulgated by international institutions. Similarly, there were fervent debates about both the concept and the content of human rights. And, above all, liberal and left-wing opinion (like others) would soon be appalled by the way in which the high hopes of 1990 would be shattered by barbaric wars and atrocities.

Yet there were also significant ways in which the progressive 'project' of this era was in harmony with perceived developments in the construction of a post-Cold War order. The *general* movement was apparently towards international co-operation with a redefinition of sovereignty, an emphasis on democratization and human rights, and an increased prominence of NGOs and civil society movements—central elements in left-liberal thinking. Nor was it naïve to believe that the world was moving in this direction, despite the setbacks and disasters. Peace settlements in Central America (Nicaragua in 1989, El Salvador in 1992 and Guatemala in 1996), the Oslo Accords in the Israel-Palestine conflict (1993), the Good Friday Agreement in Northern Ireland (1998) and, above all, the election of Nelson Mandela in the first non-racial elections in South Africa in 1994, could all be seen as positive indications that there was, indeed, progress towards a 'new world order'. It was in this general context that humanitarian intervention was also regarded as both justified and necessary.

## Humanitarian Intervention

The majority of liberal and left-wing opinion tended to view the allegedly humanitarian interventions of the first half of the 1990s through an interpretive framework closely related to the general assumptions elaborated in the previous sections. In other words, the general tendency was to argue that the crises established a moral imperative to intervene in situations where there were massive violations of human rights. But this also meant that the ethical aspect of each crisis was perceived as the issue of overriding significance, while other crucial dimensions of the evolving international order tended to be disregarded.

*Part 1: Cases.* The first case was after the Iraq war, with the provision of a 'safe haven' for the Kurds in 1991; this was followed by Somalia (1992–93) and Bosnia (1992–95). Simultaneously, there was the notorious case of non-intervention at the time of the genocide in Rwanda in 1994. In 1998–99 there was the deeply controversial NATO military action over Kosovo, followed later in 1999 by intervention in East Timor.[5] There were also interventions by the Economic Community of West African States (ECOWAS), through its military organization, the ECOWAS Cease-fire Monitoring Group (ECO-MOG), in Liberia from 1990 to 1992 and in Sierra Leone in 1997–98, which received retrospective authorization as peace-keeping missions from the UN, and which have also sometimes been regarded as humanitarian interventions (ICISS 2001, supplementary volume, p. 166). Some, but not all, of these cases are outlined below, while others, but again not all, are discussed in later chapters. It is therefore necessary to explain this uneven treatment.

The concern here is with episodes that appeared to challenge the existing international norms most extensively and played a major role in establishing the ethical doctrine, and also those that caused particular controversy. Except for a brief reference to the British action in Sierra Leone, the interventions in West Africa are not discussed because they had comparatively little international salience, despite being controversial in the region, significant in the development of peace-keeping by an African organization, and raising important issues about the relationship between a regional body and the UN (Boulden, 2003, Souare, 2006, pp. 149–96). The situation in East Timor is not discussed at all in this chapter, although it will be examined extensively in chapter 6 in relation to the post-conflict international role. It is sufficient to note here that the intervention itself was not particularly controversial at the time. Critics rather noted that the intervention had occurred nearly twenty-five years after the initial illegal occupation by Indonesia (in which there was Western acquiescence and collusion), and suggested that peace-keepers, with robust mandates, should have been dispatched *before* the referendum on independence in 1999 so that renewed Indonesian atrocities following the result might have been prevented. Rwanda is only mentioned very briefly in the main text because, despite the horrific nature of the genocide there and the subsequent impact of the international failure on debates about humanitarian intervention, it did not lead to a significant challenge to conventional doctrine

[5] There was also a form of intervention in Haiti, following the removal of the President, Jean-Bertrand Aristide, in a coup d'état in September 1991. Although the Security Council eventually authorised the use of force to restore him under a Chapter VII resolution on 31 July 1994, intercession by former President Jimmy Carter pre-empted the need for military intervention. In any case, the rationale for the proposed action was to restore an elected government to power (that is, regime change), rather than humanitarian intervention.

THE POST-COLD WAR TRANSFORMATION

at the time. However, international involvement in the pre-genocide period is discussed extensively in chapter 4.

The 1991 war against Iraq neither was, nor was generally claimed to be, an exercise in humanitarian intervention. Since the West had armed and supported Saddam Hussein throughout the 1980–88 war against Iran, despite the evidence of his brutal internal repression (including the massacres of Kurds with chemical weapons), this would have been a hollow claim. In fact, the *casus belli* was Iraq's invasion of Kuwait, although Saddam's human rights abuses were certainly used to reinforce the case for war. However, while many on the left were deeply critical of the diplomacy after the invasion in August 1990 and of the way in which the war was fought, there was little dissent about the development of humanitarian intervention after the military conquest of Iraq.[6]

The French role was particularly important in the development of the ethical argument because Bernard Kouchner, the founder of Médecins sans Frontières (MSF), was now Minister for Humanitarian Affairs. Kouchner had played a key role in promoting the idea that MSF in particular, and humanitarian organizations in general, should abandon the Red Cross tradition of neutrality and impartiality and take sides when necessary (see chapter 3). However, by the late 1980s he had gone further and adopted the concept of a duty (subsequently a right) of intervention (Kaldor, 2001, pp. 4–5)[7]—a phrase used by the French Foreign Minister in the Security Council on 5 April (Wheeler, 2000, p. 142).[8] Subsequently, the UK joined France in arguing that human rights were not simply internal affairs, the British ambassador now citing the previous example of an arms embargo against South Africa because of the apartheid system (Wheeler, 2000, p. 145).

The 'safe haven' policy was of great importance in the evolution of the doctrine of humanitarian intervention because it undermined the sanctity of sovereignty without provoking significant dissent on the Security Council. Meanwhile, acceptance of the policy by left-liberal and left-wing opinion was

---

[6] Criticism of the diplomacy focused on two major issues. First, although the war was formally authorised by the UN under collective security provisions, the US did not allow the UN to make the key decisions as to whether sanctions were working or whether there was any evidence that negotiations would succeed. Secondly, and closely related, the fact that the US (with the UK) immediately prepared for war indicated that there was a decision from the start to 'resolve' the issue through military conflict rather than peaceful means. There was also scepticism about the US motives for the war.

[7] Kouchner's controversial political evolution continued and in 2007 he became Foreign Minister in the right-wing government formed by President Sarkozy.

[8] For a concise critique of the doctrine, see Bowring (2005).

Box 1

*Iraq, 1991*

After the defeat of Iraq in the war following its occupation of Kuwait, in March 1991, the US encouraged uprisings by the Kurds in the North and Shiites in the South, which were put down with customary brutality by Saddam Hussein's Republican Guards. The immediate result was a movement of Kurds to the mountains, with reports that between 400 and 1,000 were dying every day. On 5 April the French Foreign Secretary argued in the Security Council that the Kurdish plight should lead to recognition of a 'duty of intervention' in cases where there were massive human rights violations (Wheeler, 2000, p. 142). This was not generally supported because of the fear that it would undermine the doctrine of non-intervention. However, later on the same day France and Belgium put forward Resolution 688, which was co-sponsored by the UK and the US. The Resolution *demanded* that Iraq immediately end its repression and *insisted* that it must allow 'immediate access by international humanitarian organizations to all those in need of assistance in all parts of Iraq and to make available all necessary facilities for their operations'. This, and the fact that the Resolution also claimed that the current situation posed a threat to 'international peace and security', brought it very close to a Chapter VII enforcement resolution, although it did not mention military enforcement. Media images of the dire position of the Kurds in the mountains continued to influence the evolution of policy in the US, France and Britain. The British Prime Minister, John Major, now proposed the notion of 'safe enclaves' (subsequently changed to 'safe havens') at an EC Summit in Brussels, and this was accepted by the other leaders. Bush was converted to this idea and on 11 April Iraq was instructed not to send its military forces into the Kurdish areas, where coalition officials would distribute humanitarian aid. In a further reversal of US policy, Bush subsequently announced that American military forces would be sent to Northern Iraq to protect the Kurds. This soon evolved into the creation of an increasingly autonomous Kurdish political entity, protected by the so-called 'no fly zone' policed by the US and the UK, and this led to a rapid decline in the death rates of the Kurdish population in the area. Since the proponents of intervention trod carefully, ensuring that they did not provoke a Chinese or Russian veto by specifically challenging the doctrine of state sovereignty, they had been able to bring about a form of humanitarian intervention by agreement. In general, those states that were the most concerned about the possible erosion of the doctrine of state sovereignty tacitly accepted this evolution because they believed that the postwar situation in Iraq constituted exceptional circumstances that did not create a precedent.

Box 2

*Somalia, 1991–93*

In January 1991 President Mohammed Siad Barre, who had been leader for the past 21 years, was overthrown, which led to the collapse of the central state and a clan-based civil war. After the leader of the most powerful faction, General Mohamed Farah Aidid rejected a proposed settlement, heavy fighting began in November.

On 16 January 1992 the ICRC reported that hundreds of thousands of refugees were on the brink of starvation and at the end of the month the UNHCR reported that 140,000 Somali refugees had reached Kenya, with 700 now arriving every day (Chesterman, 2002, p. 140). In the same month the Director of the Office of Foreign Disaster Assistance in the US also declared that the famine in Somalia was the greatest humanitarian disaster in the world (Wheeler, 2000, pp. 178–9). Boutros Boutros-Ghali, the Secretary-General of the UN, then proposed a two-pronged strategy. The first part was an arms embargo under Chapter VII; a Resolution on this (733) was adopted unanimously, based on concern that the situation in Somalia constituted a threat to *international* peace and security. This resolution appeared to accept that an internal situation could constitute an international threat and therefore warranted enforcement action. However, since there was also a refugee issue it was possible to argue that the consequences for stability and peace in the region (which were mentioned in the preamble to the resolution) provided a more traditional justification for a Chapter VII action (Chesterman, 2002, p. 140). The second part of the UN initiative was the dispatch of the Under-Secretary-General for Political Affairs to Mogadishu to arrange a cease-fire, which was theoretically agreed on 3 March. However, this was ineffective and the situation worsened, leading to a second Resolution (746), again adopted unanimously on 17 March. Although this was not adopted under Chapter VII, the Security Council expressed deep concern that the magnitude of human suffering in Somalia constituted a threat to peace and security. This suggested a further shift towards regarding an internal situation *in itself* as a reason for action.

On 24 April 1992, the UNSC agreed to monitor the cease-fire with 50 unarmed observers (UNOSOM I), and Mahmoud Sahnoun was appointed as special representative. Sahnoun devoted his efforts to negotiating with clan leaders, and above all General Aidid, in the belief that humanitarian assistance could reach those in need only with the co-operation of those who controlled the military forces, but in August the US presidential campaign suddenly made the situation in Somalia a high profile issue for the first time, when Bill Clinton took up the issue to highlight Bush's foreign policy failings (Wheeler 2000, pp. 178–9). This led to new media attention, with a general US perception that the warlords were holding aid delivery to ransom and that a more forcible response was necessary.

In the same month the UN agreed to send 3,500 security personnel to protect the humanitarian relief efforts (Operation Provide Relief), but the situation was clearly deteriorating. In October the Secretary-General reported that approximately 300,000 had died since the previous November and that almost 4.5 million of the total Somali population of 6 million were threatened by severe malnutrition, with 1.5 million at immediate risk of death (Chesterman, 2002, p. 141). In late November there was collaboration between Boutros-Ghali and Washington, with the US offering to provide a division as part of a multi-national force under its own control and command. The initial proposal for an enforcement action may have been made by Boutros-Ghali (Barnett, 2002, pp. 36–7), but Bush accepted the idea and lobbied the Security Council to agree to the first ever authorization of a multilateral peace-keeping mission that would not be controlled by the UN (Findlay, 2002, p. 148). Boutros-Ghali also argued that relief operations could only continue through resort to enforcement provisions under Chapter VII of the Charter combined with parallel action to promote national reconciliation.

On 3 December the Security Council therefore unanimously adopted Resolution 794 under Chapter VII, accepting the US offer to organise and lead an operation, which would use all necessary means 'to establish as soon as possible a secure environment for humanitarian relief operations in Somalia' (Chesterman, 2002, p. 142). The next day Bush ordered 28,000 troops into Somalia (out of a total at the peak of 37,000), and US Marines landed on 9 December 1992, taking charge of the United Task Force (UNITAF, also known as Operation Restore Hope) mission.

This was a coercive military action without the consent of the state in question or any specific reference to the ways in which the humanitarian crisis affected peace and security. It secured unanimous support in the Security Council for two reasons. First, there was probably a general conviction that it was a *genuine* humanitarian intervention. Secondly, the absence of any central government in Somalia made it relatively easy for states that were normally opposed to forcible intervention as an infringement of sovereignty to accept that these were 'unique and exceptional circumstances', and these words were included in the Resolution. Nevertheless, the Security Council had now gone one stage further than in the case of Iraq. There the intervention had not been authorised under Chapter VII enforcement procedures, although these had subsequently developed with the 'no-fly zones'. This time Chapter VII had been specifically used for humanitarian intervention.

The degree of success of UNITAF over the next few months remains a matter of controversy. A Refugee Study Group report in November 1994 claimed that it may have saved 110,000 lives, which would suggest that it could certainly be justified on humanitarian grounds (Wheeler, 2000, pp. 188–9). However, more recently it has been estimated that UNITAF saved only about 10,000, with approximately the same number saved by Operation Provide Relief (Seybolt, 2007, p. 54). In any case, the next phase was to be catastrophic. Despite US bravado in December, UNITAF had used minimal force and had not attempted to disarm the warlords, who had co-operated with it in the expectation that it would be followed by a UN force that would be militarily weaker (Findlay, 2002, pp. 166–84). The US, now under President Clinton, was keen to hand over responsibility to the UN and reduce its involvement. This led to a highly contradictory policy when, in March 1993, the Security Council simultaneously agreed a further, over-ambitious extension of a Chapter VII peace enforcement mandate (Resolution 814), with military engagement across the whole country, rather than the more restricted geographical focus of UNITAF, which had in practice been around Mogadishu. At the same time the size of the mission was to be reduced, as was the role of the US within it, and it was to become a UN mission, UNOSOM II.

This reduced force now attempted to disarm Aidid's forces, an action which led in June 1993 to the death of twenty-five Pakistani UN peacekeepers. This was then followed by an escalation of fighting when the US attempted to capture Aidid, leading to a battle on 3 October. In this, and other confrontations, between 625 and 1,500 Somalis (more than half of whom were women and children) were killed by UNOSOM II troops and between 1,000 and 8,000 were wounded (Seybolt, 2007, p. 59, p. 200). Two US military helicopters were shot down and eighteen Americans were killed, with the bodies mutilated and paraded in front of TV cameras. Clinton now declared that American forces would be withdrawn from Somalia by 31 March 1994. In return Aidid declared a unilateral cessation of hostilities against UNOSOM II. Other countries followed the US lead and all UNOSOM II forces were withdrawn in March 1995.

generally assured (whatever attitude had been taken to the war itself), with few raising any issues as to whether this constituted a breach of the non-intervention norm. Although there had been some initial doubts among UN officials and NGOs that were already operating in Northern Iraq, who feared alienating the Iraqi government (Kaldor, 2001, p. 123), there was a general tendency to share the view of the Secretary-General of the UN, Javier Pérez de Cuéllar, who stated in his Annual Report for 1991, 'We need not impale ourselves on the horns of a dilemma between respect for sovereignty and the protection of human rights.... What is involved is not the right of intervention but the collective obligation of States to bring relief and redress in human rights emergencies' (quoted in Chesterman, 2002, p. 205).

The almost simultaneous crisis in Somalia was viewed in a rather similar way, at least in relation to the partial erosion of the non-intervention norm. The *causes* of the Somalian situation will be considered later (see chapter 4), but Box 2 summarises its evolution and the international reaction.

Many NGOs had criticised the role of the United Nations at the beginning of the civil war, for it had withdrawn from Somalia in January 1991 on the grounds that the situation was too dangerous to guarantee the safety of its personnel. It returned in November, but the International Committee of the Red Cross (ICRC) publicly criticised its role for, in the intervening months, humanitarian assistance had depended upon NGOs (Wheeler, 2000, pp. 174–5). This was no doubt significant in prompting Boutros Boutros-Ghali to advocate resolute action the following year. The debacle that ensued would have a devastating impact on Somalia itself and on the subsequent history of humanitarian intervention. The proposals accepted by the Security Council in March 1993 were no doubt unrealistic, and the ways in which they were implemented were ill-conceived, but they were the most ambitious that had ever been proposed. They therefore led to a belief that the UN could combine military intervention, humanitarian assistance, and state building in a new form of peace-keeping. The downing of the US helicopters simply led to the abandonment of the whole mission and, in reality, the virtual abandonment of Somalia itself. What happened in Somalia also ended the US honeymoon with the UN in relation to humanitarian intervention and peace-building (Murray, 2008). All the blame for the failure was attributed to UN incompetence and in May 1994 Clinton announced a Presidential Directive that would severely restrict the conditions under which the US would participate in UN-led missions in future.[9]

Yet Somalia had raised a series of important ethical issues in relation to humanitarian intervention. First, it appeared to secure widespread agreement that (at least in these 'exceptional circumstances') a purely internal situation could justify forcible intervention for humanitarian reasons. Secondly, it opened a wider debate on whether the UN should negotiate with, warlords, about the movement of humanitarian assistance or whether it should use force and become involved in partisan alignments. Thirdly, it linked the question of intervention for humanitarian reasons with a specific project of peace-making and state building. However, the experiences in Somalia also had a major impact upon the subsequent history of humanitarian intervention. In particular, the reversal of US policy meant that it would not subsequently undertake international commitments involving the possible sacrifice of American lives,

[9] It is true that there were severe problems in UNOSOM II's organization, but the US made it extremely difficult for it to operate effectively because of its determination to maintain complete control over its own command decisions. It had therefore never sought a real co-ordination of policy (Findlay, 2002, pp. 194–205).

except when it was pursuing its own perceived interests. This would have appalling immediate consequences for Rwanda (see below) and, in the longer term, would shape the whole nature of both humanitarian intervention and peace-keeping.

The Somalia episode did not undermine the support of liberal and left-wing opinion for humanitarian intervention, although there was a minority opposition amongst the NGO sector, with the director of Human Rights Watch, and a group of others, breaking away to form African Rights in the belief that US military action could be the harbinger of a new form of imperialism (Kaldor, 2001, p. 126, citing African Rights, 1993). But in general, contemporary criticisms focused on two aspects of the intervention. First, there was the question whether the simultaneous pursuit of so many aspects of policy had been over-ambitious and had been based on sufficient understanding of Somalian society.[10] Secondly, and closely related, there was considerable criticism of the US for over-emphasizing military power and taking insufficient care to avoid civilian casualties; for its unwillingness to co-ordinate its policy with others; and for its precipitate withdrawal as soon as it suffered casualties (Findlay, 2002, pp. 204–5).[11] But these criticisms concerned the *nature* of the actions, not the justification for some form of humanitarian intervention.

The genocide in Rwanda began on 6 April 1994, and the appalling failure of the UN to do anything effective to prevent, or even significantly reduce, the massacres, was closely related to the debacle in Somalia and the almost simultaneous withdrawal of US troops from there.[12] Over the next three

[10] Those who formed African Rights felt that Sahnoun's approach had been more sophisticated and effective, even if it had meant compromising with warlords, and that he should have been supported by the UN, rather than sidelined (De Waal, A. 1994, cited in Ramsbotham and Woodhouse, 1996, pp. 208–9). For the UN's own conclusions, see 'UN, Report of the Commission of Inquiry Established pursuant to Security Council Resolution 885 (1993) to Investigate Armed Attacks on UNOSOM II Personnel which led to Casualties among them', appended to United Nations, Note by Secretary-General, UN document S/1994/653, 1 June 1994.

[11] A recent study reinforces these arguments, suggesting that humanitarian organizations had achieved a far greater proportional benefit with a small airlift before the military intervention; that the strategy of attacking Aidid was unjustified; that foreign troops may have killed and wounded as many people after May 1993 as had been saved during the UNITAF deployment; and that the violence that ensued severely curtailed the work that humanitarian organizations could do (Seybolt, 2007, pp. 54–61, p. 236, p. 270).

[12] The French mission, Opération Turquoise, was only authorised by the Security Council on 22 June 1994 (under Resolution 929) to 'contribute to the security and the protec-

months approximately 800,000 Tutsis and Hutu moderates were murdered at a rate of deaths per day that exceeded the Nazi holocaust, and Rwanda would become synonymous with an international *failure* to protect the population from appalling organised atrocities on a massive scale. Above all, this was a failure of the major states, which were aware of what was happening but deliberately played it down, to avoid pressure to intervene as (arguably) they were required to do under the 1948 Genocide Convention. But it was also a failure of the UN itself (including its highest officers), which connived with the major powers in awareness that calls for intervention would be unwelcome. In time all this would be examined and re-examined and, as more details came to light, the evidence of international culpability would increase.[13] Moreover, when the inadequacy of the response was compared with the massive resources

---

tion of displaced persons, refugees and civilians at risk, including through the establishment and maintenance of secure areas'. The motives for the French intervention remain highly controversial and its deployment was far too late to mitigate the genocide. However, it had some humanitarian benefits in limiting the refugee movement into Zaire.

[13] There have been numerous books and inquiries into the causes of the genocide itself and the international response to it. See in particular, *The International Response to Conflict and Genocide: Lessons from the Rwandan Experience*, Copenhagen: Joint Evaluation of Emergency Assistance in Rwanda, Foreign Ministry of Denmark, 1996; the Belgian Senate's 'Parliamentary Commission of Inquiry Regarding Events in Rwanda', 1997; the French National Assembly's 'Mission of Information on the Military Operations undertaken by France, Other Countries and the UN in Rwanda between 1990 to 1994' (the Quilès Commission) 1998; the 'Commission d'enquête citoyenne sur le rôle de la France durant le genocide des Tutsi au Rwanda en 1994' [2004]; the 'Report of the Independent Inquiry into the Actions of the United Nations During the 1994 Genocide in Rwanda' (the Carlsson Report), December 1999; 'Rwanda, the Preventable Genocide: The Report of the International Panel of Eminent Personalities to Investigate the 1994 Genocide in Rwanda and the Surrounding Events' (established by the OAU), July 2000. Useful brief summaries of all these reports, and full references, are in John Bolton and John Eriksson, *Lessons from Rwanda—Lessons for Today, Assessment of the Impact and Influence of Joint Evaluation of Emergency Assistance to Rwanda*, Copenhagen: Ministry of Foreign Affairs, 2004, Appendix 3.

The French role has always been particularly controversial, since France armed and supported the Habyarimana government throughout the period in which the massacres were being prepared. Its subsequent 'humanitarian intervention' following the genocide also effectively protected Hutu extremists. For two recent critical accounts, see Wallis, 2006 and Kroslak, 2007. Before April 1994 the US constantly sought to reduce the size and budget of the peace-keeping mission in Rwanda and when the genocide began, both the US and the UK tried to ensure that this word was not used to describe it (Graybill, 2002, pp. 89–90; Wheeler, 2000, p. 226).

devoted to the interventions in the former Yugoslavia, and particularly Kosovo, questions would be raised about the extent to which the Western powers were really committed to humanitarian intervention, rather than specific interventions in pursuit of their own interests. I will consider the international involvement in the conflict in Rwanda *before* April 1994 in some detail in chapter 4, and will argue that the major powers, and international political and economic policies, contributed to the situation in which genocide became a possibility. If this is so, it follows that any adequate discussion of international responsibility for the situation in Rwanda should relate not only to the failure to prevent or mitigate the genocide, but also to the longer-term international role in the years before it occurred. However, the main point here is that the *immediate* lesson of the genocide, as viewed by the majority of contemporary left-liberal and left-wing opinion, was that the international failure in 1994 *reinforced* the argument that there were circumstances in which humanitarian intervention was a duty. Rwanda was seen as the case *par excellence* in which there had been an abdication of international responsibility, and the conclusion was that this must never happen again. The *failure* in practice was therefore taken as a reinforcement of the ethical imperative for humanitarian intervention.

During the 1990s it was, of course, the wars occasioned by the break-up of Yugoslavia that gave rise to the greatest controversies over both the doctrine and the practice. And it was also over Yugoslavia in general, and Bosnia in particular, that left-liberal and left-wing opinion, particularly in Europe, would be most troubled by ethical dilemmas over humanitarian intervention. In the Cold War period, Yugoslavia had secured considerable support amongst the non-Communist left. With its international non-alignment and domestic policies of self-management and decentralization, many had seen it as offering an alternative model both to the Soviet bloc and to capitalism. This meant that the rise of exclusivist nationalisms in the republics was widely viewed with alarm, and the outbreak of violence was seen as a tragic negation of earlier hopes. This was naturally intensified by the atrocities in the war in Bosnia.

The Bosnian war caused a greater degree of controversy on the left than the previous cases reviewed here. In the light of the subsequent NATO intervention in Kosovo, there was some support for the view that the Bosnian campaign had been part of a US strategy to secure primacy over its Western allies, while simultaneously weakening the EU, marginalizing Russia and seeking to eradicate the state-led socialism of the former Yugoslavia (Gowan, 1999). But the majority of the European left and left-liberals probably viewed it quite

Box 3

*The Yugoslav context and the war in Bosnia*

The break with the Soviet Union in the 1940s led to a situation in which Yugo-slavia was the socialist state most favoured in the West, with relatively generous economic assistance until the late 1970s. However, this then began to change and the subsequent collapse of Communism in the East European states, and their rapid move towards capitalism, created an entirely new situation. By the end of 1989 it was Yugoslavia that was becoming an anomaly by retaining a socialist system. In these circumstances, it no longer retained a privileged posi-tion with the West, as was evident when the IMF provided it with a loan with harsh conditionality terms in January 1990. This, and the attempt by the Yugo-slav President to institute an austerity programme in a situation of economic decline, was to compound Yugoslavia's problems (see chapter 4). But by this time it was also evident that the political system was in crisis as the multi-national state began to unravel.

There were many warning signs of a possible disintegration of the state, accompanied by a growth of ethnic nationalism. Many have viewed Slobodan Milošević's initial exploitation of Serbian nationalist demands in Kosovo in 1987, followed by the withdrawal of Kosovan autonomy two years later, as of primary importance. Others have emphasised the significance of the rise of Croatian nationalism. Questions of social philosophy and economic organiza-tion were also involved in the evolving conflict, with Croatian and Slovenian nationalist forces favouring the introduction of capitalism, while Milošević continued to defend a form of socialism. This was also related to the fact that the two northern republics were the richest areas of the state and that nationalism there was mobilised with the claim that they were subsidizing the poor South and Serbian nationalists and Communists. But however the multi-faceted crisis is interpreted, the decisive events in projecting it into the international arena were the declaration of independence by both Slovenia and Croatia on 25 June 1991 and the attempt by the Serb-dominated Yugoslav National Army to main-tain the existing borders. Up to this point all the Permanent Members of the Security Council had favoured the continuation of Yugoslavia as a single state, but (pre-occupied by the Iraq war and its aftermath) they had done nothing of significance to increase its likelihood. After a brief skirmish Yugoslavia accepted the independence of Slovenia, but very fierce fighting broke out between Croatian forces and the Yugoslav National Army.

During 1991 the incipient tensions amongst the major powers about the Yugoslav crisis had appeared to be contained when the Security Council passed a Resolution (713) on 25 September imposing an arms embargo.[14] There was

---

[14] But this was at the request of the Yugoslav government (still formally representing all constituent Republics), and many non-Western governments made it explicit that their

also co-operation between the EC (represented by the former British Foreign Secretary Lord Carrington) and the UN (represented by Cyrus Vance, formerly US Secretary of State), who succeeded in negotiating a cease-fire, which was reinforced by a Security Council decision in December to send a peace-keeping force. Under this resolution, the Secretary-General was asked to pursue his humanitarian efforts in liaison with the ICRC, UNHCR, UNICEF and other appropriate humanitarian organizations 'to take urgent practical steps to tackle the critical needs of the people of Yugoslavia' (Ramsbotham and Woodhouse, 1996, p. 172). Following the cease-fire on 2 January 1992, the UN Protection Force (UNPROFOR) was formally launched in February and went into action in March. But by then the international disagreements over Yugoslavia had intensified.

The resolution in December had not formally recognised either Croatia or Slovenia, although by now they had *de facto* independence. Since the government in Croatia was based on exclusive ethnic nationalism, and since there was a large Serbian population there, recognition without securing pledges of minority rights would be inflammatory. However, Germany (and Austria) had become increasingly strong supporters of Croatia and Slovenia and in December 1991 Germany 'bounced' the European Community into recognition without any conditions about minority rights. This was in contradiction with the line that Carrington had been taking on behalf of the EC, and also with the position that France and Britain had been taking in the Security Council. But they acquiesced, particularly as Yugoslavia appeared to be the first test of the Common Foreign and Security Policy, which the EC was simultaneously agreeing. It was now that the centre of attention shifted to Bosnia-Herzegovina.

## The War in Bosnia[15]

Bosnia-Herzegovina was a multi-national republic, with the 1991 census showing 43.7% of the population as Muslim (often known as Bosniaks), 31.4% as Serb, and 17.3% as Croat, while the remainder included Jews, Roma and others. Approximately 25% of marriages were inter-communal and in the cities there was a secular multi-cultural climate (Kaldor, 1999, p. 42). However, there had also been a rise of ethnic nationalism, particularly in rural areas, and in the first democratic elections of November 1990, three parties that claimed to represent the three major national groups received over 70% of the votes and controlled the National Assembly. These parties now became the protagonists in the developing conflict. The Croat and Serb parties (backed externally by their fellow

---

support for this action implied no erosion of the sovereignty rule. Since the Serb-dominated Yugoslav National Army was the strongest military force in the area, the embargo itself was controversial as many viewed it as biased in favour of the Serbs.

[15] The official name was Bosnia-Herzegovina, but it became known internationally as Bosnia and this abbreviation is used here.

nationalists in Zagreb and Belgrade) called for ethnic partition, involving population transfers. The Bosnian-Muslim nationalist party, which controlled the government and formed the largest population group, generally sought territorial integrity for the Republic. The turning-point came in February 1992 when the Bosnian-Muslim government held a referendum on independence. Since late 1991 the Yugoslav National Army had been covertly arming Bosnian Serb forces loyal to the extreme nationalist, Radovan Karadžić, who now called on his supporters to boycott the election.[16] Nevertheless, there was an overwhelming vote in favour of independence by the Croat and Bosniak populations.[17] This created an extremely tense situation, and the US now forced the pace.

Having previously argued against recognition of Croatia and Slovenia, the US had reversed its position in late January, arguing that all the republics (that is, including Macedonia and Bosnia) should be recognised. This was against the EC position that Bosnia was not able to constitute a sovereign state, and also undermined its efforts, through a Portuguese mediator, to forestall war. By 18 March the EC had persuaded the three party delegations to agree on a document outlining the principles of a republic, composed of three constituent nations, each with the right to self-determination, and of a regional cantonization of territory, but without commitment to independence. But some Croatian and Muslim Bosnians, supported by the US, then encouraged Alija Izetbegović, the Bosniak leader, to go back on this agreement (Woodward, 1995, pp. 196–7). This, and the apparent US determination to persuade its NATO allies to recognise an independent Bosnia, were perhaps of decisive importance in triggering the ensuing war. The final flashpoint occurred when extremist Serb nationalist snipers fired on peaceful demonstrators, killing one student and dispersing the demonstration on 5 April (see below). The next day the US was able to persuade its allies to recognise Bosnia-Herzegovina as a sovereign state (Woodward, 1995, p. 197). This was also accepted on 20 May 1992 by the Security Council, which recommended the admission of Bosnia to the UN.

The outbreak of war led to 'ethnic cleansing'—forced movement of populations by brutal intimidation and terror tactics. Over the next three years the fighting in Bosnia would lead to the worst bloodshed in Europe since 1945. When a cease-fire, followed by the signing of the Dayton Accords in November 1995, finally ended the war, there were no firm statistics on the casualties, but

[16] Karadžić was subsequently indicted by the International Criminal Tribunal for the former Yugoslavia for war crimes and genocide, but still eluded arrest until 2008, when he was taken to appear before the Tribunal in The Hague.

[17] The Croats voted for independence in preference to minority status in a Serb dominated Yugoslavia. Subsequently, in January 1993, a separate civil war broke out when some Croats attempted to carve out a mini-state in the Croat-dominated region of Herzegovina. This led to the collapse of the Muslim-Croat alignment between May 1993 and February 1994, but it was re-established with an agreement for a Muslim-Croat Federation in March 1994 in a ceremony in Washington.

estimates ranged from 100,000 to 300,000 deaths (Bieber, 2006, p. 29), and the displacement of approximately two-thirds of their populations from their homes. There had also been appalling acts on a mass scale, including torture, rape, and detention. And the Bosnian war would also be associated with the Srebrenica massacre. This exposed the most lamentable failure of UN peace-keeping, when in July 1995 Dutch forces under UNPROFOR II stood by while Bosnian Serb militias took control of the UN 'safe area', separating and killing some 7,000 Bosniak men and boys.

The Bosnian war constantly divided the major powers on the Security Council. From the start the US regarded the Serbian leadership in Yugoslavia as primarily responsible for the war and wanted far stronger support for the Bosnian government. Many Americans therefore called for air strikes and a lifting of the arms embargo soon after the fighting began. However, both France and Britain tended to regard the events in Bosnia as a civil war, rather than a clear case of Serbian aggression, and Russia was supportive of Serbia and anxious to prevent the West from encroaching in the Balkans. Such differences were related to problems in defining the *nature* of the conflict. In theory Bosnia was now a sovereign state, but the internal conflict was obviously related to the wider crisis in the former Yugoslavia. This raised the question of whether intervention, even if requested by the Bosnian government, would simply be a partisan involvement in a political conflict or whether such considerations should be overridden by the need to protect civilians against atrocities.

All this meant that UN resolutions and mandates for peace-keepers were caught up in a constant process of bargaining that often made them contradictory and almost impossible to implement on the ground. For example, on 13 August 1992, the Security Council was able to agree on two resolutions. The first (770), under Chapter VII, authorised Member States to use all necessary means to deliver humanitarian aid to civilians. This call for *enforcement* measures was supported by Russia, but China, India and Zimbabwe abstained. The second (771) demanded that the ICRC and other relevant humanitarian organizations should be granted continuous access to all camps, prisons and detention centres within the former Yugoslavia; strongly condemned violations of international law, including ethnic cleansing; and called for a record of substantial breaches of the Geneva Convention to be compiled (Ramsbotham and Woodhouse, 1996, p. 178). However, France and Britain were providing the majority of forces in UNPROFOR II and, despite the wording of Resolution 770, they were following traditional peace-keeping methods. This meant that they were prepared to use self-defence in order to protect themselves, but would not attempt enforcement against militias to ensure delivery of supplies. In the winter of 1992–93 this protected those at risk from starvation, but did not stop Bosnian Serb forces from shelling areas where there were civilian populations. Nor, despite Resolution 771, did it prevent them from carrying out ethnic cleansing or harassing relief workers.

This led to calls for much more robust enforcement policies, particularly in the US, but in November UNPROFOR II had only 7,000 European troops, an infantry battalion from Canada, and a field hospital from the US. Its brief remained, first, to alleviate the worst consequences of the suffering by delivering humanitarian relief and, where possible by protecting civilians; and secondly, to try to help create conditions conducive to drawing up a peace settlement (Ramsbotham and Woodhouse, 1996, p. 179). The establishment of a 'safe-areas' policy, first the one in Srebrenica in April 1993 and then five others soon afterwards (Wheeler, 2000, pp. 253–4), was an attempt to conciliate those calling for stronger measures. However, this was again a compromise, with the safe areas created under Chapter VII, but without provision for enforcement action. After the breakdown of a temporary cease-fire in May and further Bosnian Serb attacks, the Security Council then authorised enforcement action in June in defence of the safe areas (Resolution 836). Yet this was still interpreted by many members as enforcement to protect UNPROFOR personnel, rather than to protect the civilians. The policy was also inherently confused, since the safe areas were not disarmed, meaning that they could be used for attacks against the Bosnian Serbs, and this reinforced the latter's view that the UN was biased against them, as Boutros-Ghali himself recognised (Findlay, 2002, pp. 231, 265–6). In April 1994 Bosnian Serb forces attacked the safe area in Goražde. In response, NATO now accepted the US position and carried out air strikes, which were intensified in August 1994 (Wheeler, 2000 p. 255). But this did not prevent the collapse of the safe areas, including, as already noted, the massacre at Srebrenica. This failure should certainly not be attributed solely to the peace-keeping forces,[18] but also followed from relatively low troop levels and constantly changing mandates, and these in turn were the result of conflicting perspectives on the war by the major states on the Security Council.

When the Bosnian Serbs attacked Sarajevo in August 1995, the US insisted on a massive bombing campaign. The French and British governments acquiesced in this and Boutros-Ghali endorsed NATO's argument that these air strikes were permitted under the Security Council resolution of June 1993. On 11 September the Russians tried to persuade the Security Council to back a draft resolution condemning the air strikes, but they withdrew because of insufficient support. By now the relative strength of the forces on the ground was also changing. The Bosnian Muslims had received covert arms supplies from several sources and were now recovering ground lost earlier in the war. Croatian forces were also receiving NATO backing, including tacit support for ethnic cleansing with the expulsion of the Serbs from the Krajina (in Croatia). The combination of shifting military forces on the ground and the intensive US air strikes therefore now

---

[18] For a balanced assessment, see Netherlands Institute for War Documentation (April 2002).

brought about a change in Milošević's position, leading to the ceasefire. The Dayton Accords, which followed, would turn Bosnia into a highly dysfunctional 'semi-state' (see chapter 5).

differently, as a result of the event that had triggered the war, and the way in which it was subsequently fought. For on the eve of the conflict, on 5 April 1992 between 50,000 and 100,000 people marched through Sarajevo to demand the resignation of the Bosnian government and the imposition of an international protectorate. Thousands more were prevented from reaching the city by both Serb and Muslim barricades. This was both an expression of a secular multi-ethnic approach to politics and a desperate attempt to prevent the slide into war and partition. Subsequently, many on the left and in international NGOs viewed the ethnic cleansing with revulsion and sought greater international intervention, more robust mandates for peace-keepers, and more effective safe areas. They also regarded the discussions as to whether this was a civil war or an inter-state war as arcane and irrelevant. Instead they believed that the international imperative was to protect civilians and humanitarian workers from paramilitary forces (see below, pp. 69–77).

In some respects, there was therefore an analogy between the situation in Rwanda and that in Bosnia. Atrocities, and particularly those in Srebenica, were seen to epitomise the ethical case for humanitarian intervention. This meant that any alternative considerations—such as possible American ulterior motives for premature recognition of Bosnia, elevating NATO over the UN, or insistence that bombing was the only way of forcing Milošević into negotiations—tended to be disregarded. The limitations of this exclusive concentration on a narrowly defined ethical dimension would be exposed by the intervention in Kosovo.

---

Box 4

*Kosovo, 1998–99*

Two factors about the immediate origins of the intervention in Kosovo were of particular significance. First, relations between the US and Russia were now far worse, with the Russian leadership convinced that the US was intending to expand its influence throughout Eurasia (Buckley, 2001, p. 160). Milošević was one of the few remaining Russian allies in East-Central Europe and this meant that Yeltsin would be much less accommodating than previously in the Security Council. Secondly, unlike Bosnia, Kosovo had never been a separate republic under Yugoslavia, although it had been granted extensive autonomy under a constitutional reform in 1974. Milošević's withdrawal of this in 1989 was a highly provocative act, particularly as approximately 90 % of the population in Kosovo were Albanians, who were overwhelmingly opposed to Serbian rule.[19] The clash of nationalisms there was always particularly intense and by the 1990s it had become intractable. Nevertheless, in constitutional terms any international intervention would clearly breach the formal position of state sovereignty.

Following Milošević's removal of Kosovo's autonomy in 1989, there was renewed discrimination against Albanians in an apparent attempt by Serbians to colonise the province (Independent International Commission on Kosovo, 2000, pp. 41–2).[20] Until 1997 the Kosovar Albanians practised non-violent resistance, but at this point the Kosovo Liberation Army (KLA) began to be active. This had begun as an alliance between nationalist groups in the diaspora, with connections to various criminal groups, including drug networks, but they were subsequently joined by people in Kosovo's villages to defend themselves. Most Kosovar Albanians sought complete independence from Yugoslavia, and dominant elements within the KLA also favoured the idea of a greater Albania. Rejecting the peaceful approach, this probably deliberately sought international intervention and carried out attacks on Serbian police, precipitating reprisals against the civilian population. The temporary collapse of the state system in neighbouring Albania in 1997 enabled it to procure arms, ammunition and training across the border and this led to an intensification of its campaign. By 1998 the situation was clearly escalating, particularly following the arrest of a KLA activist and the massacre of 58 members of his family in February (Independent International Commission on Kosovo, 2000, pp. 51–5). There was already involvement by the OSCE and a Contact Group of representatives from the USA, Russia, France, the UK, Italy and Germany, but on 31 March (under Resolution 1160) the Security Council demanded an end to the violence under Chapter VII, determining that the conflict constituted a threat to peace and security. However, it deplored the violence on both sides, calling for a peaceful settlement 'based on the territorial integrity of the Federal Republic of Yugoslavia'. There were no votes against this, but both Russia and China expressed reservations about intervention in domestic jurisdiction and the latter abstained (Wheeler, 2000 p. 259). Clearly, pressure for external intervention

---

[19] The Serbian percentage of the population in Kosovo had declined from 23.6% in 1948 to 9.9% in 1991. This was mainly the result of Serbian emigration and a high Albanian birth-rate (Kosovo Report 2000, p. 39).

[20] The Commission cited reports and monitoring by Amnesty International, the International Helsinki Federation and the Council for Defense of Human Rights and Freedoms, Human Rights Watch, the OSCE, the UN and the Humanitarian Law Center.

was now coming from the US, but there were also signs that Kofi Annan himself was inclining to this view.

On 26 June, he thus told the invited audience at the Ditchley Park conference in Britain that the events in Kosovo were 'reminiscent of the whole ghastly scenario of "ethnic cleansing" again'. Although the conflict was within a single state, he had no doubt that it was a threat to international peace and security and, after expressing his hope that it would be settled peacefully, he ended by making it absolutely clear that, if peaceful means failed, 'the Security Council will not be slow to assume its grave responsibility' (Annan, 1999, p. 15). However, by September it was increasingly evident that the divisions on the Security Council that had been festering in the Bosnian case would now erupt into a major crisis. The US and the UK were seeking a mandate for the use of force, but it was clear that this would be vetoed by China and Russia. On 23 September there was an attempt in Resolution 1199 to bridge this gap. Under Chapter VII it demanded a cease-fire and action to improve the humanitarian situation, insisting that Yugoslavia should take a series of concrete steps. It also threatened that if these measures were not taken, the Council would 'consider further action and additional measures to maintain or restore peace and stability in the region'. Kofi Annan was also asked to report the extent to which both sides were complying with the resolution and on 5 October he expressed outrage about reports of mass killings of civilians. The next day the Security Council met informally to discuss the report and the UK proposed a draft resolution authorizing 'all necessary means' to end the killings. The Russians stated that they would veto any such resolution and three days later they issued a statement 'that the use of force against a sovereign state without due sanction of the Security Council would be an outright violation of the UN Charter, undermining the existing system of international relations' (Quoted by Wheeler, 2000, p. 261).

Despite this, on 13 October, NATO announced its readiness to launch air attacks against Serbian targets, claiming that these were justified on the basis of existing UN resolutions. Faced with this threat, Milošević agreed to allow 1,700 inspectors from the OSCE into Kosovo. Yugoslavia also agreed to accept the establishment of a NATO air verification mission over Kosovo, and to comply with Resolutions 1160 and 1199 (Chesterman, 2002, p. 209). These agreements were then endorsed by the Council on 24 October 1998 (under Resolution 1203). But while the US (supported by the UK) immediately argued that the vote provided sufficient authorization for future NATO action, both China and Russia made it clear that any attempt at UN authorization of force would be vetoed (Independent International Commission on Kosovo, 2000, p. 142, citing Judah 2000, pp. 187–90 and UN Security Council Press Release sc/6597, 3944th meeting, 17 November 1998).

In fact, it was the KLA, rather than Milošević, that first broke the October agreement by moving into areas from which the Serbian forces withdrew, and there was an initial decline in Serbian violence against the Kosovar Albanians.

The KLA actions then led to full-scale counter-insurgency and the trigger for the dénouement was the massacre of 45 Kosovar Albanian civilians by Serbian forces in Račak in January 1999 (Independent International Commission on Kosovo, 2000, pp. 80–1). NATO issued a new warning that it was prepared to take military action, and under this threat, negotiations took place in Rambouillet from 6 to 23 February and in Paris from 15 to 18 March. One of the main American objectives in these discussions was probably to ensure that the agreement would be signed by the KLA and rejected by Milošević (Gowan, 1999, pp. 51–3). Certainly, in February both the US Secretary of State, Madeleine Albright, and the Assistant Secretary, James Rubin, made statements implying this, and the terms of the implementation provisions, allowing NATO to operate throughout Yugoslav territory, thereby effectively creating an army of occupation, could have been designed to provoke a Serbian rejection (Independent International Commission on Kosovo, 2000, pp. 151–9).[21] Whether intended or not, this was the result and NATO launched its bombing campaign on 24 March.

On the same day, at an emergency session of the Security Council, Russia, China, Belarus and India opposed the NATO action as a violation of the Charter. The immediate impact of the military intervention was to intensify the ethnic cleansing, as Serbian forces now marched hundreds of thousands of Kosovar Albanians out of their homes, and during the NATO air campaign approximately 863,000 civilians sought or were forced into refuge outside Kosovo, an additional 590,000 being internally displaced (Independent International Commission on Kosovo, 2000, p. 90). During the next three months, until the Russians induced Milošević to surrender, the unilateral (that is, non-authorised) intervention, through the use of devastating air power, continued to create the most serious international tensions since the end of the Cold War.

The war over Kosovo caused a crisis over the whole doctrine of humanitarian intervention. From the start the situation had raised problematic questions about the extent to which support for the Kosovar Albanians would effectively mean assisting a national movement that was seeking secession from an existing state. But it also led to still greater dilemmas about whether intervention could be justified without UN authorization, about the motives of Western policies, and subsequently about the nature of the military action. There was a widespread belief that a humanitarian action must comply with international humanitarian law, and there were concerns that NATO forces had conducted air attacks with cluster bombs near populated areas; had attacked targets that had no military purposes, such as Serb Radio and Television, heating supply

---

[21] However, the Independent International Commission on Kosovo, 2000 did not make this judgement in its own conclusions. See pp. 159–61.

plants and bridges; had provided insufficient warning to civilians of attacks; and had used depleted uranium in missile heads (Human Rights Watch, 2000, cited in Independent International Commission on Kosovo, pp. 92–4). More generally, while it was clear that the use of force would always mean casualties, many doubted whether high level bombing with a minimal risk to NATO pilots but constant potential danger to civilians could be reconciled with humanitarian principles. Many left-liberal and left-wing advocates of intervention, both opposed the specific action over Kosovo and became more sceptical about the whole doctrine as a result.[22] The Kosovo campaign also exposed an underlying tension, which had already been manifested during the Bosnian crisis, between those who were committed to non-violence and those more inclined to accept the use of force for causes they believed to be justified (Kaldor, 2001, pp. 132–3).

The divisions over humanitarian intervention amongst left liberals and the left as a whole as a result of the Kosovo crisis have still not been resolved. Subsequent chapters will provide a critique of many of the assumptions and policies implemented in the name of the doctrine in this period, and will also suggest some lessons for the future. However, there were many very plausible left-liberal and left-wing arguments supporting the development during the 1990s. The following section discusses three of these.

*Part 2: Arguments.*

a) Ethics and new norms

The most prevalent theoretical framework was grounded in an ethical position placing human rights above all other considerations. This meant that 'states that massively violate human rights should forfeit their right to be treated as legitimate sovereigns' (Wheeler, 2000, p. 12). It also followed that other states should be accorded the moral entitlement to use force to prevent such violations. However, while this fundamental proposition was straightforward, the way in which intervention was justified was often sophisticated and complex.

Asserting an ethical case for intervention obviously raised two questions. First, how was it possible to decide which of the many cases of 'massive'

---

[22] During the war itself many former left-wing advocates of intervention, including Mary Kaldor, were convinced that the bombing was unjustifiable. In a contemporary paper she (and Mient Jan Faber) wrote: 'Unless the international community changes its strategy soon and shifts from war-fighting to humanitarian intervention, the whole notion of humanitarian intervention may be discredited and, with it, the hopes for establishing an enforceable regime of international law' (Kaldor and Faber [unpublished] May 1999).

violations of human rights justified intervention? Many sought to adapt the traditional notion of a 'Just War' to help provide answers to this question. Thus Nicholas Wheeler, whose book *Saving Strangers* (2000) is a seminal work on the subject, suggests that: 1) there must be a 'just cause' (or supreme humanitarian emergency); 2) the use of force must be the last resort; 3) the means used must be proportionate; and 4) there must be a high probability that the use of force will achieve a positive humanitarian outcome. He also elaborated the problems in each of these. For example, the second point involved the need to reconcile speedy action with the requirement that force must always be the last resort, and he stipulated that, if in doubt, state leaders were morally obliged to continue to pursue non-violent means, since the use of force would always produce harmful consequences as well as good ones. Similarly, the third point raised serious issues as to whether, and under what circumstances, civilians might be killed by those intervening for humanitarian purposes, and what calculations needed to be made of whether an intervention would be more or less likely to save lives. In relation to the fourth point, Wheeler's interpretation of a positive humanitarian result was one in which the victims of oppression had been rescued and human rights were protected.

The second key question, to which supporters of the ethical case gave a variety of answers, concerned the location of legitimate authority for making the decision as to whether a particular intervention was justified. This would obviously become particularly important after 1999, with the non-authorised NATO intervention in Kosovo. This raised the issue of whether a group of states could legitimately decide that the Just War conditions obtained, or whether the only body that could do this was the UN. This also provoked the question of whether an intervention could simultaneously be illegal (because not authorised by the Security Council) but ethical.

I shall return to these debates in chapter 6, but they are outlined here simply to illustrate the most widespread form of justification for humanitarian intervention amongst a broad spectrum of liberal opinion. However, the claim was not simply that states *should* forfeit their rights to be treated as legitimate sovereigns because this was a valid ethical principle. It was also argued that this principle was being put into practice because there had been a normative shift. Once again, Wheeler argued this particularly cogently.[23] His aim was to demonstrate that the predominant view about the norms that should govern

---

[23] He continued to defend this position, though perhaps less optimistically, after 9/11 (Wheeler, 2004, pp. 48–51).

international behaviour had undergone a fundamental change since the 1970s. At that stage, the norm had been in harmony with the legal position established in the Charter—that is, non-intervention. He claimed that this was now quite different since it was *widely agreed* that, in circumstances of mass human rights violations, such interventions should take place. In this context, the words of the ambassador of the Netherlands at the UN in defence of NATO's intervention in Kosovo are significant. Acknowledging that his own government had been wrong twenty years earlier, when Vietnam had invaded Cambodia, he continued:

Times have changed, and they will not change back. One simply cannot imagine a replay in the twenty-first century of the shameful episode of the 1980s, when the United Nations was apparently more indignant at a Vietnamese military intervention in Cambodia, which almost all Cambodians had experienced as a liberation, than at three years of Khmer Rouge genocide (S/PV.4011, 10 June 1999, pp. 12–13, quoted in Wheeler, 2000, pp. 296–7).

The argument was therefore that because a normative shift had taken place, the parameters governing the relationship between sovereignty and intervention had also changed. This did not mean that Wheeler believed that states could be trusted to intervene whenever this was necessary, or that they would use justified means when they did intervene, and his book was highly critical of the policies that had been followed in several crises—above all Rwanda and Kosovo. But the lesson that he derived from this was that it was necessary to press for greater solidarity with the victims of genocide or mass murder so that governments should carry out their international responsibilities. As he concluded:

The challenge...for those working in human rights NGOs, universities and the media is to mobilise public opinion into a new moral and practical commitment to the promotion and enforcement of human rights. This change in moral consciousness will not guarantee intervention when it is morally required. What it will do is heighten awareness on the part of state leaders that they will be held accountable if they decide not to save strangers (Wheeler, 2000, p. 310).

b)  International social conflict

A second argument was based less explicitly on ethical claims (although these were certainly also present) than on a theoretical argument about the changing nature of conflict. This was analyzed very effectively by two peace studies theorists, Ramsbotham and Woodhouse, in *Humanitarian Intervention in Contemporary Conflict* (1996).

Drawing on their observations of Somalia, Bosnia and Rwanda, and also literature about other conflicts, such as those in Lebanon, Northern Ireland and Sri Lanka, they argued that 'international social conflict' had now replaced inter-state war as the predominant form of conflict.[24] These were communal conflicts, which became crises of the state and characteristically caused massive human suffering, inviting international intervention. In such conflicts there was no clear distinction between the 'domestic' and the 'international'. Instead the most useful unit of analysis in international social conflict was seen as the communal or identity group (based on religion, race, ethnicity or culture), although possession of the state was normally the 'prize' that was fought for. But social heterogeneity meant that there tended to be a discrepancy between existing state borders and the distribution of peoples and cultures, and there was also a crisis of the contemporary state (particularly in developing countries), which meant that the government became increasingly predatory, partisan and reliant on violence to maintain control. The intensity of such conflicts also tended to be reinforced by relations of belief, such as mutual perceptions of injustice and victimization, with de-humanization of the 'other', and the squeezing out of the middle ground. All this meant that violence could get 'locked in', leading to a massive increase in civilian suffering, displaced persons and refugees (Ramsbotham and Woodhouse, 1996, pp. 86–104).

These authors' analysis has obvious relevance for most of the cases considered in the previous section. However, the kernel of the argument concerned the implications of international social conflict for humanitarian intervention, for Ramsbotham and Woodhouse argued that this must be re-conceptualised. In brief, their argument was that the traditional notion connoted forcible intervention by one state against another state, but that such actions were proscribed by the UN Charter. They claimed that the new conflicts changed all this. First, humanitarian violations were not necessarily being carried out by a state; secondly, conflict inevitably affected other states because it was international, often involving identity groups that crossed boundaries and had allegiances outside the states in which they were based; and thirdly, the international involvement was collective rather than individual.[25] Furthermore, they argued that 'humanitarian intervention' could no longer be equated with

[24] An important influence on this aspect of their work, as they acknowledged, was Azar (1990).

[25] The book was written before the Kosovo war. It argued that the 'lead role' in collective international involvement was given by the Security Council and, in its framework principles for humanitarian intervention, the book stipulated that the principle of legitimacy

*military intervention*, since this was but one of a number of possible forms. Instead, they proposed that humanitarian intervention should be re-conceptualised so that it was understood to involve a whole range of instruments and actions. These covered a spectrum, with the use of military force at one extreme and aid and assistance by NGOs at the other. The objective was to create a humanitarian space in a situation of violent conflict and to use the means that were the most effective in bringing about the desired goals. This meant that in some circumstances—for example, when protecting aid workers from attack—those involved in a humanitarian intervention would need to abandon neutrality and take sides to protect the innocent (Ramsbotham and Woodhouse, 1996, p. 220). But the main goal was to maintain the principle of impartiality and non-discrimination. The purpose of humanitarian intervention was 'effective redress throughout the affected region' and the outcome 'should be to the overall advantage of those in whose name it is carried out' (Ramsbotham and Woodhouse, 1996, p. 226).

As suggested above, there was again an underlying ethical basis for this argument and Ramsbotham and Woodhouse also shared the view that a normative shift had taken place:[26]

[T]he international community, struggling into existence within the nexus of the international society of states, summoned to act in accordance with humanitarian values derived from the possibility of a world community of humankind, but at the same time having to rely on means provided by the most powerful states within the international anarchy confronts the most vicious atavistic forces unleashed by the eruption of international-social conflict. Such is the challenge of humanitarian intervention in contemporary conflict (Ramsbotham and Woodhouse, 1996, p. 224).

Nevertheless, the argument was not couched *primarily* in terms of ethics or norms, but in analytical claims about the changing nature of conflict requiring a changing conceptualization of intervention and sovereignty.

c) Progressive social values

Both of the views discussed above were based on the notion that humanitarian intervention was demanded because, in certain situations, there were massive

---

held that interveners should hold themselves accountable to the international community for their intervention, since it is from the international community that they derive the authority to intervene. This did not make the necessity for UN authorization explicit (Ramsbotham and Woodhouse, 1996, p. 226).

[26] However, it was notable that Ramsbotham and Woodhouse acknowledged that the discourse of 'humanitarianism' might be less politically divisive than that of 'human rights', and they also stressed the importance of a cross-cultural consensus.

atrocities that required action to be taken to end an intolerable state of affairs. Although Ramsbotham and Woodhouse accepted that resolving an international social conflict could take some time and require quite extensive intervention, the emphasis was still primarily upon the intervention as a form of 'rescue' operation. However, there was also a specifically left-wing version of the argument which went beyond this and argued in favour of more extensive intervention on the basis of a particular set of values. This was stimulated, above all, by the experience of the Bosnian war and the way in which this was perceived. It was given a specific form by Mary Kaldor, who played an important role in reflecting and defining a sector of left-wing opinion on the issues.

In the 1980s Kaldor had been active in European Nuclear Disarmament (END), a movement whose dominating figure had been the British historian E.P. Thompson.[27] This had sought to build pan-European opposition to nuclear weapons and had also engaged with dissidents in the Eastern bloc. At the end of the Cold War, END had reformed into a new organization, the Helsinki Citizens' Assembly (hCa). Kaldor became Co-Chair of the hCa, which defined itself as:

[A]n international coalition of civic initiatives, East and West, working for the democratic integration of Europe. Our aim is to bring Europe together at the level of society, to integrate 'from below', to create a transnational network of individuals and groups, with shared values and a shared vision of a humane and outward looking Europe. The hCa acts as a catalyst for debate and a locus for exchange and policy-making. Through a variety of activities, we seek to strengthen civil society, and to widen public debate beyond the level of political elites. In particular, the hCa supports courageous people who are struggling to keep alive civic values in situations of war, chaos and oppression[28] (Helsinki Citizens' Assembly, 1993).

The Bosnian war became a focal point for the hCa's work between 1992 and 1995, with the town of Tuzla appearing to epitomise its values. Here non-nationalist forces had won the 1990 elections and Tuzla was subsequently defended by the local police and local volunteers, continuing to promote the values of a multi-cultural civic society. Throughout the fighting, local energy sources were maintained, and even when the town was cut off the people lived off humanitarian assistance and rent in kind from UNPROFOR and taxation continued to be paid (Kaldor, 1999, p. 55). Kaldor and the hCa played an

---

[27] After leaving the British Communist Party in 1956, Edward Palmer Thompson (1924–93) became a leading member of the British New Left in its early years. His many books, above all *The Making of the English Working Class* (1963), were enormously influential.

[28] For a more substantial discussion of the role of the hCa and other civil society groups, see Kaldor (2001).

important role in helping to support activists in Tuzla and other non-nationalist oases in Bosnia, particularly as the hCa was given the status of an implementing agency by the UNHCR. This also enabled her, with others, to present views from 'below' to governments and international institutions, including the EU, NATO, the OSCE and the UN. All this led to a theoretical position that was expressed most fully in *New and Old Wars* (Kaldor 1999), which was completed before the Kosovo war.

Like Ramsbotham and Woodhouse, Kaldor argued that the new conflicts (of which Bosnia was an archetype) were quite different from traditional wars. However, there were also some significant differences in her account, for she specifically rejected the notion that the identities in whose name these conflicts took place were, in any sense, primordial. Instead she argued that they arose in an era in which the state was being eroded as a result of simultaneous pressures from above and below, and they were based on sections of elites mobilizing support through various forms of xenophobia, chauvinism and racism. The purpose was to *fragment* existing societies and communities and the deliberate strategy was terror and intimidation of civilians, rather than military engagement. The leading figures in this new form of violence constructed networks of criminal and semi-criminal activities that also undermined the notion of a public realm in which normal economic life and accountable forms of politics could be established. Amongst the early victims in such wars were those who stood for inclusive civic society and sought to resist its partition into the particular identities around which mobilization took place.

This analysis was also seen to lead to particular conclusions about humanitarian intervention. For one of Kaldor's key points was that the victims of the new wars were not simply those who were suffering and dying, but universal, inclusive values about rights, justice, democracy and multi-culturalism. This meant that her concept of humanitarian intervention went well beyond what had traditionally been understood by the term. Like Ramsbotham and Woodhouse, in 1993 she argued (with Radhar Kumar) that 'intervention has to be redefined to cope with the new type of conflicts instead of defining the conflicts to fit existing norms of intervention' (Kaldor and Kumar, 1993, p. 27). But although it was claimed that the new form of humanitarian intervention was to protect individuals, what was envisaged went far beyond this. The same article thus claimed:

The implication of our description of the new conflicts is that they can only be ended through the reconstruction of administrative authority and legitimacy. The parties to these conflicts are, by their nature, inherently exclusionary and are therefore incapable of restoring order...In an interdependent world, the demand for homogeneous closed-in states is a recipe for chronic violence. This is why the reconstruction of political authority has to come from outside, from international institutions. And this has to be the goal of humanitarian intervention...

To achieve this, the international community needs to develop new mechanisms for taking over civil authority in situations of extreme disorder....These interventions are a kind of half-house between peace-keeping interventions and a new type of humanitarian intervention. For this reason there has been a revival of interest in the idea of mandates, protectorates, trusteeships etc. These all provide frameworks in which the United Nations takes over political power on a temporary basis, until order can be restored and a democratic process re-established (Kaldor and Kumar, 1993, p. 30).

Further elaboration of the ways in which this might be carried out included discussion of whether it should be under the UN itself, or devolved to a European regional organization; the need for such bodies to nurture and interact with non-sectarian groups; the importance of transforming the content of international security expenditure to cope with such situations in the post-Cold War world; and a demand for a new kind of international economic order. But the overall conclusion was that:

Above all, humanitarian intervention requires a profound change in political morality. The rise of exclusivist movements based on identity politics is the consequence of a political vacuum. The breakdown of administrative authority is the consequence of the loss of credibility by political classes everywhere; their inability to adapt to the post Cold War world. International authority can only be established on the basis of legitimacy; that is to say, the new international authorities have to be respected. This is not just a matter of articulating a new set of humanitarian values. It also involves acting according to those values, and in cooperation with those who are known to stand for those values. This is why support for civic groups is so important. The growth of peace, human rights, women's, environmental and other groups, which are often transnational in nature.... could constitute the beginnings of a new globalist humanitarian political culture, which could provide a political constituency for international institutions. (Kaldor and Kumar, 1993, p. 33)

Certain aspects of this argument and its underlying assumptions are particularly noteworthy. First, there was a very definite view that humanitarian intervention required robust international institutions commanding effective military and civil forms of power, which needed to use necessary force against militias. Secondly, such actions should not be constrained by state sovereignty, which was in any case at least partially anachronistic in a globalizing world. Thirdly, international intervention represented (or could and should repre-

sent) a set of universal values counter-poised to the extreme forms of particu-
larist identity politics expressed in the 'new wars'.

This position involved a complex perspective towards existing international
institutions. On the one hand, there was certainly a call for more powerful and
effective institutions, with the ability to intervene rapidly, with all the necessary instruments. On the other hand, this was combined with a very critical
attitude towards both the existing institutions and their approach. In particular, they were seen to operate on the basis of traditional top-down political
'fixing', rather than engagement with civil society groups. Apart from reducing
the legitimacy of the international institutions themselves, Kaldor argued that
this also meant that political leaders lacked understanding of the nature of the
contemporary conflicts. In the case of Bosnia, this had meant that, instead of
viewing it as a 'new war' in which identity politics was expressed in violence
against humanitarian values, leaders saw it as a conflict between rival primordial nations. By the late 1990s, Kaldor therefore saw two possible scenarios
(epitomised in the different aspects that co-existed in the Dayton Agreement
at the end of the Bosnian war). One would be of partition, the legitimation of
authoritarian nationalism, and sporadic interventions to keep ongoing conflicts more or less under control with the forceful separation of warring parties.
The other scenario, based on her conception of a humanitarian approach,
would be of co-operation among international institutions and civic groups
to build a political and social alternative to nationalism, underpinned by economic reconstruction and a form of peacekeeping based on enforcement of
humanitarian law (Kaldor 1999, pp. 66–8).

## Conclusion

The arguments discussed above were all based on the assumption that the
relationship between sovereignty and human rights had changed so fundamentally that there was now a new acceptance of humanitarian intervention.
Whether the argument was based explicitly on ethical values, or combined
with an analytical claim about international social conflict, or with a call for
political engagement in support of social inclusiveness, these were liberal and
left-wing demands for a further erosion of the sovereignty principle. But this
had never been agreed internationally. Thus when such countries as China and
India accepted the interventions in Northern Iraq and Somalia, they continu-
ally stressed the exceptional circumstances and sought to ensure that no precedents were established. Even so, it was evident that the initial humanitarian

justifications were sometimes subsequently used for quite different purposes. For example, in August 1992 the so-called 'no fly zone', originally designed to protect the Kurds in Northern Iraq, was also established in the Southern zone without any explicit UN authorization, and it was used primarily to force Saddam Hussein to carry out disarmament (Chesterman, 2002, p. 199). And military action in the former Yugoslavia was *always* deeply controversial because it took place in a highly sensitive zone of geopolitical rivalries. The US might have *claimed* that its policy in Bosnia was prompted by humanitarian considerations, but many increasingly viewed this, at least in part, as a pretext for expansion into the Western Balkans while Russia was comparatively weak. The enlargement of NATO to include former members of the Soviet bloc and their involvement in the war over Kosovo reinforced this interpretation, leading to a serious crisis in Russian-US relations. And, more generally, the bypassing of the UN and the unilateral use of massive military power against Yugoslavia eroded the belief in much of the world that the US and its closest allies had any humanitarian motivation.

Certainly, there was much talk at the time about an 'emerging consensus' that intervention was justified to prevent atrocities, but this reflected aspirations and perceptions, rather than reality. This was apparent when, in a speech to the UN General Assembly on 20 September 1999, Kofi Annan argued that the conventional notion of sovereignty was dated and issued a challenge to establish a new international consensus that could combine respect for this principle with effective action to prevent violations 'that offend every precept of our common humanity' (A54/1/1999 p. 48 quoted in ICISS 2001). However, many developing countries now contrasted the treatment of Kosovo and Rwanda and came to view humanitarian intervention as a doctrine that simply served the interests of the main Western states, and particularly the US. Only eight states therefore supported Annan's position on the developing norm in favour of intervention to prevent civilians from wholesale slaughter, and most states addressing the matter were opposed to the idea (Roberts, 2000, p. 17). And when, in May 2000, the British intervened in Sierra Leone to rescue a failing UN mission that had taken over from ECOWAS, bolster the elected government, and defeat a rebel force (the RUF) that had carried out massive atrocities, some saw this as an attempt to re-colonise the country and appropriate its diamonds (Pilger 2000a, cited in Bellamy, Williams and Griffin, 2004, p. 38). It is true that an earlier phase of British involvement had been suspect, involving dealings with mercenary forces, and arms supplies (Kampfner, 2003, pp. 62–73), but on this occasion the intervention by Britain was widely accepted, although it insisted on acting in support of the UN, rather than as part of the UN force. While it was highly effective in defeating the RUF and was welcomed in Sierra Leone, it did not dispel the wider view that the West intervened only when it had material interests at stake.

By now the very term 'humanitarian intervention' had become problematic and the International Commission on Intervention and State Sovereignty (ICISS), established by the Canadian government in September 2000 in response to Annan's challenge, tried to finesse the relationship between sovereignty and intervention by replacing the concept of 'humanitarian intervention' with that of the 'responsibility to protect'. This discourse would eventually be adopted in a new UN Declaration in 2005 (UN 2005). Others, including Mary Kaldor, would eventually bury the notion of 'humanitarian intervention' within a concept of 'human security' (Glasius and Kaldor, 2004). I will discuss these ideas in chapter 6. At this stage, it is sufficient to note that these attempts at re-conceptualization followed from the crisis over the whole notion of humanitarian intervention resulting from the war over Kosovo.

But if that war brought the problems to a head, this was not solely because of the contingent circumstances of this particular crisis, but also because there were some underlying weaknesses in the way in which humanitarian intervention had been conceptualised by much left-wing and left-liberal opinion during the 1990s. These included inadequacies in exploring the relationships between human rights and humanitarianism and acceptance of a very limited interpretation of the latter; a failure to consider the negative impact of the policies of advanced capitalist countries on other parts of the world in relation to the generation of humanitarian crises; and the limited attention paid to the difficulties of the situation *after* an intervention, including the dangers of creating new forms of imperialism. The next three chapters will consider these issues.

3

# Human Rights, Humanitarianism
# and Intervention

During the 1990s humanitarian arguments were the major justification for coercive interventions, but these subsequently receded into the background as the US began to legitimise the use of force on other grounds. The war over Kosovo was of critical importance in this evolution, for Washington was clearly less concerned than its European allies about the primacy of the UN (Chesterman, 2002, p. 46, p. 234). Even Britain had worries over this; James Rubin, Clinton's Assistant Secretary of State and Madeleine Albright's adviser, subsequently recalled: 'There was a series of strained telephone calls between Albright and [Robin] Cook [the British Foreign Secretary], in which he cited problems "with our lawyers" over using force in the absence of UN endorsement. "Get new lawyers," she suggested.' (quoted in Byers & Chesterman 2003, p. 186)

This was resolved (not for the last time), by Tony Blair deciding that Security Council authorization was unnecessary. It also became clear that many European states (including Britain) were more concerned than the US to define humanitarian intervention as a distinct category. Blair's much-quoted Chicago speech in April 1999 is significant in this context. This was certainly an unconditional justification for the military action that was taking place, and a coded plea for the US to consider a ground war, but it did attempt to draw a distinction between humanitarian intervention and regime change, and suggested five principles by which to judge the justification in any particular case (Blair, 1999). Subsequently Robin Cook, on behalf of the British government, also tried to persuade the Security Council that it should try to secure some common understanding of the criteria for humanitarian intervention by producing guidelines articulating six principles.[1] This attempt secured active support from the Dutch, and the French also argued that there should be no use of the veto against humanitarian intervention when no vital interests were involved. Opposition to such proposals by China and Russia was predictable, but the US was also opposed to the British suggestion. For the US did not want any international constraints limiting its decisions as to whether or not it wished to carry out military intervention (Stromseth, 2003, pp. 264–5). In retrospect, it thus seems clear that the doctrine of humanitarian intervention had played a significant role in paving the way for the unilateral use of military force, and in American attempts to reduce the centrality of the UN as the basis for legitimacy in legal and normative terms (Matlary, 2006, p. 142, pp. 172–4).

Nevertheless, the Presidency of George W. Bush, the 9/11 attacks and the enunciation of the 'war on terror' brought about a step change. In his introduction to the National Security strategy, published in September 2002, Bush set out its themes. There was, he declared, 'a single sustainable model for national success: freedom, democracy, and free enterprise. In the twenty-first century, only nations that share a commitment to protecting basic human rights and guaranteeing political and economic freedom will be able to

---

[1] The principles were:
1. A greater commitment to prevention. Since intervention was always an admission of failure, there was a need for a strengthened culture of conflict prevention.
2. Intervention could take many forms, with armed force only a last resort.
3. The immediate responsibility for halting violence to rest with the state in which it occurs.
4. Intervention in the case of an overwhelming catastrophe with 'convincing evidence of extreme humanitarian stress on a large scale, requiring urgent relief'; it must also 'be objectively clear that there is no practicable alternative to the use of force to save lives'.
5. Proportionality and effectiveness, so that any 'use of force should be proportionate to achieving the humanitarian purpose and carried out in accordance with international law. We should be sure that the scale of potential or actual human suffering justifies the dangers of military action. And it must be likely to achieve its objectives.'
6. Wherever possible the authority of the Security Council should be secured and no single country could act on behalf of the international community.

    'Guiding Humanitarian Intervention, Speech to the American Bar Association Lunch on 19 July 2000,' by Robin Cook, quoted more fully in Stromseth (2003), pp. 262–3.

unleash the potential of their people and assure their future prosperity' (Bush, 2002).

Since freedom of speech, choice of government, religion, education, ownership of property and enjoyment of the benefits of their labour were rights for every person, in every society, the duty of protecting these values against their enemies is the 'common calling of freedom-loving people across the globe'. The US, he continued, enjoyed a position of unparalleled military strength and economic and political influence and it would use its strength to 'preserve the peace by encouraging free and open societies on every continent'. However, the first and fundamental commitment of the Federal Government was to defend 'our Nation against its enemies'. Since this was a 'war against terrorists of global reach' this would be a 'global enterprise of uncertain duration'. Furthermore, the fact that 'our enemies' were seeking weapons of mass destruction not only meant that new missile defence systems were needed, but that 'America will act against such emerging threats before they are fully formed'. Russia and China would be encouraged to advance towards democracy and economic openness, and 'Finally, the United States will use this moment of opportunity to extend the benefits of freedom across the globe. We will actively work to bring the hope of democracy, development, free markets, and free trade to every corner to the world...'

The US would also deliver greater development assistance 'to nations that govern justly, invest in their people, and encourage economic freedom'. But since no nation could build a safer, better world alone, 'alliances and multilateral institutions can multiply the strength of freedom-loving nations'. Coalitions of the willing could augment permanent institutions and the US 'welcomes our responsibility to lead in this great mission'.

The *National Security Strategy* was significant, not only because of the *practical* impact of the policy, which the world has subsequently experienced, but also because of the underlying ideological and political assumptions. With the 'war on terrorism' as the defining narrative, human rights, democracy, free enterprise, the pre-emptive use of force, an implicit support for regime change, and American leadership over coalitions of the willing were all combined.[2] Whereas Clinton had briefly included humanitarian intervention as a justification for US military action, this was deleted from Bush's National Security

[2] *The National Security Strategy* itself went further still in some areas, for example in explicitly elaborating the case for *unilateral* military action where necessary (US, 2002, p. 6) and arguing that the war on terror justified US opposition to the International Criminal Court (US, 2002, p. 30).

strategy.[3] And, when asserting the necessity for military action against Iraq in 2002–3, humanitarian arguments mainly served as a retrospective justification when no weapons of mass destruction were discovered. The next *National Security Strategy* in March 2006 reiterated many of the same themes, while defending the US record in Iraq and the 'war on terrorism', although it also asserted that there was a moral imperative to take action to prevent and punish genocide, if necessary by armed intervention (US 2006, p. 17).

In these circumstances, the argument that humanitarian intervention had simply been a mask for US-led expansion became increasingly plausible. In the immediate aftermath of the Kosovo war, Chomsky had already ridiculed the idea that the US was genuinely interested in human rights or that its interventions had anything to do with humanitarianism:

The self-described bearers of enlightenment happen to be the rich and powerful, the inheritors of the colonial and neocolonial systems of global dominion: they are the North, the First World. The disorderly miscreants who defy them have been at the other end of the stick: they are the South, the Third World—the "developing" or "less-developed countries" or "transitional economies" ...(Chomsky, 1999, pp. 11–12).

And others on the Marxist left have argued that the entire 'package' of ideas that has underpinned the case for humanitarian intervention must be rejected. David Chandler, for example, has claimed that the whole notion of human rights contained elitist assumptions that privileged the rights-based approach of Western NGOs. This, in turn, then led them to criticise non-Western governments, who were seen as responsible for the suffering of their people, thereby removing this responsibility from international capitalism and justifying intervention. This approach, he asserted, undermined the capacity for autonomy and collective rational decision-making (Chandler, 2002, pp. 118–19). However, this is surely a mirror image of the world-view of American neo-conservatives. As Amy Bartholomew and Jennifer Breakspear have argued, while it is true that human rights diplomacy can be used for imperialist purposes, it is hardly sufficient to provide a rhetorical denunciation that seems blind to the reality of appalling abuses carried out by some governments (Bartholomew and Breakspear, 2004). Similarly, in relation to Chandler's arguments, it may be asked how much capacity for autonomous self-government people have when they are being beaten to death by bru-

---

[3] For Clinton's initial (though superficial) support for humanitarian intervention and multilateralism, see Murray (2008, pp. 29–37).

tal forces prepared to carry out genocide, 'ethnic cleansing' or large-scale massacres.

The argument of this chapter is quite different. While some (on both the right and the left) insist on regarding all the ideas used to justify Western expansion as part of an integral whole, I will suggest the need for some very sharp distinctions to be made. If it is accepted that coercive intervention might be a rare necessity as a final resort, it is crucial to define the occasions on which there could be a conceivable justification as narrowly as possible, and Section 1 seeks to do this. However, it also argues that this may be achieved by elaborating an alternative notion of *humanitarianism* that helps to differentiate between an exceptional case for military intervention and unwarranted interventions. This leads to the discussion in Section 2, where it is argued that the concept of humanitarianism is traditionally defined far too narrowly and that a broader definition may be used to provide a critique of current international policies in relation to developing and transitional countries. Once again, therefore, this chapter confronts a further contradiction in recent theory and practice: between the need to accept the case for military intervention as an exceptional instance of humanitarianism and a simultaneous recognition of the fact that current policies by the rich North may contribute to the generation of humanitarian crises in the South.

## Human rights, regime change and humanitarian intervention

*Regime change.* Those who have sought to justify an extension of international intervention by the US for purposes of regime change have tended to use the discourse of human rights. This has not simply been a rhetorical device by political leaders since the end of the Cold War, for it had also been advocated earlier by some American academic lawyers, who claimed that the Universal Declaration of Human Rights was a fundamental goal of the UN, but that its implementation had been thwarted by international divisions. This was reinforced by 'legal realism', which suggested that law did not depend upon the interpretation of the meaning of the original texts, but evolved with policy and practice (Matlary, 2006, pp. 168–9; Farer, 2003, pp. 61–8). A key figure in this approach, Michael Reisman, was thus already arguing in the 1980s that it fell to states to uphold the human rights commitments of the Charter, since the United Nations itself was failing to do so (Reisman, 1984, cited in Chesterman, 2002, pp. 55–6). After the Kosovo war, he claimed that campaigning organizations and others had now made human rights protection an imperative in international law and, as the Security Council was unable to agree, unilateral action was both necessary and legally warranted in the special case of humanitarian intervention (Reisman 2000, cited in Farer, 2003, pp. 65–7).

In time this evolved into the notion of conditional sovereignty—a view that human rights were of such pre-eminence that full sovereignty was conditional upon respect for them. This was allied to the notion that full international legitimacy also depended upon the nature of the internal regime. Such notions became increasingly widespread in the post-9/11 era, and once again some academics provided justifications for the intervention in Iraq in such terms. Fernando Tesón, a legal philosopher who had argued in favour of humanitarian intervention from an ethical position based on individual rights just before the end of the Cold War (Tesón 1988), now claimed both that the overthrow of Saddam Hussein had been justified and that such actions needed to be approved solely by democratic states, since only they were truly legitimate (Tesón, 2005a, cited in Matlary, p. 105; Tesón, 2005b, pp. 392–413). US political scientists also promoted the idea of 'conditional sovereignty', dependent upon democracy and human rights. This suggested a graduated scale of sovereignty in accordance with internal conditions. It followed that intervention could be justified in cases where there was only limited sovereignty (Krasner, 2002, Keohane, 2003, pp. 275–98). Most left-wing and left-liberal supporters of humanitarian intervention will regard this as a pernicious doctrine, which provides an open-ended potential for military intervention for purposes of regime change.

One attempt to refute—or at least limit—this doctrine on the basis of liberal theory was made by John Rawls in *The Law of Peoples* (Rawls, 1999). The relevance of his work here concerns the relationships he envisaged between liberal and non-liberal societies. For he differentiated between two types of non-liberal peoples—'decent hierarchical societies' and 'outlaw states'. His argument was that the first category could not be legitimate targets for intervention, while there could be a case for this for those in the second category.

Decent hierarchical societies were not aggressive or expansionist and accepted the law of peoples (that is, international law). In their internal affairs, they accepted *some* dissent and *some* human rights, and made an attempt to implement a fair judicial system. Such societies therefore shared some features with liberal-democracy. For example, a hierarchical society might include representation of certain groups in government, or in consultations, but this would not be fully democratic and would not be based on the same underlying political principles as liberalism. Nevertheless, decent hierarchical states should be treated broadly in the same way as liberal states treat one another. This precluded both military intervention and lesser forms of coercion—for example, conditionalities in economic policy. The argument was based on a distinction between *universal* and *liberal* requirements. Those that were universal included freedom from slavery and serfdom, liberty of conscience (but not necessarily equal liberty), and the security of groups from mass murder and genocide. Other requirements, such as free elections, a multi-party system, freedom of expression and association, were part of a Western liberal tradition. There was no justification for any form of coercive intervention to promote a specifically liberal tradition, but this could sometimes be justified in relation to 'outlaw societies' that did not accept the universal requirements (Rawls, 1999, pp. 64–7).

Rawls' specification of conditions under which intervention might be justified was very sketchy, and the picture he presents is very much in the 'ideal-type' form, with little analysis of the dynamic interactions that shape societies in the real world. It also ignores state collapse in which atrocities are carried out by non-state actors. Nevertheless, partly because his position was explicitly *liberal*, it is helpful in providing some intellectual barriers against an open-ended claim that the infringement of liberal freedoms provides a justification for regime change. However, his category of an 'outlaw state' (a term that was frequently applied to Saddam Hussein's regime) still provides a basis for interventions that are essentially based on *political* considerations, rather than humanitarian ones.[4] I believe that it is preferable to attempt to distinguish fully between the notion of regime change, based on political antipathy to a particular state, and humanitarian intervention, arising from a determination to prevent particular humanitarian crimes. A judgement by the International Court of Justice against the US in 1986 is helpful in this respect.

This was during the Reagan era and the crusade against the Soviet Union, as the so-called 'evil empire'. In his State of the Union speech in February 1985 the President himself had thus enunciated the so-called Reagan doctrine as follows: '[W]e must not break faith with those who are risking their lives—on

---

[4] There is certainly an overlap between Rawls' justifications for intervention against 'outlaw states' for such crimes as genocide and mass murder and those specified here as humanitarian violations. But the mode of argument differs and, while they are certainly appalling abuses, I do not regard the existence of serfdom and slavery as sufficient justifications for forceful intervention on humanitarian grounds.

every continent, from Afghanistan to Nicaragua—to defy Soviet-supported aggression and secure rights which have been ours from birth....Support for freedom fighters is self-defense' (quoted in Chesterman, 2002, p. 93). This was his justification for blatant US support for the irregular forces (the Contras) fighting against the left-wing Sandinista government in Nicaragua. The Nicaraguan government responded by taking the issue to the International Court of Justice. This led to a clear judgement against the US in which it was held that the laying of mines in Nicaraguan waters, and American attacks on Nicaraguan ports and oil installations, all constituted the 'use of force'. The US had not denied these actions, but had attempted to justify them by claiming that it was carrying out collective self-defence on behalf of other Central American states. However, the Court ruled that none of the criteria for collective self-defence had been satisfied, as Nicaragua had not made armed attacks on Costa Rica, El Salvador or Honduras, and they had not declared that they had been attacked or invited the US to come to their aid. Nor had the US reported its action to the UN Security Council as a measure of self-defence under Article 51 (Gray, 2000, pp. 54–7, 123–43). The judgement was a rebuff to the US government, which however simply ignored it.

But the Court also made a statement that has particular relevance for the doctrine of humanitarian intervention, declaring that, whatever the US thought of the Sandinista regime:

[A]dherence by a State to any particular doctrine does not constitute a violation of customary international law: to hold otherwise would make nonsense of the fundamental principle of State sovereignty, on which the whole of international law rests, and the freedom of choice of the political, social, economic and cultural system of a State. Consequently, Nicaragua's domestic policy options... cannot justify on the legal plane the various actions the Respondent complained of (Nicaragua (Merits) [1986] ICJ Rep, 133, para 263, quoted in Chesterman, 2002, p. 93).

This has clear relevance for the situation that arose after the late 1990s. For the International Court was adamant that ideological or political opposition to a regime did not justify the use of force against it. This could be used to draw a distinction between humanitarian intervention and intervention to bring about regime change, for humanitarian intervention is designed to curtail or prevent a particular kind of *actions*, rather than to undermine a particular form of politics.

*Human rights violations or humanitarian violations?* Many genuine advocates of humanitarian intervention have sought to justify military measures in exceptional circumstances by talking of situations in which states 'massively violate human rights' (Wheeler, 2000, p. 12) or are guilty of 'flagrant and systematic violations of fundamental human rights' (Semb, 1992, p. 78). However, they often argue that it is difficult or even impossible to provide objective criteria for judging whether a particular situation should be regarded in this way. Wheeler, for example, sought to illustrate relevant cases by high-lighting genocide as the most obvious circumstance, and mentioning state collapse, with famine and the breakdown of law and order, as possible circum-stances justifying an intervention (Wheeler, 2000, p. 34). Yet it is not obvious that all these situations constitute 'massive violations of human rights'. The collapse of law and order might have this effect, but not necessarily; and while the prevention of genocide is certainly the strongest case for a justified inter-vention, it is governed by a separate international convention. Nor is it self-evident what constitutes 'flagrant abuse' or *which* human rights need to be abused to warrant an external intervention. Yet such interventions cannot be justified by gross violations of *any* forms of human rights. For example, the European Convention on Human Rights (justifiably) bans capital punishment as a violation of human rights. It might be argued that, in the case of China or even the United States, these rights are flagrantly violated. But even if military intervention against such countries were possible, it would surely not be justi-fied solely because of their criminal justice systems. Of course, few advocates of humanitarian intervention would *explicitly* argue that every form of human rights violation is equivalent. However, unless there is a specification of some kind, the potential for rationalizing unwarranted interventions will be increased.

Those who advocate intervention on human rights grounds therefore need to demonstrate both that some rights are more relevant than others and quan-tify the scale of the violations that could, in principle, justify military action. Building on work by Henry Shue in *Basic Rights: Subsistence, Affluence and US Foreign Policy* (Shue, 1980; 1996), Eric Heinze has attempted to provide a precise account of the gross violations of a restricted number of rights that could legitimately trigger humanitarian intervention (Heinze, 2004). This is very helpful in distinguishing between genuine humanitarian intervention and abuses of the argument. Heinze argued that the literature on rights (including material in UN proceedings) showed a moral and practical con-sensus that the right to life was essential for the enjoyment of all other rights and therefore the most in need of protection. Violating people's right to life through outright murder, starvation, or by any other means was permanently to deprive them of the possibility of enjoying any other right. Similarly, to violate, or threaten to violate, their physical person—through rape, torture or other abuse—potentially deprived them of this possibility. For no individual could fully enjoy any right that was theoretically guaranteed by society if there was a credible threat of bodily harm of any kind if he or she attempted to exercise such a right (Heinze, 2004, pp. 475–6). On the other hand, the denial of a civil or political right—such as the right to vote—was not *per se* a denial of personal bodily integrity.

From this Heinze concluded that it was violation of bodily rights, rather than of civil or political rights, that could, in some circumstances, warrant intervention. He also sought to identify those circumstances more precisely by defining the notion of a 'gross violation'. Quantifying human suffering or 'counting the dead' was unacceptable, for this would imply that a gross violation could not be identified until after the fact. This would also preclude preventive action when there was good evidence as to what was likely to happen. Instead he suggested three conditions under which abuses of such rights might be considered 'gross violations'. First, there needed to be evidence of *planning*, so that there was a consistent pattern of human rights violations that was the result of an intentional, coherent structure or design; normally this meant that it would be the policy of the government in question, or tolerated by the government. Secondly, there needed to be *breadth*, in the sense that the abusive elements constituted a consistent pattern with a coherent structure. Thirdly, the violations needed to occur *over time*, with repeated occurrence. This led to an overall definition of gross violations as '[T]he threatened or actual violations of life or physical bodily integrity perpetuated or tolerated by authorities in a consistent, deliberate, and widespread manner in order to establish a certain intended social, political or economic arrangement' (Heinze, 2004, p. 477).

Heinze argued that if other threshold criteria were met,[5] there was a moral case for intervention. But a particular strength of his argument was that he maintained that there was also the basis for a legal case. This arose from the very substantial agreement about both the hierarchy of rights and the definition of 'gross violations' in the overwhelming body of international law and jurisprudence. This included definitions from the principle of universal jurisdiction, the Convention on Torture, the Genocide Convention, the Geneva

---

[5] In his case, the other criteria were: (1) use of multilateral authority; (2) force as last resort; (3) proportional force to achieve desired outcome; (4) reasonable prospects for achieving this outcome.

Conventions and additional Protocols, and also jurisprudence and rulings and statutes of the post-war Military Tribunals, the Yugoslav and Rwanda Tribunals and the International Criminal Court.[6]

The importance of this argument is that it offers a relatively precise definition of the kinds of gross violations that could legitimately trigger intervention and (with the other criteria) provides some principles of universal application. Of course, this would not obviate the need for political decision-making about whether the threshold had been crossed in any particular case. But it was certainly an attempt to provide a restricted category for legitimate interventions, which would define these in *humanitarian* terms. It would, for example, be very difficult to justify an intervention designed simply to bring about regime change on the basis of the criteria suggested by Heinze.

The International Commission on International Intervention and State Sovereignty (ICISS, 2001), which will be discussed more fully in chapter 6, also sought to distinguish between warranted and unwarranted military interventions by distinguishing between different kinds of violations.[7] Moreover,

---

[6] However, he did not argue that there *was* a legal basis for humanitarian intervention. His claim was that: 'the empirical similarity between crimes prioritised by international law's prescription of universal jurisdiction, and those gross human rights violations subject to humanitarian intervention suggests a nascent legal basis for the implementation of humanitarian intervention' (Heinze, 2004, p. 486). Whether this development subsequently established a valid legal construct would depend, in his view, 'upon the international community's ability to reconcile law and morality'.

[7] It argued that, in exceptional circumstances, military intervention could be legitimate in order to halt or avert:

- large scale loss of life, actual or apprehended, with genocidal intent or not, which is the product either of deliberate state action, or state neglect or inability to act, or a failed state situation; or
- large scale 'ethnic cleansing', actual or apprehended, whether carried out by killing, forced expulsion, acts of terror or rape.

Actions covered by these definitions included:

- actions defined by Genocide Convention that involve large scale threatened or actual loss of life;
- the threat or occurrence of large scale loss of life, whether the product of genocidal intent or not and whether or not involving state action;
- different manifestations of 'ethnic cleansing', including systematic killing of members of a particular group to diminish or eliminate their presence in a particular area; systematic physical removal of a particular group from an area; acts of terror designed to force people to flee; systematic rape for political purposes of women of a particular group (either as a form of terrorism or means of changing the ethnic composition of that group);

it was categorical in *excluding* certain situations that had been claimed to justify the coercive use of military force. These included actions falling short of outright killing or ethnic cleansing (for example, systematic racial discrimination or imprisonment or other forms of repression), or a military coup carried out in spite of a population's clearly expressed desire for democracy. The ICISS regarded these as serious matters, which might in some circumstances make sanctions a possibility, but it was adamant that military intervention for human protection purposes should be restricted to situations where there was a large-scale loss of civilian life or ethnic cleansing (ICISS, 2001, paras. 4.25–4.26, p. 34). Both Heinze and the ICISS therefore provided distinctions between different categories, which could be used to erect barriers against non-humanitarian interventions.

Yet it is much less clear that the concept of human rights was necessary for this purpose. Heinze's own definition of humanitarian intervention characterises it as 'providing protection to abused individuals, which entails (1) the use of coercive force in another state by outside actors (2) for the stated purpose of halting or averting human suffering, (3) directed against the agents whose actions or negligence is the cause of human suffering ... '(Heinze, 2004, p. 472). This does not refer to human rights, but to 'abused individuals' and 'human suffering'.[8] Similarly, the ICISS used the discourse of 'basic rights', without defining these (ICISS, 2001, para. 1.35, p. 8), but also relied upon the concept of 'human security' for much of its argument (see chapter 6). It did not specifically refer to human rights violations when elaborating the circumstances in which military intervention could conceivably be warranted. There was therefore no necessity to define the gross violations with reference to the terminology of human rights. And I believe that there are major disadvantages in grounding humanitarian intervention in rights.

---

- those crimes against humanity and violations of the laws of war, as defined in the Geneva Conventions and Additional Protocols and elsewhere, which involve large scale killing or ethnic cleansing;
- situations of state collapse and the resultant exposure of the population to mass starvation and/or civil war; and
- overwhelming natural or environmental catastrophes, where the state concerned is either unwilling or unable to cope or call for assistance, and significant loss of life is occurring or threatened (ICISS, 2001, paras 4.19–4.21, pp. 32–3).

[8] It is true that some of the actions to which he referred when specifying the kinds of gross violation that could precipitate a justified intervention had been defined within international human rights law. But others were based in international humanitarian law, law on crimes against humanity, or the Genocide Convention.

One reason for this has already been mentioned: the fact that the same discourse has been used to justify regime change. But these problems are compounded when it is noted that both Heinze and the advocates of regime change used similar language to prioritise particular—but different—rights. In effect, the proponents of regime change regard civil and political rights as pre-eminent, for states that do not respect such rights are accorded only conditional sovereignty. Heinze is arguing on the contrary that, at least in relation to humanitarian intervention, liberal rights are less important than basic or fundamental rights. The discourse of rights in relation to humanitarian intervention is therefore ambiguous, when it is crucial to define a clear and restricted category.

Secondly, the *doctrine* of human rights has been highly contentious, culturally and politically, and the *practice* of Western policies, particularly in the Middle East, has provoked these disputes. This means that in much of the world human rights tend to be seen as (at best) a cover for liberal, capitalist priorities and, in some places, as a form of Islamophobia. If, therefore, humanitarian intervention is ever to be generally accepted as sometimes necessary, the prospects will be greater if it is emancipated from the discourse of human rights. Thirdly (and perhaps paradoxically), there are also some *disadvantages* in dividing human rights into different categories and giving priority to a certain set. As already argued in chapter 2, the Cold War period was vitiated by an often sterile debate as to which were the most important rights—civil and political rights on the one hand or social and economic ones on the other. It was a significant evolution in the thinking of much of the left to escape from this dichotomy and argue that the rights were, in a sense, indivisible. Furthermore, much contemporary thought about development also emphasises the importance of a holistic approach to human rights—particularly in seeking to resist the elevation of liberal rights over others.

It is therefore unhelpful to establish a hierarchy of *rights* in respect of intervention, even if it is a different hierarchy from that normally proposed by Western governments. To suggest that humanitarian intervention is justified in cases of 'gross violations of *human rights*' inevitably implies that these are the worst violations of the most important rights. However, I shall argue later in the chapter that other abuses (such as those caused by acute poverty or starvation) constitute equally important violations, even though these would not provide grounds for *forcible* intervention.

No theoretical distinction between different categories of violation will prevent a powerful state from carrying out a military intervention if it is determined to do so. And even if an intellectual case for limiting humanitarian intervention to the prevention or curtailment of a particular category of violations is accepted, it would still be possible for a particular intervention to be pursued for reasons of regime change (or other unjustifiable motivation) while humanitarian motives were claimed.[9] Nevertheless, the argument that humanitarian intervention may be justified only for the prevention or curtailment of gross violations of life or physical bodily integrity (Heinze and the ICISS) defines some important limiting conditions for its legitimate use, and it provides an intellectual barrier against the manipulation of human rights discourse so as to justify interventions that are not warranted on humanitarian grounds. Moreover, the danger of manipulation is further reduced by the fact that a state's guilt in carrying out or acquiescing in such violations is a *necessary*, but not a *sufficient* condition for humanitarian intervention (other conditions will be discussed in chapter 6).

If the major purpose of this section has been to establish the case for military intervention in precisely defined and limited circumstances, a secondary objective has been to demonstrate that the reasons for such intervention should themselves be regarded as *humanitarian*, rather than arising from considerations of human rights. For my argument is that the conviction that it is necessary to prevent or curtail gross violations of life or physical bodily integrity proceeds from a concept of humanitarianism and is a specific form of humanitarian obligation. However, in order to clarify this it is now necessary to elaborate this concept.

## Humanitarianism

The discussion in the first section sought to define the kinds of circumstances in which a coercive intervention could, in principle, be justified on humanitarian grounds. But this involved making a contentious claim, for it was suggested that the case for military intervention was based on *humanitarianism* itself. This would be contested by many, who would in fact take a diametrically

---

[9] For example, the intervention against Iraq in 2003 was undertaken for a variety of reasons, including the wish to overthrow Saddam Hussein and to advance US power in the region. Yet there certainly could have been a legitimate argument that the atrocities carried out by Saddam—particularly against the Kurdish population—constituted the category of violations that could justify intervention on humanitarian grounds. However, this case would be rather weak because the mass atrocities had occurred many years earlier (mainly in the period when Iraq had been an ally of the West) and the intervention in 2003 was clearly not designed to protect a threatened population.

opposed viewpoint.[10] For example, Fiona Terry claims: 'A "humanitarian war" is an oxymoron: it contradicts the fundamental rationale of humanitarian action to countenance killing in its name. Humanitarian action aims to minimise the harm caused by war; a humanitarian rationale cannot be invoked to justify killing one set of people in order to save another.' (Terry, 2002, p. 242)

I fully understand this position, but maintain that if, in specific circumstances, military action is regarded as the sole means to protect a population from the kinds of violation discussed in section 1, this cannot be considered the antithesis of humanitarianism. I certainly acknowledge that this constitutes an extreme position on the spectrum of humanitarian action, but I am not sure that this position is any more paradoxical than that argued by Terry. For she continues: 'This does not imply that some wars are not just: humanitarian organizations called for military intervention in Rwanda to stop the genocide because it was political, not humanitarian action that was required.' (Terry, 2002, p. 242) This implies that the prevention of genocide is required because of some (unspecified) ethical imperative. My argument is that the grounds lie in humanitarian principles themselves, and that the use of force in such circumstances would itself be humanitarian if there were good arguments for believing that no other response would be effective and that the military means were proportional and conformed to international humanitarian law.

Yet I also want to make further controversial claims about the concept of humanitarianism, arguing that conventional usage is too restrictive and that a wider interpretation entails a critique of current international policies in relation to developing countries.

*The traditional view: humanitarianism as the antithesis of politics and violence.* Although the term 'humanitarianism' is widely used, there is no agreed definition for it and there is a tendency to use it as if it is unproblematic. When it is defined at all, there are two common elements: a reference to 'humans' or 'humanity' and a relational aspect, suggesting that some agent is acting in a 'humanitarian' manner by relieving some form of suffering experienced by other human beings (Minn, 2007, pp. 2–3). More generally, I would suggest that the notion of humanitarianism is normally taken to convey that there is some human essence that links us all irrespective of our differences; and the idea of humanitarian action is seen to spring from a recognition of

---

[10] This point will be considered in chapter 6, when the framework of a 'responsibility to protect' is elaborated.

this fact. But this also effectively defines humanitarianism in terms of a double antithesis, in relation to both politics and violence. According to this view, politics accords significant differences to people based on such categories as ideology, class, nation or religion, or arising from disputes over resources, territory and power, while humanitarianism seeks to transcend such differences in the belief that there is a common humanity.

Similarly, and perhaps still more fundamentally, humanitarianism has regarded violence as its defining 'other'. This has been reinforced by the fact, noted in chapter 1, that the modern form of humanitarian action is normally seen to originate in Henry Dunant's observation of the suffering of soldiers after the Battle of Solferino in 1859, and the subsequent establishment of the Red Cross. Thus, as Birgitte Refslund Sørensen puts it:

> For him, like for present-day humanitarian workers, violence and human suffering... became the evil in which to mirror humanitarian actions. In a sense, the more inhumane the violence, the more humanitarian the attempt to stop it and heal the wounds. But ...the humanitarian and the violent, here, are constructed as two separate and opposing domains, where cruelty and malevolence is safely placed with 'the other', the soldiers, the mercenaries, and warmongers (Sørensen, 2006, p. 6).

This also leads to a construction of humanitarianism as self-evidently positive, altruistic and beneficial, bringing relief to anyone in distress, whether in situations of war or other crises, such as natural disasters or famine.

The principles of the International Red Cross and Red Crescent (ICRC) adopted in 1965 encapsulate this conception of humanitarianism, as stated in seven principles, of which four are the most central (see Box 5).[11] This has been the dominant notion of humanitarianism, evidenced by the fact that the ICRC has been granted a specific role within international humanitarian law. However, from this perspective, recent developments in the role of humanitarian organizations are widely viewed as highly problematic, as they have become increasingly involved in a *political* project and implicated in *violence*.

The most obvious form of politicization has been through the role of international humanitarian organizations in the imposition of neo-liberalism in

---

[11] The other three relate more to the Red Cross itself than to the conception of humanitarianism embodied within it. They are *Voluntary Service*, with the organization not prompted in any manner by desire for gain; *Unity*, with only one Red Cross Society in any one country open to all; and *Universality*, as a world-wide institution in which all Societies have equal status and share equal responsibilities and duties in helping each other.

---

## Box 5

### *Key principles of the International Red Cross and Red Crescent*

#### *The principle of humanity*

The Red Cross, born of a desire to bring assistance without discrimination to the wounded on the battlefield, endeavours—in its international and national capacity—to prevent and alleviate human suffering wherever it may be found. Its purpose is to protect life and health and to ensure respect for the human being. It promotes mutual understanding, friendship, co-operation and lasting peace amongst all peoples.

#### *The principle of impartiality*

It makes no discrimination as to nationality, race, religious beliefs, class or political opinions. It endeavours only to relieve suffering, giving priority to the most urgent cases of distress.

#### *The principle of neutrality*

In order to continue to enjoy the confidence of all, the Red Cross may not take sides in hostilities or engage at any time in controversies of a political, racial, religious or ideological nature.

#### *The principle of independence*

The Red Cross is independent. The National Societies, while auxiliaries in the humanitarian services of their Governments and subject to the laws of their respective countries, must always maintain their autonomy so that they may be able at all times to act in accordance with Red Cross principles.

(Source: XXth International Conference, Proclamation of Fundamental Principles, 1965)

---

developing countries. From the 1980s onwards, as the new Western orthodoxy sought to drive back the state in favour of extensive privatization and marketization, international relief and development NGOs became the favoured vehicle for carrying out this project in conjunction with the UN and UN agencies. However, of still greater relevance here is the fact that international NGOs also became the primary organizations in the international response to civil war in the 1990s (Slim 1997, p. 4, citing Duffield, 1994). Because they were already present in many of the countries concerned and were willing to take major emergency grants from Western donors and to act as sub-contractors for UN agencies, they inevitably became implicated in the multiple policies which Western governments were themselves promoting. In the 'new wars' of the 1990s, NGOs therefore developed agendas and programmes that went far beyond the distribution of emergency relief, as they became involved in such tasks as resettlement and relocation, macro-economic reconstruction and income generating activities, sanitation and health, education and vocational training, demobilization and de-mining, peace-building and human rights protection, and democracy and state-building. Nor did the NGOs, when seeking to feed vulnerable populations and protect them from armed militias in war zones, always maintain the traditional humanitarian stance of impartiality and neutrality (Slim, 1997, pp. 4–5; Sørensen, 2006, pp. 9–10).

Although some commentators and some NGOs and humanitarian workers initially viewed this trend optimistically, in the belief that it demonstrated a conversion of the 'international community' to humanitarianism, subsequently a more pessimistic consensus emerged. The fact that major powers *proclaimed* a commitment to international humanitarianism was thus termed by MSF a 'fig leaf theory' of international action, with the fig leaf worn to cover up a real political strategy of naked neglect (quoted in Slim, 1997, p. 7). However, this was coupled with the fear that, at the very least, this might lead to a corruption of the humanitarian mission because of the new roles it left for the NGO sector to pick up. For example, there was anxiety that broadening the role and interpretation of humanitarian action was likely to increase its manipulation by politicians, with the traditional values and principles on which it stood becoming eroded as humanitarian organizations simply relieved governments of their own responsibilities (Terry, 2002, p. 245). Others have also emphasised the extent to which the expansion of the humanitarian agenda in the 1990s led to a loss of political independence, and have called for a restoration of the earlier tradition (Rieff, 2002, pp. 267–335). Yet while there is no doubt that humanitarian organizations have been manipulated or used by governments (Reimann, 2005, pp. 37–53), I will argue below that the restoration of humanitarian 'innocence' is an illusory solution. Before doing so, it is, however necessary to consider one further, and still more fundamental, critique of the contemporary trend in humanitarianism.

If the traditional conception of humanitarianism defined it as the antithesis of politics and violence, the above criticisms suggest that recent trends have inadvertently forced it into a new terrain that threatens to corrupt it. However, a more radical critique has argued that the new form of humanitarianism is an integral part of the neo-liberal project for global governance, rather than an unintentional by-product of it. I will discuss a particularly influential version of this argument in the next chapter (Duffield, 2001), but several authors have argued that, in relation to many developing countries, relief operations 'are a major contributing force in creating the preconditions for violence and are indeed themselves a kind of violation' (Sørensen, 2006, p. 14). For humanitarian assistance may generate or reinforce the economic marginalization and cultural appropriation of the South, while it is kept in a structurally subordinate position, dependent on external relief and expert knowledge and subjected to different kinds of sanctions and conditions. This perspective thus

suggests that in so far as humanitarianism is part of a globalization process with a liberal agenda, it can be argued to contribute significantly to generating global and local structures of economic marginalization and inequality that may partly be responded to with resistance and violence....In addition to raising our attention to the relevance of considering structural violence, the ... perspective also includes cultural violence. This violation of cultures takes place when humanitarian organizations today stress universal goals and concepts and favour organizations and organizational practices that reflect their own worldview and interests more than they reflect local political cultures, social structures and visions for development (Sørensen, 2006, p. 19).

If, therefore, we were to accept *both* the traditional view of humanitarianism *and* this critique, it would follow that the contemporary role of humanitarian organizations constituted the abdication of universal humanitarianism (Duffield, 1997, cited in Slim, 1997, p. 11). Yet while I accept that international NGOs have indeed become involved in the liberal governance project, sometimes implicating them in structural violence of the kind noted above, I do not believe that the traditional mission is recoverable, or indeed that it was ever unproblematic.[12]

*The perennial dilemmas of humanitarian organizations.* The idea that there is—or should be—a humanitarian conscience that supersedes all differences and should soften all conflicts has an intuitive appeal. Yet there are numerous tensions within the traditional notion of humanitarianism as the antithesis of politics and violence.

---

[12] Nor, however, do I accept the all-embracing critique of Costas Douzinas, who appears to argue that all forms of humanitarianism de-humanise through pity, and this is in fact based on contempt for the 'other' and a view of Western superiority. In his interpretation, humanitarianism appears (necessarily) to be a mask for imperialism (Douzinas, 2007, pp. 51–89).

Many have accepted that there are tensions *in practice* between the Red Cross tradition and the political realm. But the idea of a *non-political* realm itself is problematic. For it is asking all to recognise that there is a sphere of common humanity that supersedes all other differences. However, it is in the very nature of some forms of politics and ideology to deny this. To take the most extreme example, Nazism did not recognise this principle because it would have contradicted its belief that Jews, Roma and people with disabilities were lesser beings who did not deserve to live. But even the very *conception* of the work of the Red Cross was incompatible with Nazism. Thus when, in November 1933, the President of the International Committee claimed that the German Red Cross (which had just become directly responsible to the German Government) would continue with the tradition of 'disinterested assistance to all who suffered', this was already barely compatible with some Nazi descriptions of charity as defeat and unselfishness as weakness (Moorhead, 1998, p. 345). In fact, as Moorhead demonstrates in *Dunant's Dream* (1998), throughout its history the key principles of the Red Cross have been denied (conceptually as well as practically) by various other regimes, including Stalin's Soviet Union, Japan during the Second World War and Mao's China. If this form of humanitarianism can be *denied* by some forms of politics, what does it actually mean to suggest that it is itself non-political? It surely means that this form of humanitarianism seeks to reach out *as widely as possible* to all who do accept the claims of a common humanity. And its chances of gaining such acceptance by bitter antagonists in conflict zones have been dependent upon the recognition that the organization is neutral and that medical care, food supplies and emergency relief will be distributed in an impartial way. Yet it exists in a political world and will be forced to make political choices.

The *practical* difficulties that can follow from a conception of non-political humanitarianism have also been evident throughout its history, particularly in relation to the principle of neutrality. For this may also lead to accusations of complicity with the perpetrators of atrocities. This was already a problem when the International Committee kept silent about the British use of concentration camps during the Boer War at the beginning of the twentieth century (Moorhead, 1998, pp. 139–48) and when it failed to speak out against the Italians' use of poison gas in their war against Ethiopia in 1935–36 (Moorhead, 1998, pp. 305–16). But the most notorious example of the possible consequences of following the principle of neutrality again concerned Nazism. The key moment was at a meeting of the International Committee in October 1942, which decided *not* to launch a public appeal on behalf of the Jews of

99

occupied Europe who were now being systematically rounded up and deported for extermination. Although the twenty-three people at the meeting were well aware of what was happening, it was agreed that such an appeal would jeopardise the ICRC's neutrality and would also be ineffective (Moorhead, 1998, pp. xxv–xxxi, 411–70). While this was a particularly shocking example of following the letter, rather than the spirit, of its own humanitarian principles, it also illustrates the ways in which an avowedly non-political stance could lead to an organization becoming complicit in the most barbaric political crime of the twentieth century. This no doubt followed from motives other than the non-political humanitarian tradition itself (including the political sympathies of some personnel, and a wish by the Geneva-based organization to safeguard Swiss neutrality in the war), but the dilemmas are inescapable.

The origins of Médecins sans Frontières lay in the belief—in fact an unwarranted belief—that during the Nigerian civil war in the 1960s, the ICRC was about to be guilty of another crime of omission. Fearing that the Nigerian government would starve Biafra into submission by denying aid organizations access to the breakaway province, a group of French doctors, of whom Bernard Kouchner was the most prominent, eventually abandoned the Red Cross to form MSF. This organization then broke with the ICRC's principles in two ways. First, it rejected the tradition of discretion and quiet diplomacy, believing that it was sometimes necessary to speak out publicly when its personnel had witnessed one side in a dispute preventing humanitarian aid reaching those who needed it. Secondly, and closely related to this, it would subsequently argue that humanitarian organizations could not be neutral in situations in which one side was clearly responsible for the atrocities (Ignatieff, 2003, pp. 52–5). However, this could obviously create other problems and political dilemmas. In this case the Biafran leadership manipulated aid organizations that continued to work in the region after the withdrawal of consent by the Nigerian government (including the ICRC, which restarted its operations there in August 1968). This work may have made the situation worse (Terry, 2002, pp. 42–3) and it has even been suggested that, by prolonging the war for 18 months, the aid agencies may have contributed to the deaths of 180,000 people (Hanlon, 2006a, p. 38 citing Smillie, 1995, p. 104).

This episode again showed that, even in the distribution of aid, humanitarian organizations are inescapably caught up in politics, and they need to make political decisions which will themselves have humanitarian consequences. In retrospect, it might have been preferable to deny humanitarian assistance on the grounds that the Biafran leader had already been defeated in the civil war and was now lavishing money on the trappings of state-building while his people were starving. But it would also have been difficult to do this, with the Biafran leadership using Western television to portray harrowing images of starvation in the region. In this case it would have been both easier, and ultimately more humanitarian, to maintain the traditional ICRC principle of not operating without the consent of the government. However, in other situations, such as the Ethiopian famine in the 1980s, this would not have helped.

The 'Concert of the Century' launched Bob Geldof to prominence and raised an estimated $ 100 million for those starving in Ethiopia. But numerous sources now argue that the principal causes of the famine in Northern Ethiopia between 1983 and 1985 were counter-insurgency measures against opponents of the government, which cynically exploited the aid so as to move whole populations (Terry, 2002, pp. 48–9). Rony Brauman, a former President of MSF, thus suggests that, by ignoring the causes of the famine and focusing on the disaster, this aid

reinforced the power of the Ethiopian government and handed it undreamed of means to accelerate and intensify its policy of transferring populations. In 1985, the distribution centres became traps where disaster victims from the high plateaux, encouraged by the presence of international humanitarian organisations, came in search of aid before being rounded up by the militia. 700,000 people were torn from their families and villages and forcibly removed to transit centres—death centres for many—before reaching the wastelands where the 'new man', the Ethiopian of tomorrow, was to be born. This radical social surgery, which killed at least 200,000 people in 1985 alone, had become the principal cause of mortality in the country (Brauman, 1997, p. 6).

Brauman certainly argues that the primary responsibility for such failures lies with political leaders, and particularly those in the major states, who *use* humanitarianism as a substitute for identifying and tackling the political causes of such crises. Yet both the Biafran and Ethiopian episodes demonstrate that, before humanitarian NGOs became deeply implicated in the neo-liberal project, their activities already had wider consequences (including political ones), which they cannot ignore. One final example illustrates the way in which this can lead to the most appalling dilemmas.

After the genocide in Rwanda in 1994, refugee camps were established in Zaire and Tanzania to house Hutus fleeing from the new Tutsi-dominated government. However, these were soon controlled by the extremists who had organised the massacres. Aid agencies were in the camps, caring for the sick (many of whom were now suffering from a cholera outbreak) and generally sustaining the population. However, the *génocidaires* were diverting aid to maintain their power and were preventing ordinary people from leaving the camps, which they wanted to use as a base against the new RPF government in Rwanda. In such circumstances, what should humanitarian organizations do? If they withdrew, it was certain that some ordinary people, who were not guilty of the genocide, would die. If they stayed they would be colluding with the perpetrators of the massacres, who were continuing to intimidate and control the population in the camps. Nor would the aid agencies be able to protect the innocent refugees if the Rwandan government and its allies attacked (which they eventually did in Zaire in October 1996, themselves carrying out massacres). Some of the agencies decided to stay in the belief that humanitarian principles meant they had a duty to support those within their care. But others thought that the conditions under which they were working were the antithesis of humanitarianism itself. MSF was divided on the issue, but late in 1994 the French section took the decision to leave.

Fiona Terry was Head of the French Section of MSF in Tanzania and favoured withdrawal. In her powerful book, *Condemned to Repeat?* she defends the decision. Like Brauman, she attributed primary responsibility to the governments of the major states for creating situations in which humanitarian organizations face such agonizing dilemmas (Terry, 2002, p. 214). But in support of the withdrawal decision, she also highlights the crucial importance of understanding the context in which any particular action takes place and the flaws in assuming that certain acts are always good in themselves. While most would agree that it is a profoundly good act to save a life, this changes in the context of a torture chamber, where a doctor is keeping a patient alive in the knowledge that another round of torture will commence. In these circumstances she suggests that, rather than carrying out an ethical act by saving the life of the patient, the doctor becomes an accomplice to torture. She continues: 'Humanitarian action is more than a technical exercise aimed at nourishing or healing a population defined as "in need"; it is a moral endeavour based on solidarity with other members of humanity. If reduced to a technical act it can be employed in the service of any kind of abuse. Thus the *consequences* of humanitarian action must be given equal weight with the *intention* ...' (Terry, 2002, p. 244, my emphasis). Humanitarian principles needed to be weighed against other values in determining which line of action promoted the best overall good. In exceptional circumstances—like those of the Rwandan refugee camps—in which humanitarian action harms those it aims to assist, refusing to subscribe to the humanitarian imperative may promote a better overall consequence for the population. 'To say "let humanitarianism prevail though the heavens fall"...is absurd' (Terry, 2002, p. 244).

In the previous section I suggested that, if humanitarianism is defined as the antithesis of politics and violence, the recent expansion of the role of international NGOs and relief agencies, particularly in the neo-liberal era, may appear to jeopardise the essence of humanitarianism itself. Yet while it is certainly true that this has reinforced the existential *angst* of those involved in humanitarian work, this section has shown that dilemmas about the relationships between humanitarianism and politics and violence have always existed. This has led some observers of repeated experiences of the role of humanitarian assistance in conflict situations to imply an almost complete erosion of the demarcation between humanitarianism and politics. Mary Anderson thus argued that 'aid too often ...feeds into, reinforces, and prolongs conflicts'. She explains:

Experience shows that aid's economic and political resources affect conflict in five predictable ways:

1. Aid resources are often stolen by warriors and used to support armies and buy weapons.
2. Aid affects markets by reinforcing either the war economy or the peace economy.
3. The distributional impacts of aid affect intergroup relationships, either feeding tensions or reinforcing connections.
4. Aid substitutes for local resources required to meet civilian needs, freeing them to support conflict.
5. Aid legitimises people and their actions or agendas, supporting the pursuit of either war or peace (Anderson, 1999, pp. 37, 39, quoted in Hanlon, 2006a, p. 41).

Anderson was not arguing that aid should be denied in situations of potential or actual violent conflict, but proposing, in effect, that it should be *political*. For relief and development agencies should be working to alleviate human suffering and simultaneously promoting a durable and just peace, 'and their aid must support systemic change toward justice rather than simply keep people alive to continue to live in situations of injustice' (Anderson, 1999, p. 7, quoted in Hanlon, 2006a, p. 45). This conception of humanitarianism is contentious (Duffield, 2001, pp. 221–4) because it implies that aid agencies should distribute assistance in relation to their own conceptions of justice and their judgements about the merits of the warring parties in conflict situations.

Yet all decisions about the allocation of resources are based upon underlying assumptions that include political and ethical judgements—even if these are often implicit rather than explicit.

To emphasise the porous boundaries between the world of humanitarianism and the world of politics is to adopt a sceptical approach to the claim that these are (or ever have been) *entirely* separate realms. Those involved in humanitarian work are inevitably caught up in all kinds of political activity. However, this is not to suggest that politics and humanitarianism are identical for, on all of the many possible definitions of each, differences remain. It is more helpful to consider political activity as *primarily* concerned with such issues as power, decision-making, the allocation of resources, and the pursuit of ideology, and humanitarianism as *primarily* concerned with the relief of suffering and the enhancement of human dignity. But inevitably these are overlapping realms, and this also highlights the fact that *all* actions and policies will have both humanitarian and political *consequences*. And even though many humanitarian organizations have recently become implicated in the neo-liberal project to restructure developing countries, there is no way of escaping this in a belief in an illusory golden age of humanitarianism untainted by politics and violence. As Hugo Slim argued several years ago: 'To operate effectively within the international, regional and local politics of today's civil wars, NGO workers must embody a combination of political sophistication, humanitarian principle and operational imagination.' (Slim, 1997, p. 13, citing Slim, 1995)

All this emphasises the inevitable dilemmas faced by humanitarian organizations and humanitarian workers in operating in contemporary world conditions. It is, however, also necessary to reconsider the underlying *concept* of humanitarianism, for this facilitates the task of both observers and participants in developing a critical analysis of current assumptions and practices.

*Re-thinking humanitarianism.* The traditional conception has focused on action to relieve suffering in an emergency, and this is the way in which the notion has tended to be embodied in international law. And there is no clearly specified legal *right* to receive humanitarian assistance except in the form of short-term emergency provisions in situations of conflict.[13] In fact, of course,

---

[13] Article 23 of the 4th Geneva Protocol (1949) refers to the free passage:

> of all consignments of medical and hospital stores and objects necessary for religious worship intended only for civilians of another High Contracting Party, even if the latter

international assistance has also been provided in response to numerous natural disasters and other crises, such as mass starvation. For example, in 2005 some $ 18 billion was devoted to expenditure that may be termed humanitarian assistance (Global Humanitarian Assistance, 2006). This represented a 91% growth in total humanitarian expenditure in the period since 1997 (Stoddard, Harmer and Haver, 2006, p. 16, cited in Weiss, 2007, p. 148), with the aid dispersed through five sets of humanitarian actors: UN institutions, government aid agencies, international NGOs, members of the Red Cross and Red Crescent movement, and local NGOs and other civil society institutions based in countries facing emergencies (Smillie and Minear, 2004, pp. 8–11). This is a substantial expenditure, but there are two major weaknesses in this form of humanitarianism. First, it means that, as far as donors are concerned, the provision of such assistance is effectively *voluntary*. Secondly, it suggests a distinction between emergency relief operations, which are regarded as 'humanitarian', and longer-term development aid. All this is related to the limited nature of the dominant conception of humanitarianism.

This tends to preclude serious consideration of the *causes* of emergencies, as indeed was the case with Dunant's original humanitarian impulse in the aftermath of the Battle of Solferino. Because the emphasis is on the immediate relief of distress and suffering, attention is diverted away from the underlying factors that may be creating the situation. The implication is that the strictly humanitarian concern is not with whether starvation and lack of shelter are caused by an earthquake or by social injustice; the task is to pay attention to the practical consequences for the victims of the crisis. However, this not only precludes discussion of *local* political responsibilities in creating a crisis (as already discussed in relation to the Nigerian civil war in the 1960s and the Ethiopian starvation in the 1980s), but also of international and structural issues. Yet the majority of situations that prompt international humanitarian action, or calls for such action, take place in developing countries, and resource issues have crucial relevance in almost all the situations in which crises arise. Thus even in natural disasters, such as earthquakes, the number of victims is affected by such factors as the quality of housing, the equipment possessed by the emergency services, the infrastructure and transport systems, and the qual-

---

is its adversary. It shall likewise permit the free passage of all consignments of essential foodstuffs, clothing and tonics intended for children under fifteen, expectant mothers and maternity cases.

Article 70 of Protocol 1 and Article 18 of Protocol 2 also specify relief action in conflict situations.

ity of healthcare. Inter-state and intra-state violent conflicts are often precipitated by disputes over scarce resources, including water, grazing land, and minerals. If these issues are not regarded as *integral* to humanitarian concerns, at best humanitarian action is addressing symptoms, rather than causes.

It is, of course, true that some of the more critical views on the recent trends in humanitarian action (discussed in the two sections above) have dealt with the negative roles of humanitarian organizations in promoting neo-liberalism and contributing to violence in developing countries. However, this has tended to provide a critique of contemporary practice on the basis of an explicit or implicit acceptance of the traditional conception. My argument, however, is that the traditional understanding of humanitarianism is itself too narrow, because of the fear that analysis of the *causes* of suffering might jeopardise its mission by appearing partisan. For example, Rony Brauman has suggested that humanitarianism 'posits a universal ethics founded on the conviction that all people have equal dignity by virtue of their membership in humanity' (Quoted in Terry, 2002 p. 19). But this ethical position surely has limited meaning in a situation of massive world inequality, where the average life expectancy in sub-Saharan Africa (the world's poorest region) as a whole has declined over the past three decades and is now 46—32 years less than that in the wealthiest countries (UN, 2006, pp. 263–4, p. 285). Nor does it appear adequate to suggest that recognition of this situation, and action to change it, belong solely to the *political* sphere, while humanitarianism is simply concerned with palliatives. In fact, it is hardly radical to suggest that there is a duty of humanitarian assistance that also embraces development.

In *The Law of Peoples* Rawls argued that 'well-ordered' societies had a duty to assist 'burdened societies'—those that lacked the political and cultural traditions, the human capital and know-how, or the material and technological resources necessary in order to become 'well-ordered' (Rawls, 1999, p. 106). Political leaders, he insisted, must attempt to secure support for this duty of assistance, even if there was limited initial motivation for it, and he hoped that, over time, the affinity between peoples in these different types of societies would become stronger so that they would eventually be moved 'by mutual concern for each other's way of life and culture' and 'become willing to make sacrifices for each other' (Rawls, 1999, p. 113).

Rawls was not using the concept of humanitarianism, and his notion of a duty of assistance is seen as inadequate by advocates of global egalitarian redistribution (Pogge, 2002, pp. 106–8, 111–12, 244). His discourse about 'well-ordered' and 'burdened societies' may also be somewhat archaic and patronizing. Yet his conception of a duty of assistance to overcome fundamental deprivation goes well beyond the notion of international aid as a voluntary reaction to emergencies; it provides a basis for linking humanitarianism with development. However, his approach also shares the weakness of the traditional focus on *emergencies*: its failure to recognise the structural connections between rich and poor countries and the responsibilities of the former in creating or exacerbating the problems of the latter (Pogge, 2002, pp. 196–215). This argument will be developed more fully in chapter 4, with particular reference to neo-liberalism, and here it is necessary only to make the point in general terms.

Concentration on the notion of humanitarian action in response to an 'emergency' implies that tragic events just arise from time to time, presenting those in the wider world with policy dilemmas. From this perspective, the relevant questions appear to take the following form. In cases of potential famine, how much relief, and of what kind, should be distributed? In cases of massacres, should armed intervention take place and, if so, by whom? It is the restrictive definition of humanitarianism that makes it seem as if these are the sole relevant questions. For it is this that presents crisis situations as a problem *there* to which *we* now need to respond in some way (Kennedy, 2004, pp. 135–41). If consideration of the impact of the structure and operation of the international system on poorer regions is regarded as an integral part of humanitarianism, additional questions are raised: in particular, could a different kind of effective action have been taken much earlier? And what has been the impact of international structures and processes on local situations? In fact, a more critical approach uncovers problems about the very notion of an 'emergency', problems that are partially obscured by the classical conception of humanitarianism as emergency assistance. This may be illustrated by the following example.

In recent years there have been constant warnings about the prospect of mass starvation in sub-Saharan Africa, with NGOs and UN agencies appealing for emergency relief. Individuals in richer countries sometimes respond generously to these warnings of crisis, particularly when they are headline news and publicised by celebrities. However, the appeals often fail to emphasise the fact that the 'normal' situation in many of the worst affected areas would be regarded as an appalling disaster should it be replicated elsewhere. For example, in Zambia 59% of adults have stunted growth because of general poverty and insufficient diet, and in Southern Africa as a whole a large part of the population is undernourished, with a high rate of infant mortality, a low life expectation, and all the other indicators of poverty. However, this is not viewed as an emergency, because of the assumption that this is the normal state of affairs for such regions (Smillie and Minear, 2004, pp. 127–32). Yet this suggests that even the way in which an 'emergency' is *perceived* is value-laden. If a particular government in a developing country begins to carry out brutal repression against civilians or if civil war breaks out, this may be regarded as an 'emergency'. If there is persistent poverty and hunger there is no emergency unless the situation deteriorates dramatically and, even then, the extent of the response is a matter for voluntary effort. Yet ongoing poverty will normally result in many more premature deaths than brutal repression or civil war, and will often contribute to the outbreak of violent conflicts over scarce resources.[14] The obvious difference is that the perpetrators of violence may be visible while it appears far more difficult to locate responsibility for long-term poverty and hunger, which are therefore regarded as endemic or even 'natural'.

All this suggests that implicit assumptions about the nature of the world are embedded in perceptions of an emergency. This is closely related to the fact that the traditional definition of humanitarianism tends to ignore the structure and operation of power and inequality in the international system (Farmer, 1997, p. 277, cited in Sørensen, 2006, p. 21). To raise such issues is uncomfortable for the beneficiaries of the current distribution of wealth. Rather than short-term humanitarian assistance being a matter of charity for those who can afford it, recognition of the impact of such factors would reinforce the notion that a commitment to development should be regarded as an international *duty*. This would go beyond the sense of duty envisaged by Rawls, since it would be underpinned by an acknowledgement that rich countries are at least partially responsible for many of the disasters and crises in developing countries.

One potential danger of this enlarged conception of humanitarianism is that it could be used by the North to *reinforce* its control over the South. The argument that those who possess a disproportionate amount of global wealth and power have a particular responsibility to alleviate poverty and inequality could appear to lead to the conclusion that they should intervene directly to micro-manage the ways in which poorer countries conduct their economic and political affairs. This case could conceivably be made either on the basis

---

[14] In fact, even in civil wars more deaths normally come about through hunger, illness and poverty, exacerbated by the violent conflict, than by the fighting itself.

of prudent financial management (rich countries would be transferring resources and therefore might claim a legitimate interest in ensuring that the money is well spent) or on the basis of allegedly superior expertise about strategies for successful development. However, the notion of an international humanitarian duty for both assistance and development does not *in principle* entail any such danger: this would depend on the way in which the duty was carried out in practice. In particular, much could be carried out through trade and debt policies involving no intervention in the domestic sphere, and the 2005 Paris Declaration on Aid Effectiveness set out some important principles designed to enhance the control of recipient countries in national development strategies (MfDR, 2005).

If humanitarianism involves a duty of both immediate assistance and long-term development support by richer countries, its implications may be expressed in two ways. It may be considered in positive terms to indicate what *should* be done. But it may also be examined in *negative* terms in relation to the damaging consequences of the failure to pursue such policies. For rather than carrying out humanitarian policies in the sense outlined above, richer countries have been *compounding* the problems, thereby contributing to the generation of conflicts. This may then create the kinds of circumstances in which a forcible intervention becomes conceivable (and sometimes necessary) on humanitarian grounds. But such interventions cannot adequately be evaluated without reference to the wider context, and to the policies of the advanced capitalist countries that may have contributed to the humanitarian crisis.

## Conclusion

It was noted earlier that both the American right and some of its critics on the left conceive humanitarian intervention, regime change, and interventions to promote human rights, democracy, neo-liberalism, and the 'war on terror' as individual parts of a single package. This chapter, however, has argued against such claims. Section 1 suggested that the category of cases in which humanitarian intervention might be justifiable needed to be very tightly defined. Part of the rationale for this was to erect a barrier (at least in theoretical terms) against interventions carried out to bring about regime change, but the aim was also to preclude forcible intervention, save in very exceptional circumstances, even for humanitarian reasons. In this Section it was thus suggested that, in the last resort, military intervention could be necessary to prevent or curtail threatened or actual violations of life or physical bodily integrity on a gross scale, and that the justifications should *not* be grounded in the discourse of human rights but in a notion of humanitarianism.

This was followed by Section 2, which explored the conventional understanding of humanitarianism and then sought to elaborate an alternative concept. It suggested that the traditional view regarded humanitarianism as the antithesis of both politics and violence, and that because of this recent developments involving humanitarian organizations in both neo-liberalism and new wars were widely regarded as the negation of the tradition. While acknowledging these dangers, I argued that humanitarian organizations had in fact had perennial dilemmas in relation to politics and violence, and that international humanitarian workers needed to acknowledge the wider context in which they were operating, rather than making unrealistic assumptions about regaining an illusory past. However, it was also argued that the traditional concept of humanitarianism has been too narrow, and that international humanitarian duties extend beyond the immediate relief of suffering and must address 'gross violations' of the human person arising from acute poverty, starvation, preventable illness, and premature death. These are certainly not the kinds of abuse that could justify *forcible intervention*, but international action should seek to eliminate them. This means that there is an international duty for both immediate assistance and long-term development.

Yet the existing policies and structural relationships between rich and poor states fail to address these issues and, still worse, they often exacerbate the strains that contribute to the generation of violent conflicts. This is the subject of the next chapter.

# 4

# Inhumanity and Liberalism

An implicit assumption in much discussion of humanitarian intervention and peace-keeping in the West is that conflicts occur in 'other' countries. Coupled with this is often the further suggestion that these are based on deep-seated hatreds, which have existed for generations and are always liable to erupt in violence. At the end of the Cold War, the tendency was to accord pride of place to ethnicity in these fault-lines of conflict, regarding these as primordial,[1] but more recently there has—for obvious reasons—been an emphasis on religious divisions. From this perspective, the task of the so-called 'international community' is therefore seen as *responding* to these conflicts, rather in the way that a doctor treats a patient. This may take the form of conservative treatment (peace-keeping), but in more extreme cases more radical intervention is required (peace-building, sometimes preceded by humanitarian intervention).[2] It is certainly true that many of the 'new wars' *appear* to be based on divisions of identity and are often fought with particular intensity and violence, with

---

[1] Note, however, that this was specifically denied by Mary Kaldor (see chapter 2).
[2] From a rather different perspective, Paul Collier also argues that particular developing countries are primarily responsible for their own problems. However, he does not explain the pathology in terms of ethnicity or religion, but claims that there is a group of about fifty failing states, mainly in sub-Saharan Africa, where civil war, a dependence on the extraction and export of natural resources, and bad governance enable corrupt leaders to reinforce poverty and create a cycle of conflict. Aid cannot help very much and the way forward is for the G8 to concentrate all their development efforts on these countries, by adopting preferential trade policies, new laws against corruption, new international charters, and calibrated military interventions (Collier, 2007).

civilians as primary targets. But what is often lacking in the analysis is recognition of the extent to which such conflicts are partially generated, or exacerbated, by changes in international political economy and the policy prescriptions that accompany them (Orford, 2003, pp. 83–120). Furthermore, this transformation, which began with the rise of neo-liberalism in the 1970s and was consolidated with the triumph of the West in the Cold War, was also evident in the diagnosis of problems once they were manifested and in the peace plans that were applied, whether or not a coercive intervention had taken place.

This chapter explores the negative consequences that policies emanating from advanced capitalist countries and international agencies may have on conflicts within developing and transitional countries. It thus develops the argument in the previous chapter about the non-humanitarian (or often anti-humanitarian) consequences of many of the orthodoxies promoted by the rich North. However, one cautionary point is necessary. In stressing the significance of this negative impact, I am *not* implying that the North has primary responsibility for the generation of the crises in all these Southern countries. In some cases this may be so, but causality is always complex and multi-dimensional and there is no suggestion here that a *general* responsibility for all ills can be located in any one place or with any one phenomenon. Nevertheless, those with the greatest power have the most options available, and alternative choices based on humanitarian principles could be made.

## Neo-liberalism and violent conflict

The new economic orthodoxy established in the Reagan-Thatcher era at the beginning of the 1980s led to a restructuring of economic, social and political relationships within the advanced capitalist countries themselves (Harvey, 2005). But the pressures to reduce the state sector, balance budgets, privatise public assets, and open markets had a far more devastating impact upon developing countries. While the earlier development model, particularly under the influence of the Soviet Union, had been based on the state, neo-liberal theory claimed that this led to inefficiency, patronage and corruption. In its place, the emphasis was on modernization through exposure to market pressures, and an end of protectionism. When all this was coupled with conditions about democracy and human rights tied to aid and loans, the destabilizing effects were sometimes overwhelming. In addition to this, poor countries suffered from the effects of falling commodity prices and a debt crisis, so that it has been estimated that between 1984 and 1989 there was a transfer from the poor South to the rich North of more than $100 billion (Hanlon, 2006b, p. 120).

The impact of such pressures was of course uneven, and it would be misleading to suggest that the impact of neo-liberalism was universally negative, but in many places the overall effect was to increase unemployment, poverty and inequalities in countries that were already amongst the poorest in the world (Harvey, 2005, pp. 98–112, pp. 152–75). Thus by 2002 even the World Bank, which had been zealous in promoting markets, noted that over the two decades up to the late 1990s some two billion people, particularly in sub-Saharan Africa, the Middle East, and the former Soviet Union, had suffered from contracting economies, while poverty had risen. It also noted that 24 developing countries had increased their integration into the world economy, with three billion people enjoying an average 5% growth rate in per capita income. But even in these countries income inequality had not been reduced (World Bank, 2002, Chapter 1, cited in Chua, 2003, p. 245). Neo-liberalism also fragmented the state sector, leading to new networks of power and patronage. These in turn reinforced competition for the control of resources and fertile land, with the effects of climate change exacerbating the problems. Such pressures were mounting throughout the 1980s, but were intensified by the collapse of the Soviet bloc. While the negative impact of these neo-liberal policies for some of the poorest peoples on the planet has been catastrophic, the focus here is on the relationship between these general external pressures and violent conflict.

The view that the conflicts are primordial and endemic is simplistic, but it is certainly true that new pressures are likely to intensify any divisions that already exist. In general, those who seek to mobilise on the basis of identities will be more successful if there are incipient tensions, and there will be a greater potential to re-awaken bitter collective memories if the current situation contains inequalities and discrimination on the basis of those identities (Stewart, 2000).[3] This may be illustrated with reference to the conflicts in Yugoslavia and Somalia.

---

[3] The nature of the more general relationship between inequality and civil war has been a subject of great controversy, particularly following the claim by the neo-classical economist Paul Collier, while director of the Development Research group at the World Bank, that conflicts arise more from greed than grievance (Collier, 2000). This was refuted by economists at the World Institute for Development Economics Research at the UN University (Nafziger and Auvinen, 2002). The evidence is assessed in Cramer (2006).

The death of Josip Tito, the main architect and leader of post-war Yugoslavia, in 1980 accentuated the increasing strains in the system. But external pressures reinforced these fissures, contributing to the re-emergence of exclusivist nationalism, mobilised by key figures. As noted in chapter 2, Yugoslavia had been the socialist state that was the most favoured by the West until the 1970s. However, at this stage aid was replaced by commercial loans, which led to accumulating debts. By 1979 there was an economic crisis and three years later an IMF Recovery Plan stipulated both liberalization and austerity, affecting the subsequent political development of the country as a whole, and intensifying competition between the republics (Woodward, 1995, p. 50; Kaldor, 1999, p. 37). The disparity in wealth between the regions was always politically sensitive, and even in 1963 per capita income in the south of the country had been less than half of that in the north (Chua, 2003, p. 171). Kosovo was always the poorest region, with per capita income in 1952 only 44% of the Yugoslav average, but this declined still further in the era of conflict, standing at 29% in 1980 and only 22% in 1990, with a 40% unemployment rate (Independent Commission on Kosovo, 2000, p. 39).

The increasing differential now meant that the economic pressures reinforced the rise of nationalism, with Slovenes and Croats claiming that they were subsidizing the poorer republics, while the latter resented the higher standard of living in the north. The federation was unable to control the money supply because the republics could print currency themselves, and by December 1989 the monthly inflation rate had reached 2,500% (Kaldor, 1999, p. 37). The IMF had constantly insisted that the federal government must reassert its economic authority over the republican governments, and the collapse of communism in most of Eastern Europe meant that Yugoslavia no longer retained a privileged position in the West (Woodward, 1995, pp. 57–74). In January 1990, the IMF therefore provided it with a loan with harsh conditionality terms, including a full shift to a market economy (Woodward, 1995, pp. 129–30). This led the last federal Prime Minister to try to institute an austerity programme based on 'shock therapy'. But the attempt to remove economic powers from the republics, coupled with a series of constitutional changes, simply reinforced the disintegration of the federal system and the mobilization of rival exclusivist nationalisms (Orford, 2003, pp. 92–6). These were exacerbated by the ensuing crises and, as argued in chapter 2, in Bosnia-Herzegovina in particular comparatively harmonious relationships between the constituent communities were fundamentally transformed in the process. The *extent* of the influence of external pressures in contributing to the crisis that ultimately led to the collapse of Yugoslavia remains a matter of dispute. However, the international political changes at the end of the Cold War, coupled with the new economic orthodoxy, certainly played a significant role in the multi-dimensional process.

Identities in Somalia were not based on ethnicity or religion, but on a powerful clan system. The establishment of a central state was largely a product of external influences attempting to mould Somalian society into a typical pattern of 'modernization'. At the height of Soviet-US competition, both superpowers sought protégés in the Horn of Africa and bolstered dictatorships in Somalia and Ethiopia, and these states exploited East-West divisions opportunistically to acquire weapons and support. Following a humiliating defeat in the Ogaden war with Ethiopia in 1977–78, Somalia soon became engulfed in civil war from the early 1980s onwards. In the midst of this ongoing political violence, the dire economic situation was reinforced by IMF and World Bank policies in the 1980s after the President, Mohammed Siad Barre, had switched from Soviet to Western patronage. This meant devaluation, a reduction of the public sector and the removal of price controls in a state that was already chaotic (Ramsbotham and Woodhouse, 1996, pp. 191–7). The ending of the Cold War, and the region's apparent lack of strategic and economic importance in these new circumstances, led to an abrupt withdrawal of external aid. These cumulative pressures resulted in the implosion of the central state, with the overthrow of Siad Barre in January 1991. But because the Cold War had imposed a particular form of state-building, with heavily militarised central power, the immediate impact was a reversion to clan-based civil war, with rival clans seeking to acquire and control as many resources as possible. Since the country had been flooded with weapons in the Cold War period, they were easily available for the use of the rival clans. The experience under Siad Barre also led to long-term opposition to the whole idea of a central state in Somalian society (Adam, 2004, pp. 253–81). Thus external pressures had reinforced the internal political crisis, fracturing the state along the lines of the traditional clan identities.

In both the Yugoslav and Somalian cases, external policies played a significant part in generating the chain of events leading to humanitarian crises and the subsequent coercive interventions. This inter-relationship between external pressures, particularly by the advanced capitalist countries, and violent conflict in weaker economies is far more general. This has been explored in three books that provide very useful, and different, insights into the phenomenon.

*Ethnic conflict and market dominant minorities.* Amy Chua worked as a Wall Street lawyer on international transactions throughout Asia, Europe and Latin America, and on the privatization of the national telephone company of Mexico. In this capacity she was thus involved in the promotion of the US model of 'free-market' democracy abroad. Her book *World on Fire* (2003) was a powerful argument against this policy, on the grounds that it bred 'ethnic hatred and global instability'.

Chua defined ethnicity as a 'kind of group identification, a sense of belonging to a people, that is experienced "as a greatly extended form of kinship"' (Chua, 2003, p. 15, citing Horowitz, 1985, pp. 51–92). This was a deliberately broad definition, leaving room for the importance of subjective perceptions. She stressed that ethnicity was not a scientifically determinable status and shifted as a result of historical and social conditions. However, she also argued that such identities were rarely constructed out of thin air and normally depended on more 'objective' traits based, for example, on perceived morphological characteristics, language differences or ancestry:

Try telling black and white Zimbabweans that they are only imagining their ethnic differences—that "ethnicity is a social construct"—and they'll at least agree on one thing: that you're not being helpful. Much more concretely relevant is the reality that there is roughly zero intermarriage between blacks and whites in Zimbabwe, just as there is virtually no intermarriage between Chinese and Malays in Malaysia or between Arabs and Israelis in the Middle East. That ethnicity can be at once an artefact of human imagination and rooted in the darkest recesses of history—fluid and manipulable yet important enough to kill for—is what makes ethnic conflict so terrifyingly difficult to understand and contain (Chua, 2003, p. 15).

Chua's definition of ethnicity is certainly open to criticism: for example, the suggestion that there are just two categories of 'black' and 'white' in Zimbabwe is a vast over-simplification, particularly given Robert Mugabe's massacre of thousands of people from the minority Ndebele in Matabeleland in the early 1980s. But the kernel of her argument is that, in certain circumstances, *perceptions* of differences in identity become the fault-lines for conflict. And her key concern is the relationship between 'market dominant minorities' and majorities whose general economic position is vastly inferior.

Her case studies, drawn from across the world, include the Chinese minority in South East Asia, the European 'white' population in Latin America, and Indian and Lebanese minorities in different parts of Africa. But she also includes different groups that both originated in the same continent, where there are market dominant minorities, such as the Tutsis in Rwanda and

Burundi, and the Slovenes and Croats in the former Yugoslavia. She makes three broad claims, which she underpins with considerable empirical evidence. First, she demonstrates that these groups have benefited from inequalities of wealth, income and power that have been upheld by dictatorships or systems that are not genuinely democratic.[4] Secondly, she argues that the introduction of democracy (under external pressures), interpreted solely as universal suffrage and majority rule, *accentuates* the divisions between the market dominant minority and the majority. While the minority will normally seek to resist majority rule as a threat to its position, the majority will often resort to ethno-nationalist mobilization against the minority. Thirdly, the promotion by the United States of neo-liberal economic policies vastly accentuated the differences between the market dominant minority and the majority. The economic elites (or some of them) were able to enter the new international political economy acquiring great wealth, while the majority population often experienced greater poverty than before. Thus the *simultaneous* introduction of a crude form of democracy and a laissez-faire form of capitalism creates an explosive cocktail. This, she argues, has led to horrific outbreaks of violence on ethnic lines, often against the market dominant minority.

Chua may be criticised for trying to squeeze too much into a single explanatory framework and combining analysis with a polemical appeal to the US government to shift its priorities. But this does not detract from her very important point about the relationship between the export of a particular form of capitalist democracy and outbreaks of violent conflict based on identity. The essence of her argument was that 'In the numerous societies around the world that have a market-dominant minority, markets and democracy are not mutually reinforcing. Because markets and democracy benefit different ethnic groups in such societies, the pursuit of free market democracy produces highly unstable and combustible conditions...' (Chua, 2003, p. 9). This meant that:

When free market democracy is pursued in the presence of a market-dominant minority, the almost invariable result is backlash. This backlash typically takes one of three forms. The first is a backlash against markets, targeting the market-dominant minor-

---

[4] In the case of Rwanda this referred particularly to the period under Belgian colonialism (see below, pp. 126–37). Nevertheless, even under the Hutu-dominated state during the Habyarimana dictatorship, many Tutsis went into the private sector, where they received preferential treatment by foreign employers. They also tended to dominate international trade, with many involved in the business sector (Prunier, 1998, p. 76, cited in Spyridaki, 2008, p. 17).

ity's wealth. The second is a backlash against democracy by forces favourable to the market-dominant minority. The third is violence, sometimes genocidal, directed against the market-dominant minority itself (Chua, 2003, p. 10).

*Global governance and new wars.* In *Global Governance and the New Wars* (2001) Mark Duffield reinforces aspects of this argument, although his approach and perspective differ from Chua's. A development specialist, who was also Oxfam's Country Representative in the Sudan for four years during the civil war in the latter half of the 1980s, he makes in this book a critique of the merging of development and security and the way in which aid agencies were incorporated into controlling of the South.

Duffield emphasises the effects of deregulation and privatization in creating new networks and relationships within developing countries. In fact, the weakening of state control sought by neo-liberalism has, he argues, led to the breakdown of the classic notion of the state itself. This has been replaced by a 'neo medievalism', with new forms of power related to emergent economic networks and agencies (Duffield 2001, pp. 161–201), which may be vast operations, involving semi-criminal activities in a shadow economy, 'regulated' by warlordism and other forms of protection. This concept of 'new wars' resembles that of Mary Kaldor (see pp. 73–77 above), but in Duffield's work the emphasis upon the interaction between North and South is much more pronounced, and his evaluation of these networks of power also differs. While Kaldor certainly attributed some responsibility for the creation of the new wars to changes in international capitalism, Duffield regards these as of overwhelming importance. While Kaldor viewed such wars negatively and believed that they should be controlled by international action (including, where necessary, humanitarian intervention), Duffield's position is quite different. This is partly because he is highly critical of such attempts, viewing them as primarily concerned to defend the interests of the North against phenomena in developing countries that are seen as 'dangerous'. But it is also because he is deeply sceptical about the possibility of controlling them—or, at any rate, doing so with the means and analytical approaches that are currently being used. For his argument is that these wars are not aberrations, but part of a transformative process, arising from changes in capitalism and the ways in which the North tries to control the South through 'global governance' (Duffield, 2001, pp. 13–16). It is necessary, he suggests, to accept that there is complexity and constant mutation and to undertake research into what is actually happening and how the new networks of power operate. Only this would make it possible to avoid constant policy failures and to act in ways that do not simply help those who already have power (Duffield, 2001, pp. 257–65).

Once again, criticisms might be made of aspects of Duffield's approach. For example, he uses a form of network theory when dealing both with power relationships and organizations. While this is interesting, its superiority over other approaches tends to be asserted, rather than demonstrated. Similarly, although he makes some very pertinent points about the ways in which NGOs have been used to advance Western neo-liberal policies, his critique does not seem entirely consistent.[5] Nevertheless, his work contains extremely important insights into the devastating impact on the South of the policies initiated in advanced capitalist countries. Its particular importance is in combining political economy with anthropology to elucidate the interaction between international economic processes, organizational change, and the life experiences of communities affected by these wider structural developments. This again refutes the idea that conflicts, or humanitarian crises, simply 'occur' in developing countries and that there then needs to be an external 'response'. Those who wield the most international power are deeply embedded in domestic systems, processes and conflicts.

*Transitions and violence.* This is also a theme of a recent work by Christopher Cramer, another development specialist, with considerable experience of applied work. The focus of his book *Civil War is Not a Stupid Thing* (2006) is given by the sub-title: *Accounting for Violence in Developing Countries.*[6] This is a wide-ranging refutation of mono-causal and reductionist theories of war, substantiated with considerable empirical detail, particularly about sub-Saharan Africa, but also drawing on experiences from Latin America. Two aspects of the argument have particular relevance here. First, he suggests that the beginnings of capitalism are always violent, particularly in the case of later transitions. This means that there are significant similarities between the

---

[5] He is, for example, extremely critical of rights-based approaches, which he views as an abandonment of the tradition of giving assistance to all those who need it. Yet he also condemns the role of NGOs in Sudan for failing to analyze the structures of power, thereby effectively serving the repressive purposes of the government in relation to the peoples in the south of the country (Duffield, 2001, pp. 202–55). However, the more traditional approach of humanitarian assistance would surely have precluded any critique of these structures, while a rights-based approach may be used to provide a radical analysis of power and policies.

[6] The title in the USA is less provocative: *Violence in Developing Countries: War, Memory, Progress* (Indiana University Press, 2006).

current situation in many developing countries and the previous historical experience of advanced capitalist countries. Secondly, he shows that the nature of the current international political economy imposes additional pressures upon developing and transitional countries, exacerbating the tendencies towards conflict.

The violence in situations of transition stems from a series of factors. First, the institutional framework that previously regulated violence now becomes unstable or anachronistic. Secondly, because of the open-ended features of change and the institutional insecurity, the stakes of the conflict will be greater in a scramble for position in a social structure whose adhesive has not yet set. Thirdly, the conflict is particularly likely to be violent in societies where there are histories of violence and groups that tend to practise it in particular circumstances. Fourthly, this is also liable to intensify if there is no credible central authority that can impose a monopoly over the exercise of force, and this is particularly common where the fiscal source for this monopoly is weak. Fifthly, in momentous transitions the crisis of uncertainty is not just about the viability or relevance of particular institutions, or even simply about the fact that power and positions are contested: the very characteristics of power are the terms of the conflict. This, Cramer suggests, was the case in the shift from feudalism to capitalism and from medieval royal power to parliamentary democracy. Similarly, in contemporary conflicts in developing countries part of the social conflict is over what power means: is it vested in traditional authorities, managed partly through 'magic', or in individual dictators or in royal dynasties, or in multi-party procedural democracy and bureaucracy? Finally, the terms of the accumulation and distribution of wealth are contested between the different classes (Cramer, 2006, pp. 215–16).

If 'violence is the norm in development' (Cramer, 2006, p. 229), Cramer's second relevant point is that contemporary transitions are particularly difficult because the states in question are entering an established global system in which the interests of advanced capitalism shape and constrain the process. This takes the form of direct market involvement, through commodities and capital flows. But it also takes the indirect form of industrialised countries 'kicking away the ladder' by making it difficult for developing countries to employ the protective state interventionist policies on which wealth creation in advanced countries was itself based:

Far from tempering the passions and cooling conflict in developing countries, the presence of advanced capitalist interests (in the form of investments, commodities supply and demand, and political pressure through the corporate and diplomatic arms of rich country nation-states, as well as through arms exports and other military goods and services) can aggravate violence (Cramer, 2006, p. 234).[7]

One final point about Cramer's analysis must be emphasised. While he seeks to demonstrate the relationship between structural change and violence, he certainly does not want to 'give war a chance'. The challenge, he argues, is to minimise the devastation caused by economic, social and economic transformations and, where there has been violence, to maximise any potential for positive change that might have arisen in the course of the conflict (Cramer, 2006, p. 288). However, he is convinced that, in the final analysis, a powerful central state is necessary (though not sufficient) to control violence and that, particularly since the 1980s, the external pressures have been in the opposite direction.

Once again, some elements in this argument may be questionable. It may, for example, be argued that some conflicts are difficult to ascribe to transition. Nor does violence only arise in situations of transition *to* capitalism: after all, attempts to establish socialism have also been accompanied by violence. Yet Cramer undoubtedly provides a penetrating analysis of the causes of conflict.

All three of the sources discussed above substantiate the main point of this section: that states and other actors based in the advanced capitalist countries have had a structural and policy impact upon the conflicts in developing and transitional economies. International neo-liberal policies have played a role in producing the humanitarian crises that always accompany violence of this kind. In these circumstances, it may seem paradoxical that the most widely advocated solution to conflict has been a 'liberal peace'. This is the subject of the next section.

## Policy prescriptions: the liberal peace

In chapter 2 the differences between peace-keeping in the Cold War and post-Cold War periods were discussed briefly, but three key points need to be highlighted. First, there was a *quantitative* increase in the number of peace-keeping missions, with sixteen during the whole period from 1945 to 1990

[7] It is also worth noting that the major arms exporters to Africa are not only in the West. In 2003, the leading supplier was Russia, and China supplied more than twice as much as the UK (Alden, 2007, p. 25).

and forty-one new ones established between 1990 and 2003 (Thakur 2006, p. 46). Secondly, there was a *qualitative* transformation. While peace-keeping had previously been more concerned with inter-state than intra-state wars, the balance now shifted.[8] Thirdly, a further shift was initiated by the reversal in the US position following the debacle in Somalia in 1993. Until then Washington had supported and promoted the new UN activism, albeit with important reservations, and at one point Clinton had even accepted the idea of a permanent peace-keeping force to which the US would contribute personnel. This now changed, and over the next decade Washington gave primacy to NATO and subsequently to 'coalitions of the willing', and other Western states tended to follow this lead. This meant that the proportion of personnel from OECD countries in UN peace-keeping missions declined rapidly and there was a proportionate increase in those from poorer countries, which also reduced the resources available to the missions.[9] However, the changes after 1993 also followed from a widely shared conviction that the UN was becoming over-extended and was unable to handle so many missions, with the prospect of several more in the future. This reinforced a tendency to sub-contract to regional organizations, where these were available, but this compounded the dangers implicit in the partial US disengagement from the UN. For sub-contracting could both weaken the UN's ability to control peace-keeping and reinforce the division between resource rich (NATO and EU) and resource poor (ECOWAS, OAU/AU) missions.

These changes are complex and the different generations of peace-keeping may be analyzed and interpreted in various ways (Bellamy, Williams and Griffin, 2004, pp. 93–185). However, the concern here is not with typology or a detailed examination of the missions, but with two features that have differentiated the whole post-1989 period from the Cold War era. First, in association with the shift from inter-state to intra-state peace-keeping, the missions have become far more interventionist. In some cases, as in Cambodia and Namibia, this could involve virtual international control over a country with the creation of new institutions. But even when the 'peace-building' presence was less extensive, multi-agency external forces have still provided a very strong

[8] This was also reflected in a transformation of the UN Secretariat, with changes in personnel committed to the new interventionist approach (Alqaq, 2006).

[9] In 1988 OECD countries provided approximately 43 % of the troop contributions; by 1999 this had fallen to just over 35 %, and by 2005 to approximately 6 % (Thakur 2006, p. 46). Of course, the sharpness of this drop in *percentages* is also partially due to the rise in the number of missions and the total personnel involved.

steer to the process. Secondly, the underlying assumption over the whole period has been that the establishment of liberal-democracy will be the best way to promote peace. The dominant viewpoint on this, partially derived from Kant's *Perpetual Peace*, has been that liberal states do not fight wars against one another. This idea, to which little attention had been paid during the Cold War, was revived in the 1980s (Doyle, 1983). This led to a flurry of studies, scrutinizing the theoretical basis for the claim and testing its empirical validity (Brown, Lynne-Jones and Miller, 1996). It also clearly formed part of the agenda of the US government in promoting liberal-democracy across the world. Claims about allegedly empirical evidence to substantiate the view that liberal institutions are beneficial for peace *within* states (as well as *between* them) also played a role in introducing such ideas into peace-making. Thus R.J. Rummel argued that democracies were considerably less likely than non-democratic states to experience violence (Rummel, 1997, p. 85, quoted in Paris, 2004, p. 43) and that in democratic countries:

social conflicts that might become violent are resolved through voting, negotiation, compromise, and mediation. The success of these procedures is enhanced and supported by the restraints on decision makers of competitive elections, the cross-pressures resulting from the natural pluralism of democratic....societies, and the development of a democratic culture and norms that emphasise rational debate, toleration, negotiation of differences, conciliation, and conflict resolution (Rummel, 1995, p. 4, quoted in Paris, 2004, p. 43).

Yet support for democracy as a peace-making approach also rested on normative beliefs and, as suggested in chapter 2, these were shared by civil society movements and many on the left. For there is a long tradition, stressed by radical peace theorists, of arguing that genuine peace cannot be achieved through repression, or even through power alone. Instead the idea of a 'positive peace' based on social justice, representation, inclusiveness, human rights and the dispersal of power has been favoured. Democratization as a peace policy has therefore had a wide appeal. This does not, of course, mean that the *form* of democracy, or the *ways* in which it has been implemented, conformed to these aspirations. And, in practice, rapid democratization (of a crude kind) coupled with economic liberalization has been markedly unsuccessful in establishing peace after wars.

In *At War's End* (2004), Roland Paris subjected the liberal peace thesis to a comparative analysis, based on eleven case studies. His overall conclusions reinforce the points made in the previous section about the ways in which both economic and political liberalization can reinforce conflict in vulnerable societies.[10]

But the concern here is not with the failures of peace-building *per se*, but with peace processes that made the situation worse and contributed to a humanitarian crisis. Paris deals with both Angola and Rwanda in this way. I will consider Angola very briefly, but examine Rwanda in depth because of its tragic significance in relation to humanitarianism and intervention.

*Angola.* Two years after the Portuguese revolution of 1974 and the subsequent withdrawal from Angola, the Movimento Popular de Libertação de Angola (MPLA) defeated a smaller liberation movement and was left to confront the União Nacional para a Independência Total de Angola (UNITA) for total control of the country. The MPLA was supported by the USSR and Cuba, which sent 50,000 troops, while the USA and South Africa backed UNITA. Attempts to negotiate a peaceful settlement failed in the early 1980s, but the changing climate of East-West relations in the Gorbachev era led to a breakthrough in December 1988, with provision for a cease-fire, the withdrawal of Cuban troops and the ending of South African support for UNITA. However, George Bush Senior continued to give covert military support to Jonas Savimbi, the UNITA leader, and this may have reduced Savimbi's incentive to make peace (Ohaegbulam, 2004, p. 161). In any case, despite a UN presence, fighting continued and it was only in May 1991, with Soviet and US

[10] He highlights the fact that liberal-democracy is a system in which conflict and competition are integral in both the political and economic spheres, but that in well-established systems these are constrained by institutions. However, in transition regimes, these constraints are not present or are very weak, and he identifies five possible pathologies leading to violent conflict. First, in contrast to the assumptions of many advocates of democratization, civil society groups are not always a positive force. There can also be 'bad civil society'—that is, groups that intensify conflict and preach hatred. Secondly, there may be 'ethnic entrepreneurs' who seek to perpetuate ethnic divisions rather than build any kind of unity. Thirdly, elections, which are often regarded as the culmination of the democratization and peace-building approaches, are instead often focal points for harmful competition. Rather than being viewed as a way of sharing in power or temporarily holding power, they are seen as a means of winning and keeping total power in a zero-sum game. Fourthly, there may be saboteurs, who apparently support democracy, but actually use it to consolidate power and prevent any real transition. Finally, as discussed above, economic liberalization can reinforce inequalities or threaten those who have held power, leading to intensification of conflict. Overall, the failures stem from the attempt to institute the liberal model in the situation of *extreme vulnerability* that normally prevails in a society emerging from civil war, where there are intense social conflicts, weak conflict dampeners, and ineffective political institutions (Paris, 2004, chapter 9).

observers and Portuguese mediation, that the parties initialled a comprehensive peace accord at Bicesse, on the basis of a liberal democratic system. This commitment to multi-party democracy was a shift in MPLA policy; it had previously sought a one party state, but this had changed with combined pressure from the US and the Soviet Union. Similarly, the MPLA now also accepted liberalization of the economy in place of the previous belief in central planning, since this, and a settlement with UNITA, would facilitate the securing of external investment and aid, which could not come from the Soviet Union, now in its terminal crisis. However, when the elections finally took place at the end of September 1992, only 65% of the MPLA's and 26% of UNITA's forces had been processed to return to civilian life (Paris, 2004, p. 66). This meant that both sides (and particularly UNITA) could easily return to armed conflict if dissatisfied with the results of the voting.

In mid-October, when the results showed that the MPLA had won both the legislative and presidential elections, Savimbi denounced the results and tried to take control of the country. There were certainly reasons for distrusting the MPLA whose militias had killed some of UNITA's senior members during the elections (Ali, Matthews and Spears, 2004, p. 298). But once again Savimbi no doubt felt encouraged by the fact that Bush blamed the post-election violence on MPLA forces and their 'winner-takes-all' attitude. The US refusal to offer immediate recognition to the newly elected government may therefore have reinforced Savimbi's confidence in resuming the fighting (Ohaegbulam, 2004, p. 185). On the other hand, Savimbi continued his war after May 1993, when Clinton recognised the government, lifted the US embargo on the sale of military hardware to the MPLA, and called for sanctions against UNITA. In 1994 there was a further attempt to broker a ceasefire and peace agreement, but this also failed. Once again UNITA had some grievances about government behaviour during the ceasefire (Ali, Matthews and Spears, 2004, p. 298), but the major factor in the breakdown of the proposed settlement was probably Savimbi's own character. The civil war therefore continued, with the withdrawal of the UN peace mission in February 1999, and fighting ended only after Savimbi was killed in 2002.[11]

In the two years following the 1992 elections approximately 300,000 people were killed, more than the estimated numbers in the previous eighteen years of fighting. Several factors had contributed to the failure of this settlement

[11] Savimbi was killed on 22 February 2002 in a battle with Angolan government troops. It has been claimed that he was murdered by Western-backed forces as the major obstacle to peace.

and the subsequent violence and humanitarian crisis, including US ambivalence and the fact that the control of diamonds by UNITA and oil by the MPLA provided both sides with resources to buy arms (Ali, Matthews and Spears, 2004, p. 300). But the most important single reason was that the two parties had approached the 1992 elections as the continuation of war by other means without offering any prospect of subsequent reconciliation or co-operation. This was reinforced by their fear that there might only ever be one election (Ali, Matthews and Spears, p. 300) and Savimbi, in particular, had no intention of renouncing armed conflict unless he was elected president. The notion that elections (the central component in the international peace-making project) would channel violence into a political process was therefore flawed and superficial, for in fact they triggered the resumption of the civil war. Instead of the concentration on rapid elections, the chances of success would have been enhanced by a sustained international presence, focusing on other elements, including disarmament, economic support and a more gradual approach to institutional development (Paris, 2004, pp. 63–9; Ali, Matthews and Spears, 2004, pp. 300–8). The peace process did not simply fail: it contributed to the deaths and suffering that ensued.

*Rwanda.* The external involvement in the situation in Rwanda was both more complex and still more tragic, as it was the immediate background to the genocide. My concern here is not with international responsibility at the time of the genocide itself, but with the external role in the earlier period, although, of course, the two are closely related.

The crisis in Rwanda in the early 1990s resulted from a complex interaction between at least four elements. First, the reawakening of bitter collective memories in a situation of civil war; secondly, a weakening of the regime; thirdly, enhanced external influence because of the economic and political situation; and fourthly, insistence by the international forces on a particular solution—a liberal peace.

The bitter memories were rooted in the colonial period and its immediate aftermath. Hutu and Tutsi identities had been comparatively unimportant in pre-colonial times when clan membership was of greater significance. However, colonialism, particularly by the Belgians, introduced ethnic categories and claims about racial hierarchy, with Tutsis (around 14% of the population) treated as superior to the Hutu majority (accounting for around 85%).[12] This

[12] The Twa people, a pygmy group, account for the other 1 % of the population. They have tended to suffer from ethnic prejudice and exclusion by both the dominant groups.

policy was suddenly abandoned following a revolution in 1959, leading to the abolition of the monarchy and the overthrow of the Tutsi structures through which the Belgians had previously ruled. The Tutsi ruling group attempted to maintain authoritarian control and drew up plans to eliminate the emergent Hutu elite. However, the Belgians refused to support these ideas and now supported the Hutu revolt (Jones, 2001, p. 20). This led to a reversal in the power relations between Tutsis and Hutus, which was confirmed by the results of parliamentary elections and a referendum on independence. Overt violence began when the leader of a Hutu party was assaulted by Tutsi youths, an act that led to a Hutu uprising and the killing of hundreds of Tutsis. This was a preface to repeated acts of violence against Tutsis, which increased in scale, with the worst phase taking place at the end of 1963 (the year after independence), following armed attacks by Tutsi exiles from Burundi. Catherine Newbury explains the ethnic violence as follows:

[T]he salient fact was that virtually all those who controlled the state (before 1959)—the chiefs and the sub-chiefs—were Tuutsi [sic], and here is where the ethnic factor becomes important ...[A]n appeal to Hutu solidarity became, for Hutu leaders, the most effective rallying point for revolutionary activity. Although Hutu could and apparently did distinguish among Tuutsi of different types and attitudes, the fact that the chiefs and other African agents of the state were seen as exploiters, and that virtually all of these were Tuutsi, made an appeal to ethnic solidarity potent where an appeal to "all poor people" may have been less so. Because colonial policies had repeatedly pressed upon Hutu their inferior, excluded status, even poor Tuutsi did not experience quite the same form of discrimination as did those classified as Hutu (Newbury, 1988, p. 213).

It was in this period that Rwanda most resembled the clash between a previously dominant minority and a majority population, as described by Amy Chua. These years would remain an important reference point for collective memories amongst both Hutus and Tutsis, which were reinforced by experiences over the next ten years. Democratic pretensions were soon abandoned and by the early 1970s power was concentrated around the presidency and a small group of politicians from central Rwanda. As the post-independence government lost popularity, it sought to reinforce its position by inciting a new round of anti-Tutsi violence in 1973, which was rationalised with reference to the massacres of Hutus by Tutsis in Burundi (see chapter 1).

These successive waves of violence and the purging of Tutsis from positions of power led to a very large refugee population in neighbouring countries. Their total number (including their descendants) by the early 1990s was approximately 600,000, which was about half the size of the Tutsi population that remained within Rwanda. The refugees in Uganda would play a critical role in the civil war and the pre-genocide crisis.

In 1973 a military coup led to a change of regime, bringing Juvénal Habyarimana to power. Although his power base was amongst the Hutus in the north, whose attitude to the Tutsi tended to be particularly hostile, he prevented further massacres so long as Tutsis renounced any political ambitions. From then until 1990 Habyarimana retained dictatorial power while the state was reconstructed on a basis of authoritarian Hutu power, implemented through a single party, the Mouvement Révolutionnaire National pour le Développement (MRND). While Habyarimana was consolidating his dictatorship, Tutsi exiles played a very significant role within Uganda, contributing combatants to the rebel army that brought Yoweri Museveni to power in 1986. Subsequently, he supported the establishment of the Rwandan Patriotic Front (RPF) at the beginning of 1988 (Sellström and Wohlgemuth, 1996, p. 22). This was a highly motivated and well-trained force, including up to three thousand soldiers who had belonged to the Ugandan army and now took their weapons with them into the RPF army. However, while Museveni helped to build up military forces against the Rwandan government, his support for an indigenization movement in Uganda also pushed the RPF into action, for the Tutsis were no longer able to remain there as before (Mamdani, 2002, pp. 182–4). In October 1990 the RPF invaded Rwanda, creating a civil war.[13]

[13] There is an aspect of external involvement in the Rwandan tragedy which remains highly controversial, with many questions still unanswered: the role of the French rivalry with the 'Anglo-Saxon' powers in the ensuing crisis. French support for the Habyarimana regime and the Rwandan army is well-documented and there is no doubt that France played a crucial part (aided by Belgian and Zairian forces) in halting the initial incursion by the RPF. It also remained hostile to the RPF throughout the civil war, despite publicly presenting itself as a mediator (Kroslak, 2007, pp. 98–152). The position of the US is less clear. The RPF military commander (and subsequent President of Rwanda, Paul Kagame) was at a US military college when the invasion took place and quickly returned to take control of the campaign. The French government, particularly in military and intelligence circles, believed that there was an 'Anglo-Saxon' plot to enhance Anglophone influence in the area through support for the RPF, which was English-speaking because so many Tutsi refugees had settled in Uganda (Barrett, 2002, p. 171; Wallis, 2006, pp. 25–6). Some still argue that the US and the UK sought regime change in Rwanda and used the RPF deliberately for this purpose (Friesecke, 2004; Mamdani, 2007). However, both the RPF and the US have denied that there was American support (Kroslak, 2007, p. 111) and it has also been argued that the British government may have kept a particularly low profile in Rwanda, partly so as to remove any grounds for French suspicions (Melvern and Williams, 2004, pp. 8–9, p. 18). A report by the French National Assembly in 1998 concluded that there had been no Anglo-American plot, and

This took place in a rapidly deteriorating economic situation, which was also weakening Habyarimana's hold on power.

Until the second half of the 1980s, there had been some positive economic developments in Rwanda. In 1976 the country had been the poorest of the five states in the region but it subsequently surpassed its neighbours, attracting external aid and NGO activity, even becoming known as 'the Switzerland' of Central Africa (Barnett 2002, p. 53). However, economic strains then developed, with the proportion of the population in extreme poverty rising from 9% in 1982 to 15% in 1989. This was largely because of a scarcity of land under current crop patterns, reinforced by environmental degradation, but there were also external economic problems.[14] Tin had accounted for 15% of export earnings, but in 1985 the last tin mine was closed. Of far greater significance was the fact that between 1986 and 1992 there was a 75% decrease in coffee prices, and since coffee accounted for around 66% of export revenues, this meant a fourfold increase in the debt-service ratio (Sellström and Wohlgemuth, 1996, p. 23).[15] All this was coupled with severe drought in 1989–90

---

some sources in the French government subsequently claimed that it was President Mitterrand himself who had interpreted the conflict in this way (Kroslak, 2007, p. 112). On the other hand, the loss of French influence in Rwanda has certainly been a consequence of French policy both before and during the genocide, and competition for influence in the region remains intense. This aspect of the situation will not be explored any further here, both because of the uncertainty of the evidence and because it is less relevant to the main theme than the *combined* impact of the major external forces on the crisis. For highly critical accounts of French policy before, during and after the genocide, see Wallis (2006) and Kroslak (2007). For a brief judicious discussion of the rivalries, see Cilliers (2001).

[14] An over-simplified argument that the violent conflict in Rwanda was caused primarily by environmental factors (Nancy Gibbs, 'Why? The Killing Fields of Rwanda, *Time*, 16 May 1994) has been convincingly refuted (Percival and Thomas Home-Dixon, 1995; Uvin, 1998, pp. 180–201). Yet there was certainly a complex inter-relationship between population pressures, environmental degradation and the other socio-economic causes of the crisis (Ohlsson, 2000).

[15] The collapse of coffee prices was also related to neo-liberalism. In 1962 the International Coffee Agreement (ICA) had been a Cold War initiative promoted by President John F. Kennedy to prevent destabilization in Latin America due to low coffee prices, but in 1989 the ICA collapsed because of the pressures of the large coffee traders, bringing about an immediate fall in coffee prices. Furthermore, structural adjustment policies in developing countries, including Rwanda, also required production to be geared to commodity exports, causing a simultaneous flooding of coffee markets by all coffee-producing economies, with a collapse of prices. International pressures for liberalization also prevented the Rwandan government from taking protective measures to assist the coffee producers (Spyridaki, 2008, pp. 28–32; Kamola, 2007).

(recurring in 1991 and 1993) and diseases affecting two staple crops, which led to half a million people experiencing food shortages and malnutrition (Sellström and Wohlgemuth, 1996, p. 24). The rapid progress of the RPF army, which soon secured control of much of the country, reinforced the economic problems; for example, an attack in the most fertile part of the country at the beginning of 1993 led to displacement of 13% of the country's total population and a drop of 15% in marketed agricultural production in a year. By 1993 the proportion of the population in extreme poverty had increased to 31% (Sellström and Wohlgemuth, 1996, p. 23).

It was in this precarious economic situation that the international involvement became so important. As the Rwandan situation deteriorated, international aid had increased by about 60% between 1989 and 1991, and this level was sustained until the end of 1993 (Sellström and Wohlgemuth, 1996, p. 24). However, in September 1990 the World Bank and the IMF negotiated a structural adjustment programme, with involvement in joint financing and co-financing from seven bilateral donors, the African Development Bank and the EU. Habyarimana had resisted this for several years, but could no longer do so with the crash in coffee earnings and a trade and budgetary deficit. In return for funding, a package of austerity measures and privatization was approved in June 1991. The *direct* economic impact of these measures upon the crisis is difficult to determine. Clearly the pressures to liberalise and reduce expenditure in a situation of increasing poverty were liable to reinforce the growing tensions and violence. And although the government did not comply with the terms at first (with the budget deficit increasing from 12% of GDP in 1990 to 19% in 1993), in response to this the World Bank then withheld the second tranche of the structural adjustment credit and the real incomes of coffee farmers fell. This exacerbated the worsening conditions for the rural population resulting from the reduction in food production caused by drought, crop disease and massive population displacement (Sellström and Wohlgemuth, 1996, pp. 23–6). Furthermore, instead of being used for social expenditure, revenue from devaluation was diverted to military expenditure, reducing those funds allocated for health expenditure for the poorest groups in the population. A freeze on public sector wages combined with reductions in real purchasing power after the devaluations also had a negative impact upon the position of the civil service. All this contributed to the rapidly growing tensions.

In addition to their *economic* impact, the fact that foreign donors were subsidizing some 70% of public expenditure also made them key *political* actors in the Rwandan crisis. Their negative role had two main aspects. The first, which has been analysed in depth by Peter Uvin in *Aiding Violence* (1998), was to uphold the privileges of the Hutu political elite in a situation of increasing inequality, alienation and popular unrest. The International Financial Institutions remained unwilling to consider any but neo-liberal indicators of budgetary control, and the aid agencies did not change their policies either, despite the ever growing discrimination and violence against the Tutsi in a situation of acute political crisis (Uvin, p. 44, pp. 88–94).[16] This meant that international finance and aid were upholding an increasingly unpopular repressive regime and helping it to sustain the state infrastructure and military spending that would subsequently enable the genocide to be carried out (Orford, 2003, pp. 102–10).

Furthermore, international NGOs also often exercised a negative influence. This was partly indirect, in that the overwhelming majority of their assistance went to the elites rather than the poor (Uvin, 1998, pp. 122–4). But it was also because of a tendency to believe that any growth of civil society movements was automatically positive, while in reality Rwandan NGOs and the church were as divided by ethnic conflict, exclusion and hatred as the society as a whole. In general, the international NGOs defined their mandates in strictly apolitical terms and therefore supported groups that were sometimes controlled by Hutu extremists who ultimately took part in the genocide (Uvin, 1998, pp. 172–8). The second negative role concerns the way in which both international donors and governments chose to use their influence with regard to the liberal peace theory.

From the late 1980s political opposition had been developing, and although Habyarimana had previously ruled out any alternative to the one-party system, the RPF military campaign now forced the pace of political reform and small new parties (with little ideological differences between them) were formed during 1991. Habyarimana had hoped to build a united front against the RPF, but most of the new parties remained opposed to the MRND-dominated state. In April 1992 a new transitional government was established, including the smaller parties, but their relations with the MRND (renamed MRDNDD, with 'et la Démocratie' added) remained tense. Without external pressure, it is unlikely that the one-party state would have ended in 1991 or that the power-sharing government would have been established the following year, for the changes were propelled by a complex international peace process. This

[16] After the genocide the World Bank continued to demonstrate a similarly narrow view in its retrospective judgements as to what had gone wrong (Williams, 2004, pp. 108–12).

involved France,[17] Germany, the United States, Burundi, Zaire (now the Democratic Republic of Congo), Uganda, Tanzania, and representatives of the UN and the OAU. Major aid donors (Britain, Canada, the Netherlands and Switzerland) also followed the negotiations, and the whole process was facilitated by Tanzania and mainly took place in Arusha (Jones, 1995, p. 241).

The Arusha Peace Process played a major role in precipitating the crisis that would lead to the genocide, with the potential for disaster reinforced by the negotiating process. There had already been some African mediation attempts, followed by those of the US and France during 1991 (Jones, 2001, p. 57), but the first key stage began in June 1992 when a stalemate in the war led the two warring parties to convene in France to establish the terms for the Arusha peace process. The Tanzanian facilitators adopted an incremental approach, beginning with the least contentious issues, and this resulted in an almost immediate ceasefire. But the third stage agreement on a new 'Broad-Based Transition Government' drastically curtailed the powers of the president, and by now there was a clear trend, followed in the final three phases of the process, in which the government of Rwanda made all the concessions. These meant that Habyarimana's party could subsequently become a minority in government and that the RPF (which was overwhelmingly Tutsi) would share power in the army (Scorgie, 2004, pp. 68–9, Jones, 2001, p. 93). Such results meant that the government as a whole (and not only its most extreme elements) constantly regarded the negotiating process as one of defeat, rather than compromise.

There were two fundamental reasons for the RPF's 'victory' in the negotiations. First, it was a united and determined team, while the Rwandan government was divided. Secondly, the RPF was winning the war. This meant that it could simply leave the negotiations and make rapid military progress, creating havoc and further economic damage, as it did in February 1993. For the RPF fighting and negotiations thus constituted two options, while the government

[17] In the French case, there were both mixed motives and mixed policies for using influence in this way, but the predominant view, particularly in the Foreign Ministry, was that a settlement was the best way to preserve French influence. Otherwise the fear was that the Anglophone RPF would win an outright victory (Quilès Commssion, 1998 and Commission d'enquête citoyenne, quoted in Bolton and Eriksson, Annex 3; Jones 1995, p. 242). However, the public role of the French in promoting the multi-party system was contradicted by the continuing support for Habyarimana, particularly in military circles (Kroslak, 2007, pp. 72–152).

really had little alternative but to accept whatever was on offer in the bargaining process. The final agreement in August 1993 thus included: the principle and creation of the rule of law; power-sharing, the enlargement of the transitional government, with the inclusion of the RPF, and the creation of a transition parliament; the reintegration of refugees and internally-displaced persons; and the establishment of a national unified army. It read 'like a victor's deal, rather than a general settlement between relatively equal sides' (Adelman and Suhrke, 2000, p. 149, quoted in Scorgie, p. 70), and it threatened the whole Hutu dominated power system.

Almost eighteen months earlier, Hutu extremists had set up a new party, the Coalition pour la Défense de la République (CDR), to prevent any such eventuality, and a Hutu extremist militia, the Interahamwe, was also established. Both were openly inciting violence against Tutsis, and during the Arusha discussions the RPF insisted that the CDR was excluded from subsequent stages of the negotiations and from any future government. Once the civil war had begun, Habyarimana himself had also increasingly treated all Tutsis as enemies, and state-directed atrocities against Tutsis had resumed. A human rights report held the President personally responsible for the deaths of at least 2000 people in the period between October 1990 and January 1993 (Fédération Internationale des Droits de l'Homme, 1993, cited in Sellström and Wohlgemuth, 1996, p. 31). Nevertheless, he was probably less extreme than many of those surrounding him, including his wife and her family, who were determined to uphold Hutu power and had links with the CDR and the militias (Wallis, 2006, pp. 51–2). The transition government established in 1992 had already meant a partial loss of control, but the Arusha process would constitute a far more fundamental change. By late 1992 the CDR was probably already preparing massacres on a new scale, and in July 1993 a private radio station (Radio-Télévision Libre des Mille Collines, RTLMC) began to broadcast hate propaganda that incited violence. At every stage Habyarimana tried to procrastinate in the peace process or to subvert agreements that had been reached. These tactics no doubt reflected his own wishes, but he must also have been aware of the probable results if the Arusha Accords were signed and implemented. However, the outcome was *not* simply determined by the relative strength of the two sides in the negotiating process, but also by the role of the external forces.

International support for the liberal peace thesis was so strong that external influence and pressure were directed solely to bringing about this result, and there was a linkage between financial support and the peace process. Thus, in

March 1993, a threat to cut aid following the publication of the damning human rights report (mentioned above) probably induced Habyarimana to resume the peace talks (Sellström and Wohlgemuth, 1996, p. 27). Similarly, in July 1993 international donors, working with the World Bank, told him that international funds for the government would be terminated unless he signed the final version of the Arusha Accords, and he did so the next month (Human Rights Watch 1999, cited in Paris, 2004, p. 71). Given the extreme dependence of the Rwandan government on international financial support this meant that donors were, in effect, coercing him to accept an agreement that involved a total demolition of the state system, which had been constructed on the basis of Hutu power from his own region. The international forces were not *directly* responsible for the terms of the agreement, but there was no co-ordinated external attempt to amend those terms so as to make them more acceptable to moderate Hutu opinion, and Tanzania, France and the US interceded to restore the agreement over the army when Habyarimana initially refused to accept it (Jones, 2001, pp. 84–5).[18] Yet the terms of the Arusha agreement made it far more likely that the extremists would be able to mobilise support (Jones, 2001, pp. 157–77).

The international peace-makers regarded Habyarimana himself as the major obstacle to change. Once the CDR had been excluded from the talks it was effectively ignored subsequently by the external financial and political forces involved in the peace process. This continued over the next few months as the most extremist groups, which remained firmly implanted in the state structure, prepared to massacre the Tutsi population in the attempt to maintain their power base. It is, of course, uncertain whether an alternative approach by the external actors could have averted this. One route for reform within Rwanda would have been through increased human rights and minority rights protection, and it is therefore possible that a threat to withhold aid unless there was progress in these realms could have been effective. In 1991 this was tried and probably achieved the release of 8,000 to 10,000 arbitrarily detained Tutsis, and the following year a handful of development NGOs spoke out about deteriorating trends, publishing a declaration against the massacres, and called for sanctions. There is also some evidence that similar threats in 1993 had some success (Uvin, 1998, p. 90, p. 96, p. 230). However, it is perhaps unlikely that negative conditionality of this kind would have brought about major concessions, and it would certainly have done nothing to overcome the

---

[18] The French, Americans, Tanzanians and even Ugandans opposed the exclusion of the CDR and the deal over the army (Jones, 2001, pp. 90–1; Mamdani, pp. 211–12).

frustration of the Hutu masses suffering from the privations caused by the civil war and economic hardship. In this situation the use of aid resources to *strengthen* the underlying social and political conditions for improved policies might have been more effective (Uvin, 1998, pp. 236–8). But instead of seeking reforms in this way, international forces were simultaneously using their influence to institute neo-liberal economic policies and to establish a liberal peace that would undermine the whole basis of the Hutu power structure.

The external forces were equally myopic once the Arusha agreement had been signed. This involved the deployment of an international peace-keeping force, the establishment of a transitional government including the RPF, and multi-party elections to be held no later than 1995. Most African states in the region were well aware of the importance of a robust peace-keeping mission, given the antagonisms within Rwanda, but when the issue was presented to the Security Council the US applied further pressure. In the immediate aftermath of the Somalia debacle, with Congress hostile to participation in further missions when American interests were not directly involved, the US sought to reduce the size and expense of the mission, and to restrict its mandate. This led to further delays and the eventual deployment of a poorly resourced and small peace-keeping force of 2,500, under a strict Chapter VI mandate, with the first contingent arriving in late October. The mind-set reflected in this belated deployment of an inadequate force then continued.

This meant that there was no appreciation of the impact in Rwanda of events in neighbouring Burundi where, on 21 October 1993, Tutsi soldiers assassinated the first democratically elected Hutu President. This led to tens of thousands of deaths, with 70,000 Hutu refugees fleeing to Rwanda, and it also reinforced the potency of the Hutu extremists' message that the Tutsis would never accept majority rule.[19] Although General Dallaire, who was the force commander of UNAMIR, experienced the reaction in Rwanda to the crisis in Burundi (Dallaire, 2003, pp. 98–9), the continuing view in UN headquarters was that Arusha was a successful example of a democratic peace process that would end the civil war. In addition, it was maintained that the parties to the dispute must implement the agreement, with UNAMIR playing a

---

[19] Later estimates placed the deaths at between 35,000 and 50,000, split equally between the two ethnic groups, but the initial reports were of 150,000–200,000 deaths, mainly of Hutus massacred by Tutsis (Jones, 2001, p. 36). The lack of any response by the UN to the situation in Burundi (on the grounds that there was no peace process there for it to uphold) probably also reinforced the belief by the Hutu extremists that no international action would be taken to prevent genocide in Rwanda.

minor role in the background. The extremist Hutu forces were filtered out of this vision and Dallaire was hardly aware of their existence when he first visited Rwanda in August 1993 (Dallaire 2003, pp. 57–79). Even when he tried to warn the UN about the preparations for massacres early in 1994, Habyarimana's further procrastination in implementing the agreements was still viewed as the main obstacle to progress. He was therefore presented more than once with the threat that the UNAMIR force would be withdrawn unless there was immediate progress to the next stage (Barnett, 2002, pp. 95–6). Finally, on 5 April he flew to Arusha for further discussions, and it was on his return the next day that his plane was shot down and the genocide was initiated.[20]

It is possible that this would have occurred if the Arusha process had never been instituted and the civil war had simply continued without a peace process. Nevertheless, there was certainly a degree of collective *external* responsibility for the ensuing holocaust. There are three elements in this judgement. First, the role of externally driven economic liberalization in exacerbating the political and economic problems in poor countries with deep conflicts was again evident. Secondly, the Rwandan experience reinforces the earlier points about the dangers of following mechanistic formulae about the liberal peace thesis in situations of acute conflict. Rather than following such policies, international donors and governments might have used their power to seek reforms over a prolonged period, and in 1992–93 they could have attempted to moderate the Arusha agreement, rather than simply acquiescing in the RPF's negotiating victory. Thirdly, external forces (specifically international donors and the World Bank) were, in effect, coercing Habyarimana into signing and then implementing the power-sharing agreements. Certainly, he was a dictator who had upheld Hutu supremacy and was guilty of extreme human rights abuses, but he was no doubt also aware of the dangers in the agreement (and may have been assassinated because of it). After international pressure of this kind in such a perilous situation, it might be expected that the major

---

[20] US sources, including the State Department, the CIA and the Defense Intelligence agency, have argued that Hutu extremists were responsible for the attack on the plane, but this remains disputed. In 2004 a French anti-terrorist magistrate, Jean-Louis Bruguière, claimed that the assassination had been carried out on the orders of Paul Kagame, the RPF leader and current President of Rwanda. Bruguière repeated this charge in a second report in November 2006, leading to Kagame breaking off diplomatic relations with France. A major source for Bruguière's accusation appears to be the testimony of Abdul Ruzibiza, a defector from the RPF.

powers would also commit themselves to policing and protecting the settlement. Instead they devolved full responsibility for implementation to the parties who had signed it. The genocide was carried out by internal forces, but Rwanda had effectively been abandoned before it began.

## Conclusion

This chapter has argued that the combination of neo-liberal economic policies and pressures to democratise can contribute to the generation of violent conflicts in developing and transitional countries. It has also demonstrated that this impact can continue when the same general policy prescriptions are translated into peace-making processes.[21] In other words, a broadly liberal approach by advanced capitalist countries can contribute to the most inhumane results. This does not mean that any of the key actors *intend* to bring about a situation in which violent conflict will arise. Nor would I suggest that the effects are always predictable. In the Rwandan case, for example, few predicted genocide, although warnings of massacres were certainly disregarded.[22] And, while Rwanda was in no sense typical, it provides the most terrible warning about the way in which external policies can constitute links in a chain of events leading to dire consequences. Furthermore, this also involved many NGOs, which participated in this process without any coherent strategy, in an apparent belief that civil society developments were positive in themselves. This reinforces the point made in the previous chapter about the need to *assess* the probable consequences of all actions, rather than simply assuming that peace and humanitarianism will follow from peaceful or humanitarian intentions.

[21] There are some signs that, at least in theory, the World Bank has recognised this (Collier *et al.*, 2003, pp. 87, 123, 154–6, 166, 177, cited in Hanlon, 2006b, p. 133). It is less clear that its practice has changed substantially.

[22] However, the possibility had been raised in a report by the UN special rapporteur on extrajudicial, summary or arbitrary executions, which was never seen by the Security Council (Barnett, 2002, pp. 63–4).

# 5

# After Intervention

Humanitarian intervention has traditionally been viewed as a brief episode of military incursion, followed by almost immediate withdrawal once the gross violations have ceased. In fact, a speedy exit has been regarded as a defining characteristic of a genuine humanitarian intervention. Otherwise it would be suspected that the motives were more likely to be non-humanitarian, such as a military occupation to bring about regime change or to control resources. In practice, however, many allegedly humanitarian interventions of the 1990s were not followed by this kind of rapid evacuation. It is, of course, possible to interpret this in various ways. One argument would be that the continuing external presence *confirmed* the original definition and refuted the suggestion that the interventions were genuinely humanitarian. However, an alternative interpretation would be that the original definition of humanitarian intervention was based on simplistic assumptions.

Many of those who advocated such interventions tended to consider the consequences in an unduly narrow way. There was much discussion, often with reference to the traditional Just War notion of 'proportionality', of the need to assess the likely outcomes when considering the justification for an intervention. However, these were normally evaluated in terms of immediate deaths and suffering: that is, would a coercive intervention save more people than it would harm? Comparatively little attention was paid to two other equally crucial issues. First, it was surely naïve to assume that in complex situations an intervention could be followed by almost immediate withdrawal or that, if this did occur, this meant that it could be regarded as a success.

This may be illustrated with reference to the intervention in Somalia. Whether or not the military action there had any positive consequences in saving lives—and, as noted in chapter 2, this is still disputed—following the abrupt withdrawal after the debacle in 1993 the country was effectively abandoned, with continuing rule by warlords and territorial secessions.[1] Little international interest was taken in the country until after 9/11 when the US began intervening again on suspicion that Islamic groups were funding terrorists. Subsequently the increasing power and domestic popularity of the Islamic Courts Union, widely regarded as the first force to begin to unite the country since 1991, led to a counter-attack by the Transitional Federal Government, established by prolonged negotiation among the factions. Ethiopia supported this counter-attack, partly as a proxy for the US in the 'war on terrorism' at the end of 2006, and in early 2007 the US itself undertook military action in support of the Ethiopian government, and was still launching sporadic attacks against alleged Islamic extremists in March 2008. This meant that the country was once again engaged in a violent conflict, with hundreds of thousands of refugees moving out of Mogadishu. Meanwhile, Somalia remained one of the poorest countries in the world, with 43% of the population in extreme poverty, 73% in general poverty (less than $2 per day), only 18% enrolment in primary schools, and an overall adult literacy rate of 19%, with the male rate almost double that of females (UN, 2007a). In these circumstances, the rapid withdrawal in the early 1990s contributed to negating any positive humanitarian effects of the original international intervention. But the whole notion of humanitarian intervention as a military operation, followed by rapid evacuation, is problematic in other ways.

In *Reading Humanitarian Intervention* (2003), Anne Orford notes the analogies between fictional heroic masculine warriors rescuing the innocent, particularly in films, and the militaristic virtues that are (implicitly) extolled in contemporary interventions. In Hollywood films, the star may save ordinary people from the local gangsters and then ride off into the sunset leaving a tranquil community living in harmony and contentment! Orford's main concern is with the ideological and emotive impact of such ideas and their political effect in representing the powerful states as virtuous and pure saviours. But there is no similarity between the fictional vision and the complex-

---

[1] The civil war led to continued fragmentation of the state, with various degrees of separation. The most serious are those of Somaliland, the former British protectorate, which declared itself fully independent in 1991, and the adjoining province in Northeastern Somalia, which declared autonomy as Puntland in 1998.

ity of any real society. Thus even if a regime carrying out brutal repression were defeated militarily in a genuine humanitarian intervention, there would be no guarantee that it would not resume such actions immediately after withdrawal, or that other social and political forces would have the resources to re-establish a functioning non-repressive governmental system in the short term. And, without this guarantee, it could be argued that once an intervention has been carried out the external forces may be able to succeed in achieving their original objectives only if they *do remain* after the initial military victory, and that they may have a duty to do so. On the other hand, they then inevitably become actors within the society, affecting its pre-existing distribution of power. They become a factor in the political, social and economic conflicts of the country, favoured by some forces and opposed by others.

Nor is it conceivable that international forces would be entirely neutral, for there would almost certainly be reciprocal hostility between those who intervened and those who had benefited from the previous set-up. And since interventions in the real world are carried out for mixed motives, the political preferences of those who intervene are likely to be still more pronounced. This means that a prolonged international presence contains precisely the dangers that the traditional view sought to exclude: that an allegedly humanitarian intervention will become imperialistic. This chapter will consider such issues in relation to Bosnia, Kosovo and East Timor, but it is first necessary to consider more general questions about the nature of, and legitimacy for, this kind of international tutelage.

## International administration or liberal imperialism?

In earlier chapters it has been argued that forcible intervention to protect a population from massive violations may be justified in exceptional circumstances although this certainly transgresses the doctrine of state sovereignty. However, a sustained international presence after the military defeat of the perpetrators of such atrocities constitutes a still more radical transgression of the principle of sovereignty. For the suspension of self-government violates traditional liberal and left-wing ideas. Since the whole notion of external rule suggests imperialism and the inequality of peoples, international control appears to call into question the assumption that decolonization, national liberation and the formation of new states constituted an era of progress. Similarly, it contradicts the idea of the sovereign equality of states, seeming to indicate that some states have only a limited right to sovereignty—or a right to limited sovereignty.

Some revisionist and right-wing historians and politicians certainly seek to reappraise the imperial era positively and, from this perspective, the new international governmental regimes are therefore unproblematic. However, much of the left has naturally been deeply concerned about this recent trend and many developing countries have feared that it means a reversion to imperialism. Once again, such fears have been exacerbated by the post 9/11 'war on terrorism' and both the theory and practice of regime change. For example, in September 2003, Paul Bremer, the Head of the Coalition Provisional Authority in Iraq, promulgated four orders that included 'the full privatization of public enterprises, full ownership rights by foreign firms of Iraqi businesses, full repatriation of foreign profits...the opening of Iraq's banks to foreign control, national treatment for foreign companies and...the elimination of nearly all trade barriers' (Juhasz, 2004, quoted in Harvey, 2005, p. 6). The orders were to apply to all areas of the economy, except oil, while strikes were effectively forbidden in key sectors, unionization was restricted, and a highly regressive taxation system was imposed. This was followed up with laws specifying, in minute detail, the operation of the free market and free trade systems, and when the interim government, appointed by the US, was declared 'sovereign' in June 2004, it was not permitted to change the existing laws. The occupation has therefore not simply precipitated violence and the establishment of a new base for Al Qaeda, but may justifiably be regarded as neo-imperialist—in line with the war itself. Some critical perspectives have regarded the international regimes following interventions in Bosnia, Kosovo and East Timor as essentially similar, the aims in each case being peace maintenance, economic restructuring and discipline, and socialization into the Western system (Freeman, 2006, pp. 171–4). While accepting that there are certainly common features of this kind, once again I want to distinguish between humanitarian intervention and the interventions in Afghanistan and Iraq. Yet even if the latter are excluded from the analysis, the notion of post-conflict international control poses major ideological and conceptual problems.

In general, defenders of international governmental regimes in such situations are anxious to argue that they are not advocating a new form of imperialism or even unequal sovereignty. Some seek to embed the whole phenomenon in a new post-Cold War framework, arguing that a 'solidaristic' international society has replaced the inter-state system based on sovereignty (Knudsen, 2006, pp. 159–60). Instead, they argue, new international forms of governance are responding to a concern to defend populations and minorities as well as states. Such notions can be helpful, but seem unduly optimistic about the nature of economic and political structures of power in the current era. More frequently it is suggested that international governmental regimes are exceptional and temporary. The international role is justified on preventive and transitional grounds in situations where there has been violent conflict and/or where there is not yet a functioning state. The objective is seen as nurturing the emergence of a viable and self-sustaining polity that will operate through political, rather than violent processes. Most supporters of the international regimes also resist any analogy with post-colonial transitions, arguing that the raison d'être of international governance, its multilateral character, and the relationship with the domestic actors differ fundamentally from imperialism (Caplan, 2005, pp. 20–33).

The post-war occupation regimes in Germany and Japan are also sometimes seen as a reference point, but this raises some awkward issues. First, these followed from total victory in inter-state war, with the occupation justified on these grounds, but the international regimes in Bosnia, Kosovo and East Timor were not occupations of enemy territory. Secondly, the objective in both Germany and Japan was quite explicitly one of regime change, with the goal of transforming warlike states into peaceful liberal-democracies, with exceptional forms of demilitarization. In practice, as argued below, this has also been a major element of the current international governmental regimes, but the normative basis for the attempt is much weaker than in the post-war occupations. At that stage it was justifiably believed that Nazi Germany and the militarist regime in Japan were primarily responsible for the devastating war that had just ended, and that the occupation forces were entitled to attempt to change the nature of the societies. Bosnia, Kosovo and East Timor have not been international aggressors and the justifications for establishing a particular kind of political system are correspondingly less widely shared.[2]

A more common analogy for the current wave of international forms of governance has been with previous episodes of international trusteeship over disputed territories, including the League of Nations mandate system (Chesterman, 2004, Chapter One). This implies both that the international presence is temporary and that it is acting as a trustee for a society that will take full control of its own affairs in the near future. Yet these notions are also problematic. The UN World Summit in September 2005 took the decision to

[2] Of course there was no agreement between the Soviet Union and the US as to the kind of regimes that should be established in the defeated Germany (and the Soviet Union was excluded from influencing post-war Japan). However, both wanted to eliminate the possibility of renewed militarism.

terminate the UN Trusteeship Council because the whole idea was seen as colonial in many parts of the world. Furthermore, the trustee system may be regarded as part of a neo-imperial order. That is, it can suggest that the territory in question is being prepared for emancipation from direct colonial rule into a system in which it will continue to be exploited, but in less direct ways. It has certainly been argued that this is a rather precise description of the regimes that were instituted in Bosnia, Kosovo and East Timor (Orford, 2003, pp. 140–3), but this is not what the defenders of the trusteeship analogy have intended.

In fact the whole idea of international control is deeply problematic. For some of the most radical critics, it is simply one of the many ways in which imperialism seeks to disguise itself (Chandler, 2006). But a recent study, which is broadly sympathetic to the enterprise, nevertheless concludes that in practice it has sought to impose Western standards of economic and political liberalism, and that the underlying assumptions have resembled nineteenth-century beliefs that such intervention is justified by a civilizing mission (Zaum, 2007, pp. 229–32). It is even difficult to find an appropriate terminology to describe this kind of international presence. Any term including the word 'imperialism' will have negative connotations for most of those who would describe themselves as liberal or left-wing. On the other hand such terms as 'international governance' or 'international administration' suggest benevolent or neutral intentions and practices, and this may be misleading (Bain, 2006, pp. 526–30). It is true that, whatever else they have been trying to do, at least *two* objectives of the international forces have been simultaneously to foster non-violent political entities *and* to prepare the way for some form of self-government. But, if this is so, what is (or should be) the relationship between these two goals, and how may it be encapsulated linguistically? Sometimes this is conceptualised in terms of a balance between the elements of trusteeship and the elements of domestic ownership. However, even apart from the neo-colonial connotations in these terms, it may be argued that any such notion of balance is misconceived because the two ideas are incompatible. The notion of trusteeship does not involve any reference to the wishes or democratic claims of the future beneficiaries. The only element of accountability is to those who established the trust—for example, the UN, NATO, the EU or all of them collectively. On the other hand, the notion of ownership or control by the society in question contradicts that of trusteeship. It has therefore been argued that the whole idea of balancing two incompatible objectives is both unworkable and senseless in normative terms (Bain, 2006, pp. 530–4). If so, it might seem to follow that a choice has to be made between the two principles. If trusteeship is adopted, the implication is that the interests of the 'internationals' are placed above the goal of self-determination. But according to Bain this inevitably constitutes 'a denial of human dignity' through 'subjection to alien rule' (Bain, 2006, pp. 537–8). This interpretation, which is not from a left-wing perspective, appears very close to that which views international administration as a form of imperialism.

Some advocates of an international presence have been prepared to accept this label. By 2003 Michael Ignatieff, an early proponent of intervention in Yugoslavia, was prepared to accept that humanitarian intervention was a form of imperialism and that the US was an empire, which acted in precisely the same way as previous empires (Ignatieff, 2003). This, he argued, meant neither that the interventions themselves were unjustified nor that the international regimes established in their wake were inimical to the interests of the societies in which they were based. Accepting that this appeared to contradict the whole notion of self-determination, he claimed that the problem was that some nations did not have the capacity to establish what they needed:

[T]hese nations, by themselves, cannot heal their own wounds, self-inflicted or otherwise. It is a delusion, even for those who believe fervently in the equality of peoples and their right to rule themselves, to believe that they can always succeed in nation-building on their own. Those who imagine a world beyond empire imagine rightly, but they have not seen how prostrate societies actually are when nation-building fails, when civil war has torn them apart. Then and only then is there a case for temporary imperial rule, to provide the force and will necessary to bring order out of chaos (Ignatieff 2003, p. 125).

For Ignatieff the problem was not that this new kind of imperialism denied the right for peoples to rule themselves. It was, on the contrary, that it was 'Empire Lite' (*sic*), lacking the determination for a long haul, unsure of its own legitimacy, and wanting a quick exit and low-cost strategy. The implication was that, where necessary, international personnel had to be willing to regard themselves as trustees, guaranteeing the best long-term interests of their beneficiaries without being too worried about acting decisively without reference to domestic opinion. This is a view that seeks to pre-empt criticism by claiming to be comfortable with the idea of international governmental regimes as liberal imperialism. Yet this is too complacent about the real problems, in both the concept and the practice. Kreilkamp has sought to avoid these by contrasting a neo-colonial model with a consent-based model, arguing in favour of the latter (Kreilkamp, 2003, pp. 620–3, pp. 666–70). Yet there remains a fundamental contradiction between the notion of international control and that of domestic ownership. Even if it is accepted that there are situations in which it is *temporarily* impossible for a society to rule itself *totally*—and I do accept that this was so in Bosnia in 1995 and Kosovo and East Timor in 1999—there is certainly no justification for external control in the long run. In the immediate aftermath of a crisis involving an international intervention, a form of international control may be unavoidable, but in the long run the idea of trusteeship is untenable and equivalent to a contemporary form of imperialism. There must therefore be a progression from international control to local ownership, and the extent to which this dynamic element occurs provides one essential criterion for evaluating success. Others include the progressive reduction of violence and assessment of whether this appears sustainable without international policing or military control; the extent to which international forces avoid imposing particular models on the territory in question; the amount of popular, rather than elite, support on which the new structures are based; and the degree to which a stable political, social and economic entity emerges at the end of the process.

This means that the term used to describe the nature of the international presence should, in my view, have neither negative nor positive connotations. The attitude taken towards it should follow from the degree of its success in relation to the criteria noted above. For this reason it is characterised here by a neutral term, as an *international governmental regime*.

## International governmental regimes: three case studies

The nature of the international governmental regime, and the relationships with domestic society, differed in Bosnia-Herzegovina, Kosovo and East Timor. Each is first discussed separately, but with the following common themes emphasised: the relationships between the international and local actors; the extent to which there was an attempt to impose a particular kind of solution; the degree of success in nurturing a sustainable peace; and the prospects for the future.

*Bosnia-Herzegovina.* Bosnia[3] has been the most complex of the three cases. It has involved a multiplicity of international actors interacting with a highly

[3] It will be referred to as Bosnia, as is now customary, although officially it remains Bosnia-Herzegovina, which is often abbreviated as BiH.

complex set of domestic power relationships. Many of the contradictions that have characterised the situation have followed from the Dayton Accord of December 1995. This effectively accepted the ethnic separation that had been created during the civil war. While it may have been impracticable to try to reverse this immediately after the violent conflict, there were certainly many who argued that the Dayton system was a recipe for failure (Kumar, 1997).

The Accord set out the responsibilities of the Bosnian parties and the international agencies. National elections were to be held for new pan-Bosnian political institutions, including a three-member presidency (one representative from each of the three major ethnic groups) and a bicameral parliament. The country was also divided into ethnic sub-units, with the areas controlled by Muslims (known as Bosniaks) and Croats forming the 'Federation of Bosnia and Herzegovina'. This was itself an international creation, following the attempt by the US and others to unite the Croats and Bosniaks into a single unit in 1994 (Caplan, 2005, pp. 110–11). The second sub-unit, in the Serb areas, was the 'Republika Srpska' (Serb Republic). Each of these 'entities' would also possess its own democratically elected political institutions. A draft Constitution set out the division of powers between the national and entity-level governments. In addition to various measures for demilitarization, the parties were to ensure the free movement of civilians throughout Bosnia, including the return of refugees, of whom there were then about 1.2 million in other countries and 1.1 million displaced persons within Bosnia itself (Bieber, 2006, p. 29). They were also to co-operate in the investigation and prosecution of war crimes. This Constitution was an attempt simultaneously to accommodate Serbian separatism and the aspirations of the Bosniaks for a single state, but it meant that the central government was weak from the start, while nationalist parties were given a territorial base from which to mobilise. However, the difficulties were reinforced by further complexities in the international control regime itself.

The US had insisted that the multi-national military forces policing the Dayton settlement must be under its control, and the UN was not the legal authority. Instead the key figure was the so-called High Representative, but, again at American insistence, he did not control the military forces. There was also a dispersal of international civilian power, with other actors including the OSCE, the President of the European Court of Human Rights, and the IMF all playing roles. Above all, the Peace Implementation Council (PIC), which included 55 countries and organizations, was established in 1995 to sponsor and direct the peace implementation process; however, the PIC Steering

Board, comprising the G8, Turkey and the EU Presidency, was the key body, and the PIC as a whole effectively ceased to function in 2000 (Zaum, 2007, p. 69). The Steering Board nominated the High Representative, who was endorsed by the Security Council, and there was an informal understanding that the High Representative would always be European, and that one chief deputy would be from Germany and the other from the US (Chesterman, 2004, pp. 128–9). The Office of the High Representative was funded by the PIC, with the Steering Board providing the High Representative with 'political guidance' (Orford, 2003, pp. 129–30). In effect, then, the West was firmly in control of the international institutions established to preside over Bosnia. Nevertheless, the diffusion of international power was a significant weakness in the crucial early stages of the international governmental regime.

US insistence that military forces would not undertake civilian tasks meant that the High Representative could only call upon an unarmed International Police Task Force for law enforcement. This enabled Serbian nationalists to intimidate Serbs into moving out of Bosniak areas, with acquiescence by the Bosnian government (Caplan, 2005, pp. 47–8). Thus ethnic separation was reinforced despite the presence of international forces. Furthermore, the High Representative did not have full responsibility for law enforcement, and the police forces that already existed were themselves penetrated by, and effectively answerable to, the ethnic nationalist parties. This meant both that their enforcement was partisan and that there was reluctance to co-operate across the lines of division between the entities. There were similar obstacles to most other aspects of state-building that could dilute ethnic separation, such as reform of the judicial system, the return of internally displaced persons, and the establishment of minority participation. While the Constitution prevented a particular group from securing overall political control, it also meant that Bosnia could not function as an effective state. Joint institutions were weakened by the rotation of chairs, threats to use veto powers and a proliferation of autonomous powers in the two entity level governments, leading to different laws, tax codes and administrative procedures. National criteria as the basis for election and appointment to public office simply entrenched ethnic division (Caplan, 2005, pp. 112–13).

Such problems were reinforced by the insistence on early elections. Despite warnings that these would consolidate the nationalist parties, they were held in September 1996, less than a year after the end of the war. This was because of US pressure, and many suspected that it was related to Clinton's domestic schedule for the imminent presidential elections (Paris, 2004, p. 100; Caplan,

2005, pp. 121–6), but the consequences confirmed the worst fears. The most nationalistic parties in each of the three communities triumphed in the legislative elections at both national and entity level and in the elections to the tripartite Bosnian Presidency. As the US negotiator of the Dayton Accords put it, 'the election strengthened the very separatists who had started the war' (Holbrooke, 1998, p. 344, quoted in Paris, 2004, p. 101). This tendency continued throughout the next year and was reinforced by municipal elections the following September, and even within the Muslim-Croat Federation the Bosnian Croats attempted to retain separate institutions, rather than merging with the 'entity level' government (Paris, 2004, pp. 101–3).

The ongoing priorities for the PIC were 'deepening economic reform and creating the conditions for self-sustaining market-driven economic growth', accelerating the return of refugees and internally displaced persons, and 'fostering functionally and democratically accountable common institutions supported by an effective, merit-based civil service and a sound financial basis' (quoted in Orford, 2003, p. 130). By 1997 it had become clear that the combination of relatively weak authority for the High Representative with a diffusion of responsibilities amongst international agencies and the devolution of powers to the entities and nationalist politicians was not conducive to achieving these goals. The first phase had been based on an assumption of 'local ownership', although this was a pretence, for the most significant element in the international presence at this stage was the fact that 60,000 troops (including 20,000 from the US) were stationed in the country. Now there was a move towards far stronger international control—but this caused new problems.

More progress towards multi-ethnicity took place in institutions that were either directly controlled by international bodies or were partly immune from party politics.[4] Similarly, progress towards the establishment of minority representation in entity police forces (an aim of the Constitution) was far greater in the special status territory of Brcko District, where the internationally appointed Supervisor had sweeping powers, than in the rest of the country.[5]

---

[4] This was reflected in such bodies as State Border Control, the Independent Media Commission (later becoming the Communications Regulatory Agency), the Central Bank and the Human Rights Ombudsman. All these were initially run by international bodies with the participation of members of the local community selected by the transitional authority (Caplan, 2005, p. 92, Bieber, 2006, p. 59).

[5] Brcko District, with a population of 87,000, was established with a special regime because it was a multi-ethnic area. The reform of the police was more successful than elsewhere

Western frustration with the reluctance of the three main nations to share power there led to a reversal in policy with an accretion of authority by the High Representative, whose Office became the most influential institution in Bosnia. This operated without democratic principles or power-sharing, although Paddy Ashdown, the High Representative from 2002 to 2006, opened up some higher positions to Bosnian staff and was blocked by the German government when he wanted to bring in a Bosnian instead of a German as his senior deputy (Ashdown, 2007, pp. 224–5, pp. 274–5). The key decision-making powers therefore continued to be held by international staff, and between 1997 and 2005 the Office of the High Representative enacted over a hundred laws, passed several hundred decisions and dismissed more than 180 public officials, including the President of the Serb Republic and the Croat representative in the Bosnian Presidency. In June and July 2004 alone Paddy Ashdown dismissed 70 officials in the Serb Republic (Bieber, 2006, pp. 83–5). This power to bar elected or appointed officials from office did not require the production of evidence or include any right of appeal (Caplan, 2005, pp. 188–9).

After the initial simplistic view of elections as the key to democracy and peace, there was a substantial shift from 1997. Instead of remaining neutral in the elections, in 1998 and 2002 the international agencies and High Representative intervened with funding, and heavy-handed attempts to rig the process so as to favour more moderate politicians and undermine exclusivist ethnic nationalism (Paris, 2004, pp. 103–5; Caplan, 2005, p. 127, pp. 180–2). In 2002 Ashdown admitted:

We thought that democracy was the highest priority, and we measured it by the number of elections we could organise. The result seven years later is that the people of Bosnia have grown weary of voting. In addition, the focus on elections slowed our efforts to tackle organised crime and corruption, which have jeopardised quality of life and scared off foreign investment (Ashdown, 2002, quoted in Chesterman, 2004, p. 207).

And in his subsequent account of his four years as High Representative, he justified various forms of political manoeuvres as essential to bring about the

---

and a multi-ethnic police force made up of 45% Serbs, 37% Bosniaks, 16% Serbs and 2% others was established in 2000. The International Supervisor also imposed de-segregated education, beginning in 2001, although some subjects were still taught separately. Nevertheless, even here a strongly nationalist atmosphere remained and it was not clear how the situation would evolve after the reduction of the power of the International Supervisor, following the October 2004 elections. (Caplan, 2005, pp. 57–8; Bieber, 2006, pp. 133–43).

necessary changes, although he argued against manipulating elections (Ashdown, 2007, pp. 238–47).

A similar trajectory was evident in economic reform (Zaum, 2007, pp. 98–107). Thus in 2000 the previous High Representative, Wolfgang Petritsch, rewrote the Serb Republic assembly's legislation so as to reduce unemployment benefit, arguing that the higher rate would have caused financial difficulties to enterprises, thereby jeopardizing the privatization process, current employment, and the viability of enterprises (Caplan, 2005, p. 188). He subsequently defended his actions with the claim that 'the laws concerning economic reform and development are essential, and they simply have to be passed' (Petritsch, 2001, quoted in Orford, 2003, p. 131). The emphasis upon market reform and conversion of Bosnia into a single economic space was accentuated by his successor, Paddy Ashdown, who declared that his ambition was to turn Bosnia into the most business friendly country in the region, replacing the international community's military presence with its business representatives (Orford, 2003, p. 132).

Another key priority after 1997 was the strengthening of the High Representative's role in relation to the whole area of human rights and ethnicity. This involved direct intervention in the entity Constitutions, attempting to provide more rights for minorities and to weaken ethnic territoriality (Bieber, 2006, pp. 114–15). There was a serious attempt to involve all the main parties in this process during 2002, and they did carry out much of the groundwork, although the High Representative imposed a constitutional amendment when they failed to agree on the details. Similarly, civil service reform was driven by the High Representative, overriding parliamentary objections, and he also took various initiatives to facilitate free movement and to eliminate major barriers to 'minority returns' (Zaum, 2007, pp. 107–13; Caplan, 2005, pp. 183–4). A million displaced persons had returned by September 2004, but more than a million remained outside—either in Serbia or Croatia, or in a new location in Bosnia in their majority ethnic areas—and the return statistics were also misleading as some returned simply to sell their property and move away (Bieber, 2006, pp. 111–13).

The general direction of the international governmental regime had been evident from the beginning, but it was only in January 2003, after the transfer of many responsibilities from the UN to the EU, that the Office of the High Representative devised a Mission Implementation Plan. The core tasks were defined as to: entrench the rule of law; ensure that extreme nationalists, war criminals, and organised criminal networks could not reverse the peace implementation; reform the economy; strengthen the capacity of Bosnia's governing institutions, especially at the state level; establish state-level civilian command and control over armed forces, reform the security sector; pave the way for integration into the Euro-Atlantic framework; and promote the sustainable return of refugees and displaced persons. This was accompanied by 21 action plans, with each identifying a transition point which could be judged complete or in a position to be handed over to Bosnian authorities (sometimes jointly with another international organization). However, it also clarified the overall aim as to ensure that 'Bosnia and Herzegovina is a peaceful, viable state on course to European integration' (Caplan, 2005, pp. 173–4).

This confirmed the role of European integration as the primary external state-building/peace-building vehicle. Ashdown's formal title, unlike that of his predecessors, included the words 'European Union Special Representative', and in 2002 Bosnia was also granted entry into the Council of Europe. In 2004 the European Commission announced willingness to start negotiations leading to a Stabilization and Association Agreement, and the EU also took over the peace-keeping role from NATO.[6] By now the EU was adopting a carrot and stick approach to Bosnia. In 2005 talks on the Stabilization and Association Agreement began after the leaders agreed in principle to unify the police forces. The final technical round was completed in December 2006, but Bosnia was subsequently warned that progress in establishing closer ties would be slowed down unless the desired reforms were completed, and a major crisis erupted in the autumn of 2007. In October, after a further defeat of police reform measures, the sixth High Representative, Miroslav Lajcak, introduced procedural reforms to streamline parliamentary and ministerial voting pressures and declared that he would introduce these by decree unless they were accepted by the beginning of December. This led to the resignation of several Serb officials and politicians, the threatened resignation of the Prime Minister of the Serb Republic, and veiled threats of a referendum on secession (although this was prohibited under the Dayton agreement).[7] In this tense atmosphere

[6] The next year a high level International Commission on the Balkans, chaired by the former Italian Prime Minister Giuliano Amato, argued that the prospect of entry into the EU was essential for the future of Bosnia. It cited the evidence of a survey indicating that no ethnic group was now intent on threatening the existence of the Bosnian state, although the same survey also showed that more than half the Serbs still preferred the idea of separation. It recommended passing authority from the Office of the High Representative to an EU negotiator and shifting other responsibilities to the Enlargement Commissioner in Brussels (International Commission, 2005, p. 17, p. 18, pp. 23–5).

[7] This was in the context of the imminent declaration of independence by Kosovo, but, more generally, observers still claimed that in 2007 Bosnian Serb public opinion

renewed violence appeared possible, but a compromise was reached just before the December deadline when both the High Representative and the Prime Minister modified their positions. This was followed immediately by the initialling of the Stabilization and Association Agreement, although the EU made it clear that this would not be signed until the elusive police reform legislation had been agreed. In April 2008 this was introduced into the Bosnian parliament, making signature of the Agreement very likely.

How, then, should the international governmental regime of Bosnia be evaluated? In 2007 the former High Representative, Ashdown, had no doubt, describing progress, measured by the timescales of peace-building, as miraculous. In fact, he claimed that peace and stability had already been basically assured by the time he began his work there in 2002 and that the main task was now state-building (Ashdown, 2007, p. 220). He was similarly upbeat about progress in this direction by the time he had completed his term of office in January 2006:

...VAT was up and running, the customs services had been unified into a single state-wide service, the Bosnian judiciary was working under a single state-wide framework of law, the courts were beginning to try even the highest in the land for corruption, the economy was growing at 5 per cent (albeit from a very low base), a single army was operating under state control, a single state intelligence service, accountable to parliament, had been created and the country had entered on to the long road that, hopefully, will lead it to Europe (Ashdown, 2007, p. 296).

Progress had certainly been made. The international presence had controlled the violence, but this is obviously a minimum requirement and, as Kofi Annan recognised in 2001, any worthwhile criterion for success must include some confidence about sustainable peace without a continuing international presence (UN 2001).

Dayton had accepted ethnic partition and the international governmental regime had subsequently sought to dilute this, primarily from 'above', with a programme based upon an image of an inclusive, multi-ethnic society. But the forces in favour of inclusiveness were too weak a basis on which to construct the state after the horrors of the war, and only the Bosniaks supported any strengthening of the central institutions. The result has been a polity in which ethnic separation and mutual suspicion continue to predominate, making effective government difficult for the foreseeable future (Bieber, 2006, pp. 144–51). Yet the strengthening of nationalist parties in the first post-

---

overwhelmingly favoured leaving Bosnia and that secessionist sentiment had been revived after Montenegro's vote for independence (Fawn, 2008, p. 277).

Dayton elections had led to a complete change of direction in international policy, which was highly paradoxical. In effect, it now operated on the assumption that, in order to secure the goal of an inclusive liberal-democracy, it was legitimate for the High Representative to veto choices that had been made democratically. David Chandler, a vehement critic of the international governmental regime, has argued that the three communities would have been more inclined to seek mutually beneficial co-operation had they been left to make their own choices (Chandler, 1999, pp. 196–9). This is arguable, but the attempt to manipulate democracy to bring about particular results certainly tended to foment alienation, rather than participation.

Nor was the international economic regime a success. By late 2002 per capita GDP in Bosnia was only half the pre-war level, despite seven years of international aid that, on a *per capita* basis, surpassed the assistance Western Europe had received under the Marshall Plan (Chesterman, 2004, p. 244; Bieber, 2006, pp. 34–5). Both the criminal networks and the profiteering that had been a prominent feature of the violent conflict continued after the war, tending to reinforce the inequalities that had already been created in those years. There were also increased disparities between ethnic groups, largely because of the geographical distribution of resources. In 1997, the average gross wage in the Serb Republic was therefore only 51.7% of that in the Federation. Subsequently, a less nationalist government in the Serb Republic secured greater international aid (which had previously mainly gone to the Federation) and, perhaps partly as a result, by 2002 wage levels had increased to 71.9% of those in the Federation (Bieber, 2006, p. 36, p. 38). But there was now an economic hierarchy of the three major communities, with Croats at the top and Serbs at the bottom. As argued in the previous chapter, neo-liberal policies tend to have particularly de-stabilizing effects in situations of transition, when there are obvious differences between the status of the ethnic groups. Florian Bieber suggests that the inequalities in economic development have not yet been an important factor in ethno-nationalist discourse (Bieber, 2006, p. 40), but neither will they do anything to achieve stronger Serbian support for the new state. As usual, market-driven international policies have also accentuated development gaps within Bosnia, particularly between Sarajevo and the rest of the country. Overall, the disparities are attributable partly to the incoherence of the funding programmes and the absence of a regional approach, but also to the inadequacy of Bosnia's institutions and the difficulties of trading between the entities (Chesterman, 2004, p. 244, Bieber, 2006, pp. 144–51).

The negative impact of attempts to institute a 'liberal peace' in vulnerable societies was discussed at length in chapter 4, and the Bosnian experience provides further relevant evidence for this. But the work of the international governmental regime there also provides other lessons. It was argued earlier that such regimes could be justified by immediate post-conflict situations, but that they needed to make themselves redundant through a clear trajectory to self-government. In some respects, Bosnia went in a reverse direction. On the basis of his thorough comparative study, Richard Caplan has argued that the first six to twelve weeks are the most critical period for establishing a secure environment and the credibility of an international peace force (Caplan, 2005, p. 55). However, this was the time when the international control regime was at its most inadequate in terms of security policies. Instead the emphasis was upon premature elections. Subsequently, there was a stronger attempt to *induce* an acceptance of a single state, based on human rights, minority rights and inclusion.[8] Liberal and left-wing opinion will sympathise with the aim, but it is highly unlikely that it can be achieved through *force majeure* by those wielding international power. This is particularly so when war memories are very recent and people seek security by living in majority ethnic areas. Excessive intervention may also have a negative impact upon both public opinion and political parties: if it is known that the real power is *international* there is a reduced incentive to participate actively or for politicians to bargain and negotiate. Finally, there are contradictions even in the notion of eventual EU membership as the primary external peace-building device. Certainly, this is a goal about which there is considerable agreement in Bosnia, but the state constructed at Dayton may be too weak to push the integration process forward successfully (Bieber, 2006, p. 146).

The international control regime has certainly brought about a degree of stability, reflected in the sharp decline in the number of peace-keepers stationed in the country. By 2002 the initial NATO force of 60,000 had already been reduced to 12,000, and there was a further reduction when the EU replaced NATO in 2004. At the end of February 2007, EU leaders announced that a reduction from the current level of 6,800 to 2,500 would take place over the next few months. Yet the crisis in late 2007 demonstrated that the situation remains volatile. Nevertheless, poverty and unemployment, rather than secession, are now the dominant themes in political life, and there has been

[8] It is also notable that, even after the constitutional amendments passed at the insistence of the High Authority, the rights of minorities other than the three major groups (above all the Roma) remain very poorly protected (Bieber, 2006, pp. 115–16).

incremental change in strengthening the state and weakening the entities. The system of government remains highly complex, with a continuation of ethnic dominance, and control through elites, rather than reliance on popular support and participation. But the prospect of eventual EU membership, and the combination of pressure and bribes that this involves, may stabilise Bosnian politics and create more functional co-existence between the entities. It remains to be seen whether this will eventually lead to EU membership and the termination of the international governmental regime.

*Kosovo.* In Bosnia a recognised state already existed when the High Representative arrived. However, the very status of Kosovo was a matter of dispute. At the Rambouillet conference of February 1999 the Americans had insisted that a referendum should be held on independence within three years, but this proposal had been one of the causes of the Yugoslav government's rejection of the proposals, leading to the NATO attack. Although the Kosova Albanians had hoped that the result of the war would be independence, this did not happen. Both because China and Russia insisted on Kosovo's legal status as part of Yugoslavia and because the West hoped that a less hostile ruler might succeed Milošević in Belgrade, the ultimate status of Kosovo was left uncertain.[9]

This meant that the international presence in Kosovo from 1999 onwards was always in a paradoxical position. The Albanian majority, accounting for some 90% of the population, was overwhelmingly in favour of independence and totally opposed to any continuing relationship with Serbia. Having regarded NATO, and particularly the US, as liberators, the Albanian Kosovars therefore expected the peace-keeping troops to support their demands. They were therefore bitterly disappointed to find that this did not occur. At the same time the KLA, which was the main activist force amongst the majority population in the aftermath of the war, was fiercely nationalist

[9] UN Security Council Resolution 1244, adopted on 10 June 1999 at the end of the war, embodied the ambiguity, with numerous references to Yugoslav sovereignty coupled with conditions ensuring that Belgrade had no control over Kosovo. Annex 2, paragraph 5 encapsulated the contradictions, specifying the 'Establishment of an interim administration for Kosovo as a part of the international civil presence under which the people of Kosovo can enjoy substantial autonomy within the Federal Republic of Yugoslavia, to be decided by the Security Council of the United Nations. The interim administration to provide transitional administration while establishing and overseeing the development of provisional democratic self-governing institutions to ensure conditions for a peaceful and normal life for all inhabitants in Kosovo.'

and supported violence to secure independence. In response to Serbian forces' atrocities against them, including forced mass migration at the beginning of the war, KLA forces now undertook reprisals against Serbian and other minority populations. These ran counter to international claims that the objective was to establish a multi-ethnic Kosovo in which Serbs would remain permanently settled. At the same time, the international forces also faced two additional, and inter-related, problems in achieving that goal. First, part of the Serb minority, in co-ordination with Belgrade, was attempting to create a *de facto* division of Kosovo in the north of the region, with the partition of Mitrovica; secondly, the minority also resisted any moves towards the independence of Kosovo.

Because of the difficulties in the situation, the international governmental regime always tended to veer towards an imperial role in Kosovo. This time the UN had legal authority through the Special Representative of the Secretary-General (SRSG), at the head of the United Nations Mission in Kosovo (UNMIK). However, differences between the various agencies involved, as well as between national authorities, weakened UNMIK. Nor was the SRSG in a position of authority over the whole mission. Thus when the SRSG came to believe that Serbs might be more supportive of UNMIK if 25% of its staff moved from the mono-ethnic capital to the Serbian area of Northern Mitrovica, his orders were defied (King and Mason, 2006, pp. 249–53). Once again, there was a separation between the multi-national military forces under NATO control (KFOR) and the SRSG, who had no control over them. However, KFOR did take responsibility for the maintenance of internal security, rather than leaving this to the police as had been done in Bosnia (Caplan, 2005, p. 39, p. 48). Simultaneously, the SRSG sought to establish institutional capacity. As there had been no separate institutions since Milošević had revoked Kosovan autonomy in 1989, the assumption (or illusion) was that it was possible to build up a civil and political society without making any decision as to whether this would be within Serbia or independent from it.

Although Bernard Kouchner, the first SRSG, appeared to favour independence, his successor, Hans Haekkerup, kept more closely to the mandate of procrastinating on the ultimate status (Chesterman, 2004, p. 134). And in general UNMIK sought to establish non-partisan institutions and build up judicial capacity, their major success in this area being the establishment of a new police force, which was 16% female and 15% from minority communities, including 8% from the Serb community (Caplan, 2005, p. 59). Another key concern was to dilute the power of the KLA, and this was partially achieved in the first local elections in October 2000, when the party of Ibrahim Rugova, who believed in a peaceful road to independence, easily defeated the party that was closely linked to the KLA. The KLA was formally dissolved by being incorporated into the new Kosovo Protection Corps and acting as a mainstream political party.[10] Nevertheless, former KLA members still practised violence and remained powerful, and Serbs were opposed to the establishment of the Kosovo Protection Corps, which they regarded as a provocative step towards the creation of a Kosovan Albanian army (Caplan, 2005, pp. 93–4). In fact, the issue of final status was the major political concern, which dominated everything else. Although UNMIK set up the Kosovo Transitional Council in order to secure local representation and enhance its legitimacy, for the Albanian majority the failure to say anything about the final status of the territory undermined any notion of local control or democracy. Meanwhile, UNMIK constantly noted the lack of participation by the Serbs and Belgrade's continuing influence over those in the North (UN, 2007b)

Albanian frustration with the slow progress towards independence led the UN to accelerate the establishment of self-governing institutions in 2001. This was to involve the transfer of authority to provisional institutions in the executive, legislative and judicial fields following elections for a Kosovo-wide assembly in November 2001. These again resulted in a victory for Rugova, who became the first President in March 2002. But the Kosovar Albanians initially rejected this framework for provisional self-government because it did not include a commitment to independence or a referendum on the issue (Caplan, 2005, pp. 116–17). Similar problems arose with the currency. Using the dinar would enable Belgrade to control the economy, but the initial use of the deutsche mark, followed by the adoption of the euro in 2002, again led the Serbs and Belgrade to suspect movement towards independence (Caplan, 2005, pp. 140–2).

There were also complaints about the lack of democracy by the international authorities. The office of Ombudsperson had been established to protect human rights and freedoms, but the US had insisted that KFOR was excluded from its purview (Caplan, 205, pp. 200–1). In addition to this, UNMIK authorised judicial panels in which international judges were in the

---

[10] This would eventually lead to success in the elections of November 2007, when the party secured 34 % and Hashim Thaçi, the leader of the KLA at the time of the 1999 war, became Prime Minister and subsequently declared independence for Kosovo (see below).

majority (to overcome local bias) and also used executive orders to detain criminal suspects without legal processes, as, for example, in February 2001 when they detained Kosovar Albanians suspected of bombing a bus (Caplan, 2005, pp. 61–5). However, actions of this kind led the Ombudsperson to issue a scathing report in 2002:

UNMIK is not structured according to democratic principles, does not function in accordance with the rule of law, and does not respect important international human rights norms. The people of Kosovo are therefore deprived of protection of their basic rights and freedoms three years after the end of the conflict by the very entity set up to guarantee them (Ombudsperson Institution in Kosovo, 2002, quoted in Chesterman, 2004, p. 126).

While such criticisms were no doubt valid, UNMIK's behaviour also followed from the structural contradictions in its position. Thus, when drafting the framework for Provisional Self-Government, it felt the need to resist Kosovar Albanian attempts to include a reference to the 'will of the people', because this effectively referred only to the majority ethnic group. Furthermore, while there is no justification for an international body to infringe human rights, sections of the Kosovar Albanian population were prepared to use violence to secure independence.

As in Bosnia, the problems were exacerbated by the economic situation and international economic policies. Kosovo had already been desperately poor by European standards long before the eruption of the violence, and its formal GDP had contracted by an estimated 50% between 1989 and 1994 (Pugh, 2006, p. 117), while the economic devastation was again worsened by the war. At Rambouillet there had already been an insistence that the economy in Kosovo should function in accordance with free market principles, and neo-liberalism was incorporated into the constitutional framework promulgated by the SRSG in May 2001 (Pugh, 2006, p. 123). This was moderated by the recognition that there was a need for some measures of social protection (Pugh, 2006, p. 122, p. 125), but these had little impact upon a region in which there was very poor rural infrastructure and a gross imbalance in wealth and opportunity between rural and urban areas. Despite major concerns about the legality of UNMIK permanently changing property rights in an area in which it was not the sovereign power, privatization was also pushed through after 2003, with the SRSG taking the lead in this, while the UK Department of Trade and Industry and USAID were involved (Zaum, 2007, pp. 152–67). Yet unemployment and poverty remained the critical problems, with the International Commission on the Balkans claiming that unemploy-ment levels were approximately 60–70%, up to 90% in minority areas (International Commission 2005, p. 20).[11] Two years later, the IMF estimated Kosovo's GDP at only 1,200 euros per person per year, and GDP growth generally hovered at around 3–4% per year after 2002, although it was negative in 2005 (IKS, 2007, p. 12). Kosovo, like Bosnia, included a thriving criminal economy, but some of this was also a means of survival for ordinary people. International policies, insisting on privatization and balanced budgets, enriched the criminal networks, but simply drove others towards the shadow economy for protection (Pugh, 2006, pp. 116–17, 127–9).

In this situation there was constant resentment by both the majority and minority populations, and a tendency to try to take direct action to precipitate change. The international governmental regime, on the other hand, constantly procrastinated so as to avoid making any declarations about the final status of the territory. In December 2003 UNMIK thus officially adopted 'standards for Kosovo' with which to evaluate the achievement of certain benchmarks, but still without any guarantees as to how progress on the standards would help to resolve the sovereignty issue (Kristensen, 2006, pp. 135–56, Knudsen, 2006, pp. 160–1). Such delaying tactics fuelled discontent, which erupted over two days in March 2004 when violent rioting took place throughout Kosovo, involving an estimated 51,000 participants. The aim, both in cities and in small villages, was to rid these areas of all remaining vestiges of a Serb presence, with other minorities, including the Roma, also targeted. This led to a damning report on both KFOR and UNMIK by Human Rights Watch, concluding that ethnic Albanian extremists now knew that they could effectively challenge the international security structures, while the ethnic minorities had lost any remaining trust in the international presence (Human Rights Watch, 2004). The impact of all this was to convince many key international actors that decisions on the final status of Kosovo needed to be expedited.

The high-level International Commission on the Balkans in 2005 was deeply critical of the Kosova Albanian leadership for doing nothing to counter the public mood that favoured an ethnically homogeneous Kosovo. But it also condemned UNMIK, concluding:

The international community has clearly failed in its attempts to bring security and development to the province. A multi-ethnic Kosovo does not exist except in the bureaucratic assessments of the international community.

[11] The IMF estimate was much lower, estimating that 22–30% of the active labour force was unemployed (RNISS, 2007, p. 12).

The events of March 2004 amounted to the strongest signal yet that the situation could explode. Since then UNMIK has demonstrated neither the capacity nor the courage to reverse this trend. Serbs in Kosovo are living imprisoned in their enclaves with no freedom of movement, no jobs, and with neither hope nor opportunity for meaningful integration into Kosovo society. The position of the Serbian minority in Kosovo is the greatest indictment of Europe's willingness and ability to defend its proclaimed values (International Commission 2005, p. 19).

The Commission also noted the weakness of the economy, the fact that UNMIK itself was viewed as corrupt and indecisive, and the failure of Kosovo to make sufficient progress on human rights, respect for minorities, and law and order. But its overwhelming concern was that the status quo was unsustainable and could drive the whole region towards highly dangerous instability. Its objective, clearly shared by major Western powers, was to try to resolve the final status, while also protecting minority rights. Once again, as in the case of Bosnia, the proposed strategy was to offer the prospect of eventual membership of the EU. In this case the Commission also recognised that the best prospect of securing the agreement of Belgrade (and therefore, probably, that of Russia and China) was by offering a similar future to Serbia.

From the beginning of 2006 until March 2007 the former Finnish President Martti Ahtisaari tried to negotiate this strategy on behalf of the UN. The Commission had suggested a four-stage process, with the culmination as independence within the EU. Similarly, Ahtisaari's proposal suggested that, as a first stage, Kosovo should have the right to negotiate and conclude international agreements, including the right to seek membership in international organizations. However, the status proposals also prescribed the main features of the constitution, which would include guarantees to minorities in a multi-ethnic state that would have no official religion. Once again, the role of the EU was also given particular prominence and it was proposed that the main international figure with authority over Kosovo should combine the title of International Civilian Representative with that of EU Special Representative (UNOSEK, 2007).

Yet there were formidable obstacles to this strategy for stabilizing Kosovo. On 10 March 2007, after a meeting in Vienna, Ahtisaari issued a statement saying that this concluded the negotiations held over the past fourteen months, which had included seventeen rounds of direct talks and twenty-six expert missions to Belgrade and Pristina. He expressed regret that 'there was no will from the parties to move away from their previously stated positions', but he was also convinced that there was no common ground and concluded that the potential of negotiations was exhausted (UNOSEK 2007b, Press release 10 March 2007). Since the reactions of the two sides in Kosovo were also predictable, with the Albanian majority denouncing it as too limited, and the Serbian minority as tantamount to independence, the only hope was that Serbia might be persuaded to accept it in return for fast-track membership of the EU.[12] But unless Serbia acquiesced, there would be no agreement on the status proposals in the Security Council, particularly as there was a serious deterioration in relations between Russia and the West.

In July 2007 the EU and US failed to secure Russian support for a resolution at the UN, despite various drafts designed to demonstrate that 'supervised independence' for Kosovo would not undermine the principle of state sovereignty. Nor were the Serbians and Kosovar Albanians able to reach any agreement, and talks between them broke down at the end of the year. Following elections in November, the former KLA leader, Hashim Thaçi, became Prime Minister at the beginning of 2008. With support from the US and the EU, it was clear that independence was imminent, and this was announced on 17 February. Although it is too early to make confident judgements about the eventual impact of this development, certain elements in the situation were immediately clear, and, as had been the case for the past ten years, the external and internal aspects of the situation were intertwined (International Crisis Group, 2008a). The Ahtisaari plan had envisaged the rapid termination of UNMIK, with some of its functions transferred to the Kosovo government and others to the International Civilian Representative and the EU. However, this strategy was undermined when Russia backed Serbia's insistence that both the declaration of independence and the EU mission in Kosovo were illegal. This meant that there could be no smooth transition and that both the UN and the EU remained in the region, but without a clear basis for co-operation because of the disagreement in the Security Council.[13] This difficulty was compounded by a second problem: direct action by Belgrade and the 50,000 Serbs in Northern Kosovo to thwart the West's project. For within a month of independence, particularly after violence against UNMIK and KFOR

---

[12] In March 2007 there were reports that the European Council was divided on this issue (Balkan Investigative Reporting Network 16 March 2007, 'EU Split on Fast-Track Serbian Membership').

[13] The EU sent its rule of law mission (EULEX) and a special representative the day before the announcement of independence. EULEX was the largest civilian mission yet established by the EU under the framework of the European Security and Defence Policy, with around 2,000 police, judges, prosecutors and customs officials.

forces on 17 March, there were many indications that Belgrade, in collaboration with Serbs of the Mitrovica area, was intent on seeking a *de facto* partition. And despite claims by the International Civilian Representative that the EU mission would operate throughout Kosovo, it was not clear that EU or KFOR forces would be prepared to risk military confrontation to prevent this Serbian action. In such circumstances, approximately 70,000 Serbs in enclaves to the south of a post-partition border could be in a very vulnerable position.

How, then, should the international presence established in Kosovo in 1999 be evaluated? Even Ian King and Whit Mason, two former members of UNMIK, have argued that the only successes of the international governmental regime in Kosovo were in tackling the immediate humanitarian crisis in 1999, organizing elections, and partially refurbishing basic infrastructure. In their view, it failed almost completely in improving inter-community relations or protecting minority rights, and merely presided over a reversal of positions between Serbs and Albanians (King and Mason, 2006, p. 239, p. 261). It barely met the minimum conditions of preserving peace and security. Yet international forces put twenty-five times more money and fifty times more troops, on a per capita basis, into post-conflict Kosovo than they did between 2001 and 2004 into Afghanistan (International Commission, 2005, p. 7). It never appeared probable that this would lead to a sustainable peace. Of course, the international regime was operating in substantially the same situation after the intervention as before it: that there was no basis for agreement between the Serb and Albanian communities. Any attempt to satisfy one would almost inevitably alienate the other. Instead UNMIK tried to push through legal and economic reforms, based on its own liberal model, without any local 'ownership'. But this failed to satisfy either community, and the Western-led international forces then increasingly acceded to the Albanian demands because of local pressure, rather than because the international standards had been met (Zaum, 2007, pp. 166–8).

The intractability of this conflict was reinforced by the lack of *international* agreement about whether any solution should be imposed without the consent of Belgrade. This also raises wider questions about the notion of humanitarian intervention. In theory, this is designed to protect a population from violations, but the Kosovo situation involves two further issues. First, the 1999 violations were against a majority in a province that sought territorial separation from the state exercising legal sovereignty over it. But the creation of a new state by an external decision would always be a *political* act, and the controversial nature of this step was indicated by the fact that only 40 states had recognised Kosovo's independence three months after the announcement. Secondly, after 1999 humanitarian principles required protection of the Serb minority, although the defence of the Albanian majority had been the justification for the original action. Thus the international governmental regime had always operated without any agreed principles to help it to suggest a solution (Kristensen, 2006, pp. 138–40, pp. 149–51; Knudsen, 2006, pp. 162–6). Western support for 'supervised independence' in 2008 was, at best, acceptance of a particular solution through pragmatism, rather than principle. Nevertheless, despite Serbia's bitter hostility about the loss of Kosovo, in November 2007 Belgrade and the EU initialled a Stabilization and Association Agreement, which was signed the following April. As in the case of Bosnia, it is therefore *possible* that a regional EU enlargement could eventually provide a basis for the resolution of the ongoing conflict. But at present only a reckless gambler would bet on this.

*East Timor/Timor-Leste.*[14] Until recently the UN mission which was in East Timor from 1999 until 2002 was widely regarded as a success, although many analysts were highly critical of aspects of its policy. However, a major political and social crisis erupted in 2006, followed two years later by assassination attempts on the President and Prime Minister by the leader of a rebel army. Few had predicted developments of this kind, and the links between the policies of the international government regime and the subsequent crises were not immediately obvious. Yet, as I will argue below, there were some clear causal connections between them, and the continuing social and political instability in Timor-Leste was closely related to failures during the transition period.

The international presence in East Timor followed the final stage in the prolonged crisis arising from the Indonesian occupation that began in 1975, after the withdrawal of the Portuguese colonial forces. The occupation and resistance are estimated to have led to the deaths of up to 10,000 members of the Indonesian forces (Dee, 2001, p. 19, n. 5; Shwarz, 1994, cited in Bellamy, Williams and Griffin, p. 179) and one-third of the total population of East Timor (180,000 people), either directly in the fighting or as a result of occupation-related hunger and illness, with 55% of the population displaced at some point, and there was also a high incidence of torture, rape and detention (CAVR, 2005, cited in Norad, 2007, p. 13). As noted in chapter 1, the Indo-

[14] East Timor became Timor-Leste with independence in 2002.

nesian occupation had been accepted—even encouraged—by the West, but after the end of the Cold War, the changing international climate had also transformed the context for East Timor. A new President in Indonesia in 1998 appeared more responsive to international pressure and agreed to hold a referendum on independence. Indonesia insisted that it was the sovereign power in East Timor and, although most states had never accepted the legality of this claim, the UN initially acquiesced and abandoned its original plan to oversee the transition to independence. But after 78.5% voted for independence in the referendum, Indonesian-backed militias began a new wave of murder. This resulted in the displacement of 75% of East Timor's population and the destruction of 70% of its physical infrastructure (Dee, 2001, p. 4, cited in Bellamy *et al.*, p. 225). However, Australia, which was one of the few states that had recognised Indonesian sovereignty, now called for an international intervention. Following US pressure through the IMF, with supporting action by the UK and Japan, Indonesia now accepted this (Martin, 2001, pp. 107–9). In September 1999 the UN authorised an international military force under Australian leadership—the International Force in East Timor (INTERFET)—with the task of halting the violence so that a UN administration could then facilitate the transition to independence. By the end of the next month, the Security Council decided that INTERFET had succeeded in creating a secure environment and established UNTAET (United Nations Transitional Administration in East Timor), which was given overall responsibility for administration, with full legislative and executive authority. Sergio Vieira de Mello became the Secretary-General's Special Representative and Transitional Administrator with power to enact new laws and regulations and to amend, suspend or repeal existing ones (Bellamy, Williams and Griffin, 2004, p. 180; Orford, 2003, p. 137).[15]

---

[15] In purely legal terms, it is questionable whether the international action in East Timor should be regarded as one of humanitarian intervention. If this is defined as forcible intervention without the consent of the state in question, this was not the case. Indonesia was not generally recognised as the legal sovereign and it was therefore arguable whether it needed to give its consent. In any case, with some arm-twisting from the US it acquiesced in the mission and withdrew all claims to the territory. Since there was no government or state there in 1999, the issue of East Timorese consent hardly applied in a strictly legal sense and there was widespread support for the intervention. Yet even if the intervention rested on formal consent, it was certainly *forcible*, for the first task of INTERFET was to disarm and defeat the militias that had certainly been supported by elements in the Indonesian government in the immediate past. In this sense, it was a humanitarian intervention.

UNTAET appeared to have a potentially easier task than its counterparts in either Bosnia or Kosovo. There was widespread support for it internationally, with no opposition from any of the permanent members of the Security Council, and authority was concentrated in one body, rather than dispersed between several agencies. Furthermore, the overwhelming majority of the population welcomed it after almost a quarter of a century of Indonesian oppression. Nor were there any existing structures of government with which it was necessary to share power, as in the case of Bosnia. The objective was also clear: to oversee the transition to independence. Yet there were also formidable problems. East Timor was a desperately poor country with a very rudimentary infrastructure, and unemployment remained around 80% throughout the transition period (Caplan, 2005, p. 135). Furthermore, UNTAET was constrained by the attitudes of the Security Council, particularly the United States, which never contributed its own personnel but maintained a very small separate military mission, and appeared content to rely on Australian leadership. It also sought to limit the time-scale of the UN's involvement in capacity and state-building in ways that seemed unrealistic to the Secretary-General and the mission itself (Norad, 2007, p. 5, pp. 48–9). Both this wider context and the attitudes of some of the international personnel would undermine the success of the mission and exacerbate the tensions that led to the crisis of 2006.

The first weakness in this approach was the underlying assumption that there was already a *nation* and that the task was to create a *state* (Norad, 2007, pp. 25–6). Superficially, there was a basis for this since the struggle against the Indonesian occupation had created some sense of national identity, but this was very recent and the Portuguese (who had exercised various degrees of control over the island for more than 400 years) had ruled by exploiting ethnic, tribal and linguistic differences. Unless there was consolidation of the embryonic sense of nationhood, it could easily disintegrate once again. But instead of facilitating the building of a national identity, UNTAET tended to weaken it.

One way in which it did this was by appearing to discount the importance of traditional culture. There was thus a tendency to misunderstand local systems and seek to impose a pattern of behaviour that was familiar to UN officials. For example, there were traditional political and judicial processes that were highly valued in the local culture, particularly during the Indonesian occupation when the justice system was seen as abusive. Village councils functioned on a peer jury system, and consensus-based decision-making was often successful as a tool for reconciliation, where members of the local community who had joined the militias were forgiven and allowed to rejoin the village (Freeman, 2006, p. 180). For the local custom was to judge actions in terms of the consequences for the welfare and survival of the community, rather than as an issue of individual rights and punishment. However, the system certainly presented some challenges as it did not conform to Western models of justice and was highly patriarchal, particularly in relation to issues of rape and domestic violence (Kerr and Mobekk, 2007, p. 159, p. 170). In this situation, international personnel appear to have oscillated between two extremes. At times UNTAET and the UN Civilian Police relied on the traditional system, even in rape cases, to the consternation of human rights observers. Yet they also sometimes showed disdain for the system and a fear that the traditional authorities could manipulate it for their own advantage (Zaum, 2007, pp. 203–5). Above all, there was a failure to reconcile the two legal orders— for example, by allowing the traditional informal mechanisms to deal with the more minor offences that did not contravene international human rights law. Moreover, the fact that UNTAET also decided to continue the Indonesian legal system further alienated local opinion. All this impeded the reconstruction of the judicial system and in May 2005, three years after independence, the Court system continued to rely on international judges and prosecutors, while much of the population still regarded the traditional system as more legitimate (Zaum, 2007, pp. 195–206).[16]

Cultural misunderstandings also meant that the first attempt by UNTAET to introduce a civic education programme was rejected by the Timorese because it had not valued their own interests and capacities (Chesterman, 2004, p. 136). Still more fundamentally, local concepts of legitimacy were based on ideas of sacred and ancestral authority, but because these differed from conventional assumptions about the state and political power, they were not understood by the international governmental regime (Caplan, 2005, p. 120). Part of the problem was the pressure of time, but the failures also resulted from a lack of familiarity with the culture and languages of the territory and the inappropriate assumptions on which UNTAET's policy was based. Many of the key personnel had previously worked in the Balkans, and saw it as an urgent necessity to secure control through decisive action. But this was unnecessary given the initial goodwill towards the mission. The need was to entrust more authority to the Timorese and to value their experience

---

[16] For a valuable comparative discussion of the role of traditional informal justice mechanisms in conflict transformation, see Kerr and Mobekk (2007), pp. 151–72.

(Caplan, 2005, p. 119). But the failure to do so was also based on deep-rooted cultural assumptions about the superiority of the Western liberal model. This was coupled with stark differences between the lifestyles of the 'internationals' and the local people, which reinforced the local alienation. That was certainly not entirely (or even primarily) the fault of UNTAET itself, which was constrained by the rules and procedures of the UN. In fact, Vieira de Mello (who was subsequently killed in the attack on UN headquarters in Iraq in 2003) was sensitive to many of the problems. As he wrote:

The UN mission in East Timor had over 500 vehicles for its staff, but it was only by breaking rules that a meagre dozen vehicles could be released for Timorese political leaders. The UN spent millions of dollars on offices and accommodation for staff, but the rules had to be bent again to allow us to do up a limited number of public buildings which were not for use by staff. The rules also do not allow one to give lifts. In a country where transport is lacking, such rules (luckily often broken!) make the UN appear arrogant and egotistical in the eyes of those whom we are meant to help (Vieira de Mello, 2000, p. 8, in Caplan, 2005, pp. 102–3).

Only about 10% of UNTAET's annual budget of over $500 million actually reached the Timorese, and this certainly contributed to the increasing sense of frustration, particularly given the very limited opportunities for participation in the development of the new institutions (Chesterman, 2004, p. 183).

The international governmental regime also undermined the construction of national identity by attempting to construct a centralised state, rather than building on local variations—an approach that led to a crisis within UNTAET itself. In theory, the country was divided into thirteen districts, with each district structure composed of a peacekeeping force, humanitarian aid, a local government administration, and civilian police. Each was also to consist of a sub-district, village and hamlet level of administration. Finally, there was to be an elected council in place, with each hamlet electing a representative to a village council, which in turn would elect a representative to the sub-district level. The villages would then submit proposals for how they wanted money spent, with their own representatives at the sub-district level making the decisions. Jarat Chopra, the Head of District Administration, was convinced that this model would simultaneously reverse the previous colonial system of government and the failures of centralised forms of international governmental regimes by the UN (Chopra, 2000). However, in March 2000 Chopra resigned, claiming that 'Stalinist' and 'colonialist' practices by several senior members of UNTAET, and particularly the Head of Territorial Administration, were jeopardizing the UN mission. The central issues in the dispute concerned the extent to which democratically elected sub-district and village-level officials should be allowed to determine their own development and reconstruction priorities in a World Bank-funded community empowerment project. However, this was part of a wider difference in theory and practice about the way in which UNTAET should be structured and its relationship with the Timorese, and Chopra's resignation was followed a month later by those of all thirteen District Administrators (Caplan, 2005, pp. 97–8). In general, the mission was highly hierarchical and centralised in the capital without sufficient knowledge of, and input from, the wider society. The only exception to this was in UNTAET's Division of Health Services. This transferred responsibility to the Timorese a year after the start of the operation, while maintaining control over the budget, and thus a successful partnership was created between UN health officials and locals (Caplan, 2005, p. 87, p. 103). But in general the UN appeared to fear that a local democratic input might result in a loss of control and concentrated on construction of a central state apparatus, a tendency also reinforced by international economic assistance (Norad, 2007, p. 67). This led to a greater sense of alienation and marginalization by the provinces.

A further weakness in the international governmental regime—implicit in its disregard for East Timorese culture and its centralizing emphasis—was the fact that it worked through the political elites rather than at grassroots level. But this again tended to reinforce the division between the rulers (both national and international) and the masses. A litmus test was in relation to language policy. Decisions on this would inevitably be difficult, for there are 16 languages and numerous dialects spoken in the country. Tetum was used by 50–80% of the population, with Indonesian as the second language, spoken by about 30% of Timorese. Although Portuguese is now spoken by only 5% of the population, it was identified as the language of resistance. Portuguese and Tetum were therefore designated as the official languages, but the decision to give Portuguese this status exacerbated the feeling that a particular identity was being imposed by an elite without consultation amongst the population as a whole (Norad, 2007, pp. 56–7).[17]

---

[17] It also led to a demand for language training that could not be met and could create a greater sense of distance from its closest neighbours, Australia and Indonesia. However, the situation would have been still worse had English been made an official language, since this is spoken by only 3 % of the population.

UNTAET attempted to increase the legitimacy of its rule by establishing a consultative body, the National Consultative Council of East Timor, but Vieira de Mello sought to reinforce this by establishing a special relationship with Xanana Gusmão and the National Council of Timorese Resistance (CNRT). Gusmão had remained in East Timor throughout the Indonesian occupation, gradually building up a broadly based resistance movement (CAVR, 2005, Part 5). Despite being captured and imprisoned by the Indonesians in 1992, he had remained a dominant figure, although there were also significant divisions within the resistance movement (see below). The partnership with the CNRT seemed natural to UNTAET because it shared many of its aims and had popular support in the early period. However, there were also some tensions in this collaboration. Almost as soon as UNTAET had begun its work, Gusmão submitted proposals for a mixed Timorese-UN transitional administration, but these were ignored, and when the UN drew up its own plans, there was little attempt to explain them to the local population (Caplan, 2005, p. 168). And because there was so little opportunity for the Timorese to participate effectively, many of them, including Gusmão, frequently threatened to resign from the consultative bodies in an attempt to bring about change (Chesterman, 2004, pp. 136–40).

As the level of Timorese frustration became apparent, the UN Security Council decided to move more quickly to independence than had been planned originally. In 2001 the focus now moved to the holding of elections as the final step towards independence. This also led to some tensions in the discussions about the drafting of a Constitution, for although UNTAET privileged the CNRT, it also wanted to establish a multi-party state. This led Gusmão to claim that the UN was attempting to impose a universal system that was not suitable for East Timor (Chesterman, 2004, pp. 140–3). Nevertheless, the CNRT was dissolved in June 2001 to make way for political parties (Chesterman, 2004, p. 135). Elections took place in August for a Constituent Assembly (which became the Parliament in January 2002), and the Revolutionary Front of Independent East Timor (FRETILIN) achieved a resounding victory.

The dispute with Gusmão over the establishment of a multi-party system was related to an international failure to appreciate the extent of the divisions within Timorese political forces.[18] In particular, there were long-standing dif-

---

[18] However, the UN Missions were far more conscious of this than other observers and reported on these divisions as early as 2000 (Norad, 2007, p. 26).

ferences between the leader of FRETILIN, Mari Alkatiri, and Gusmão that would impede the construction of both national identity and state formation and play a key role in the post-independence political crisis. These divisions originated in the resistance movement.

In the brief period between Portuguese withdrawal in 1974 and Indonesian occupation the following year, many parties had engaged in a contest for power. However, FRETILIN had taken over the government in August 1975 after its armed wing, the Armed Forces for the National Liberation of Timor Leste (FALINTIL), had won a military victory, which led to the deaths of between 1,500 and 3,000 Timorese (CAVR, 2005, cited in Norad, 2007, p. 40). The Indonesian invasion at the end of that year led to further divisions, with many FRETILIN leaders going into exile in Portugal or Mozambique. Meanwhile, the overwhelming majority of the FALINTIL fighters were killed within the first six years of the Indonesian occupation. In this situation a split occurred, which would become more pronounced as time went on. The dominating ideology of FRETILIN had been a form of Marxist revolutionary ideology and, in theory at least, this was continued by the political leadership in exile in Mozambique, with Mari Alkatiri ultimately emerging as the dominant figure in the so-called 'Maputo group'. However, in East Timor Gusmão had gradually separated the resistance movement from FRETILIN and Marxism. By 2001 it was not entirely clear how far apart Gusmão and Alkatiri were ideologically, but there was continuing mutual suspicion between them. However, as FRETILIN was the majority party in the Constituent Assembly it was able to draw up a Constitution, which gave the main role in the government to the Prime Minister—a position which was now assumed by Alkatiri. When presidential elections were held on the eve of independence in April 2002, Gusmão, who stood as an independent, was endorsed by nine parties and comfortably elected. However, neither FRETILIN nor Alkatiri supported him. There was therefore a bifurcation at the highest level of leadership that would be at the heart of the political crisis four years later.

In May 2002 Timor-Leste was recognised as an independent state. Given the weak legitimacy for prolonged rule by international governmental regimes and the growing tensions between the Timorese and the 'internationals', continuation of UNTAET's rule would not have been acceptable. However, that and total independence were not the only two possibilities. In the Security Council debate a year earlier, there had been general agreement with Kofi Annan's warning that a long-term UN and international presence would be necessary even after independence (UNIS, 2001) so as to help Timorese society to achieve socio-economic development. The words of Jarat Chopra, when resigning as Head of the Office of District Administration in 2000, were also very pertinent. He argued that UNTAET should have fixed a date for independence, organised early elections to a Constituent Assembly, and transferred power, but should then have remained in East Timor to assist with long-term capacity building. Instead, he feared that the mission would simply hold an election as an exit strategy and would leave the Timorese with no genuine capacity built and 'we will have replicated the overnight decolonisations of decades past' (Dodd, 2000). This was prescient, for the mission had established a skeletal structure, based loosely on a model of political and economic liberalism, in the hope that this would be sufficiently robust to withstand the internal and external pressures that would be placed upon it. The Security Council seemed to accept that this might be excessively optimistic when passing a resolution noting that continuing international assistance would be required after independence, and in the establishment of the much smaller UN Mission of Support (UNMISET) to succeed UNTAET in May 2002 (Caplan, 2005, pp. 222–6). The UN also negotiated with Australia in an attempt to ensure that the new state benefited from the exploitation of marine oil and gas reserves, but Australia strongly 'encouraged' the new government to grant it approximately 70% of the revenues from the Timor Straits (Pilger, 2000b, cited in Bellamy, Williams and Griffin, 2004, p. 246).[19] Neither this nor the continuing role of the World Bank and IMF provided the kind of support that was needed, and the international failures in relation to socio-economic development were the most obvious link between the pre- and post-independence situations.

The attempt to restructure political life on the island had been accompanied by an attempt to incorporate its economy into the international system, with the World Bank playing the lead role. In East Timor the Bank did provide funding for health, education and public sector infrastructure (Caplan, 2005, pp. 168–71). Nevertheless, its plans followed neo-liberal priorities in seeking to ensure that East Timor had a limited public sector, with contracting out of service provision, particularly to foreign investors (Orford, 2003, pp. 135–6). By 2001 some improvements had certainly been made, with the reconstruction of over thirty major public buildings and the provision of basic infrastructure and services, including roads and the supply of electricity and

[19] After years of disputes an agreement was finally signed in January 2006, but the lion's share of the revenues still went to Australia, as the settlement was based on a maritime boundary of 1972 that has never been recognised by Timor Leste.

water in urban areas. Yet many critics were already arguing that the influx of foreign investors and UN and aid workers had created a dual economy, with a new form of colonialism that was deepening divisions within the society (Orford, 2003, pp. 137–8). In 2006, four years after independence, Timor-Leste still ranked 142nd out of 177 countries (below Congo and Sudan) in the Human Development Index, with more than 40% of the population living below the poverty line (UN 2006b, Unicef 2007). This raises the fundamental question of whether the international economic involvement increased or decreased stabilization. A very thorough Norwegian Review of Development Cooperation in Timor-Leste in October 2007 (Norad, 2007) suggests the latter, although it is also critical of the policies of the post-independence government. While ensuring the recovery of agriculture had originally been viewed as the major priority in order to reduce poverty for the 75% of Timorese working in this sector, this was not carried out. In fact, the report suggests that limited attention was given to most of the sectors directly affecting the lives of ordinary people, and the overall focus of assistance reinforced the defects of the international governmental regime's general approach: it concentrated on the central state apparatus and accentuated the concentration of activity in the capital, Dili. As one informant told the Norwegian project: 'We were so focused on building the best possible Government that we forgot about the people' (Norad, 2007, p. 34).

The failure of either the international governmental regime or the subsequent government to lead to tangible improvements in everyday life created the potential for a social and political explosion, particularly amongst rural dwellers who had been forced to move to the city and amongst youth.[20] This latent unrest was reinforced by failures during the transition period. As already noted, the general assumption was that there were no serious cleavages amongst the population, except perhaps in relation to a minority who had collaborated with Indonesia. Yet during the crisis in 2006 there appeared to

[20] The young are the largest and best educated segment of the population, having benefited from the expansion of public services in education and health. However, this service expansion had not been complemented by new opportunities in the labour market, participation in political processes or adequate expansion of post-secondary education and training. Timorese youth therefore faced high unemployment and this was accompanied by a massive internal migration to Dili. However, youth unemployment rates in the capital remained significantly higher than those elsewhere, with 70% of male teenagers and 50% of 20–24 year old males unemployed in 2007 (Norad, 2007, pp. 61–2; IGC, 2008). This also led to a strong sense of alienation, reflected in an extremely high membership of martial arts groups and gangs.

be a very serious division between 'Easterners' and 'Westerners'. This left many analysts uncertain whether this had long historical roots or was a very recent development that had simply been manipulated and exploited by political leaders (International Crisis Group, 2008b, p. 7). However, the sudden eruption of these conflicts was related to the rudimentary sense of national identity and widespread alienation from the political process. As the Norwegian review expressed it:

The concept of the Timorese nation was not given the opportunity to evolve as large sectors of the society felt marginalised and distant from their leaders. Rather than a new sense of "nation" to confront the challenges of development, what emerged were diverse and competing narratives. Many of these were based on the old rivalries, ideological cleavages and recalled betrayals: Who were the "true" resistance fighters? Who collaborated with the Indonesians? Who deserved the spoils of war and benefits of peace? Who sat out the war in exile, and did not suffer?

The narratives highlighted old cleavages and divisions. They diminished the contributions of the "other" and, therefore, the right of opposing groups to be full participants in building the new nation. This was a key element in the East-West divisions. Efforts by the political elite to develop a Lusophone identity were often seen as an imposition, particularly among youth who had no affiliation with the colonial past and Portuguese language or culture. Historically-based concepts of identity did not incorporate the experience of the youth population, further alienating them from the older leadership.

As a consequence, Timor-Leste looked like a state in search of a nation by 2006 (Norad, 2007, p. 50).

Such tensions might have been less explosive had there been a united political leadership, but after independence both Alkatiri and Gusmão sought to strengthen their own positions, constructing separate bases of power. The fact that international development assistance, both before and after independence, promoted a centralised state provided Alkatiri, as constitutional head of government, with particular advantages in this respect, and he used his control over parliament to establish an increasingly autocratic system of government with little popular participation and declining support (Norad, 2007, pp. 42–3). Gusmão's institutional position was much weaker, but he remained more influential and popular in the wider society. By 2006 the relationship between them had deteriorated further, with Gusmão criticizing the government for its slow progress in relation to development goals. In this context, a further failure during the international government regime would now become relevant: the fact that no coherent overall security system had been established. For the two leaders had also played a key role in establishing rival security forces with different loyalties, with Alkatiri as the main focus for the National Police Force of Timor-Leste (PNTL) and Gusmão for the Timorese Defence Force (F-FDTL). It was in this situation that the crisis erupted.

In January 2006, 126 soldiers from the F-FDTL submitted a petition to a Brigadier General and to Gusmão (but not to Alkatiri) complaining of mismanagement and discrimination. When the government failed to respond, the petitioners left their barracks at the beginning of February and began a series of protests. The Brigadier General, with the support of Alkatiri, then dismissed 594 members of the F-FDTL (almost 40% of the army's total strength) in mid-March. The dismissals led to an escalation of the protests and on 28 April five people were killed, with at least 37 more violent deaths in the next few weeks. But this also sparked off the underlying social crisis, with an estimated 155,000 people—15% of the Timorese population—fleeing from their homes. On 24 May the Foreign Minister, José Ramos Horta (a close associate of Gusmão), sent official requests for military assistance to Australia, New Zealand, Malaysia and Portugal, and the first forces arrived the next day. Finally, on 30 May, Gusmão declared a state of emergency for 30 days, giving him sole command of both military and police forces and personal responsibility to liaise with the international forces. He and Horta (who now became Prime Minister) also effectively forced Alkatiri out of office in late June by threatening to resign unless he went.

The crisis led to a reversal in UN policy. UNMISET had been due to withdraw, but as soon as the situation was first discussed in the Security Council on 5 May, there was general agreement (with the sole exception of the US) that the current UN presence in Timor-Leste needed to be strengthened so as to ensure that the new state would be sustained. There was also widespread concern that the work done by UNTAET between 1999 and 2002 could not be allowed to fail (UN, 2006c). In August, Kofi Annan's report pointed to a series of underlying social and political problems that had not yet been resolved in the country, and also to the way in which poverty and associated deprivation had contributed to the crisis. This again highlighted the need for long-term development assistance. As a result, it was agreed on 25 August to establish a new integrated mission in Timor-Leste (UNMIT) for an initial period of six months (subsequently renewed), with a civilian component, including some 1,600 police personnel and up to 34 military liaison and staff officers (UNMIT, 2006). However, this did not lead to any resolution of the underlying social or political crises.

Gusmão had used the military petitioners to force a confrontation with Alkatiri, and Alkatiri's endorsement of the petitioners' dismissal was equally confrontational, for he was clearly attempting to gain total control over the security forces. But there were also some important international dimensions to these events. Gusmão had already been criticizing Alkatiri's policy to external donors and, although the intervention was subsequently endorsed by the UN, the appeal for military assistance had been directly to *governments* (with Australia playing the leading role). This meant that particular external forces were reinforcing the power of Gusmão against the elected government. There were also some unavowed issues about national identity and international orientation in these events. The choice of Portuguese and membership of an international Lusophone identity were particularly associated with Alkatiri and the Maputo group, but the major international funders did not speak the language. Australia had played the leading military role in attempting to stabilise Timor-Leste, and clearly supported Gusmão and Ramos Horta. In effect, there had been a coup against Alkatiri and FRETILIN, with external backing for the President.

There were further outbreaks of violence in the autumn of 2006 and the spring of 2007, and the presidential and legislative elections took place from April to June 2007 in a tense climate with the political division unresolved. José Ramos Horta was now elected President and in August named Gusmão as Prime Minister in a coalition government. This gave them effective control over the government, but FRETILIN, with more seats than any other party, declared the new government illegal and announced a parliamentary boycott. This led to renewed violent protests and arson attacks. Furthermore, 10% of the total population remained internally displaced, with approximately 30,000 living in 51 camps in Dili and 70,000 living with relatives or friends. This concentration of IDPs and youth in the capital meant that the situation remained potentially explosive (IGC, 2008b, pp. 3–6). However, the culmination of the prolonged crisis came with events related to the confrontation over the security forces almost two years earlier. In February 2008 a former high-ranking soldier, Alfredo Reinado, who now led a rebel army, was allegedly behind an attempt to assassinate both Gusmão and Ramos Horta. Gusmão escaped unhurt and Reinado and another rebel soldier were killed by the presidential bodyguards, but Ramos Horta was seriously injured and taken to hospital in Australia. A state of emergency was declared, which included a night curfew and bans on gatherings and rallies, but the government did not secure control over the rebel army until the alleged co-leader of the assassination plot surrendered at the end of April.[21]

It is paradoxical that a UN mission that had been viewed as successful in 2002 had left a situation in which unresolved tensions had erupted so soon after independence. The international governmental regime could not be accused of becoming imperialistic by staying too long. But if the term 'neo-imperialism' suggests informal external control over a weak newly independent state with a limited capacity to resolve its domestic problems, this may well describe the situation in Timor Leste.

## Assessments and lessons

Peace theorists have formulated some concepts that may be used to provide insights into the theoretical and practical dilemmas facing international governmental regimes. First, there is an important distinction between two notions of peace, highlighted in the work of Johan Galtung (Galtung, 1985). While the terms have been defined in various ways, in general 'negative peace' suggests a situation in which overt *violence* between the parties to the conflict has ceased, or is at least greatly reduced. However, it does not necessarily imply elimination of the potential for revival of violence. 'Positive peace' is a far more ambitious goal, for it suggests that social relationships are such that forms of 'structural' violence embedded in oppressive, unjust and unequal power relations have also been eliminated (Galtung, 1969). Moreover, as Galtung later argued, it is also necessary to eliminate 'cultural violence', which may be used to legitimise both direct and structural violence—as for example in racist, ethnic-nationalist, or patriarchical discourse and attitudes (Galtung, 1990).

It may be argued that an entirely 'positive peace' represents an aspiration, rather than a reality, and that all existing societies contain elements of structural and cultural violence even when there appears very little likelihood of overt violence on any extensive scale. It is partly for this reason that the term 'sustainable peace' has become widely used in recent years. Yet the notion of a continuum, with negative peace at one end, a sustainable peace somewhere in

---

[21] In May 2006 Alfredo Reinado had joined the soldiers who rebelled after their dismissal by Alkatiri. Although at that time he was a supporter of Gusmão, this changed when Reinado was pursued for murder and Gusmão relied on Australian forces to capture him. When Reinado's co-leader (Gastao Salsinha) surrendered in April 2008, he denied that there had ever been an assassination attempt.

the middle, and positive peace at the other end, can be useful in considering situations in societies emerging from overt violent conflict. In such circumstances, the notion of advancing far towards a positive peace seems an unrealistic aspiration in the short term, after all the hatred and bitterness fuelled by years of fighting and atrocities. Yet a considerable transformation in relationships will be necessary if there is to be any sustainable peace, and there are inherent tensions between the notions of negative and positive peace in practice (Miall, Ramsbotham and Woodhouse, 2005, pp. 188–94). For example, in the immediate aftermath of violent conflict security is normally the most urgent necessity, and this may require a strong policing and military presence. A heavy reliance on security forces, which is integral to negative peace in the aftermath of violent conflict, will also be a normal precondition for any movement along the scale towards a positive peace. But any domination of the society by the police and military sectors may inhibit development of the forces on which a sustainable peace would ultimately depend—thriving political and social movements. Furthermore, left-liberals and the left share Galtung's convictions about the need to eliminate (or at least drastically reduce) both structural and cultural violence. Much emphasis has also been placed in recent peace research upon the importance of constructing peace from below through civil society movements. This places particular emphasis on the importance of women in effecting change, since they are normally major victims of violence, but not its perpetrators (El-Bushra, 2006). Once again this often contradicts the approach of negative peace, which tends to seek to manage and contain violence primarily from above. The establishment of a sustainable peace is thus dependent upon the ingredients of both the negative and positive approaches, which may be partially sequential but also in constant tension with one another.

These theoretical and practical difficulties in peace-building become still more complex in relation to the situations discussed in this chapter. In these circumstances, as noted earlier, the international presence is based on a denial of the current capacity of the territory to exercise sovereignty, but its only justification for continuation must be its success in facilitating the attainment of an autonomous sustainable peace. In other words, in addition to the inescapable tensions in any peace-building situation, in the immediate aftermath of the violent conflict the international governmental regime is the key component in the construction of negative peace from above, for it controls the main security forces. The issue then is whether it will be willing and able to help foster the shift in power relationships—both between itself and the host society and within that society—necessary for movement along the scale towards a positive peace. The case studies discussed above do not provide a basis for great optimism in this respect.

In Bosnia, both the war itself and the Dayton Accords left the most nationalist forces in each of the communities in a powerful position, and the progressive transfer of authority to local control could simply empower the forces of exclusive nationalism. In Kosovo, while the intervention was justified on the basis of protecting the Albanian population, it was subsequently the Serbs (and other minorities) who were the main victims of violence, intimidation and discrimination. In Bosnia, in the initial stages, the tendency was to follow the mantra of a liberal peace policy, but then to put this into reverse once elections entrenched the power of the most nationalist forces. In order to strengthen the central state and secure minority rights, including the right of return, the High Representative then acted decisively *against* local power interests. But, having begun by deferring to an electoral process, these subsequent actions also caused resentment and alienation. In Kosovo, where the international governmental regime had a monopoly of institutional power (unlike Bosnia where this was shared with the local institutions), the problem was different, for there was a divergence between its aims and those of the majority Albanian community. The latter sought support for rapid independence, while the former wanted to avoid any discussion of final status and to strengthen minority rights. When the Albanian majority was dissatisfied with progress, some were inclined to create 'facts on the ground' by intimidating the Serb minority. This left the international governmental regime and, still more, the peace-keeping forces with the question of whether they were prepared to take decisive action against the majority population that the original intervention had (allegedly) been designed to protect. In March 2004 it appeared that they were not. Finally, in East Timor, the problems were again different. Whereas in both Bosnia and Kosovo a major issue had been how to balance the goal of eventual local control with the need to prevent this leading to entrenchment of ethnic exclusivism, this was not a primary concern in East Timor. Here the need was to help build capacity across the whole territory and to be prepared to involve the local population through genuinely participative bodies from the start. Instead the tendency was to maintain tight control as if the situation was similar to that in the Balkans.

As Richard Caplan has shown, some of the shortcomings of the missions were attributable to organizational problems, the specific features of the regions in which they were located, and the degree of regional and international support on which they were based (Caplan, 2005, pp. 252–3). However, there were also theoretical and strategic weaknesses in their approach. In particular, it is now widely agreed to be more urgent to build up security and institutional, civil and judicial capacities than to focus on early elections, which can simply exacerbate conflict or reinforce extreme nationalisms (Chesterman, 2004, pp. 180–2, p. 234; Paris, 2004, pp. 179–207). The UN belatedly recognised this in 2001 in 'No Exit without Strategy' (UN, 2001). However, security is not simply a matter of law and order, but also involves such issues as economic and social security.

The attainment of sustainable peace is facilitated by balanced economic development. However, all three cases considered above concerned weak economies, which had been devastated by war, and their subsequent experiences provide further evidence that neo-liberal policies are destabilizing in transition and post-conflict societies. Chesterman has also pinpointed some key differences between the way in which Marshall Aid was co-ordinated with US political objectives in the post-war period and the approach to international economic reconstruction since the end of the Cold War. First, American aid was targeted at relatively wealthy countries, while the current recipients tend to be fragile, usually of limited long-term interest to donors, and unable to absorb a sudden influx of aid in a short period. Secondly, such aid has often been short-term emergency relief, rather than development assistance. Thirdly, there are now many more actors involved, with the rise of NGOs and competition between them. Fourthly, Marshall Aid took place in the era when government intervention was generally accepted as beneficial, whereas the current orthodoxy is that governments should simply facilitate market conditions. There is therefore little strategic vision involved in the distribution of assistance. Finally, aid often comes with conditions attached and, despite grandstanding by governments at the time of the initial crisis, in many cases it never arrives at all. All this means that the general recognition that state-building and peace-building require buttressing by development assistance is rarely matched by practical action of the right kind (Chesterman, 2004, pp. 185–98). As argued in previous chapters, this demonstrates the necessity for a radical shift in international economic structures and relationships, but even a restoration of Keynesian economic principles would almost certainly be beneficial to post-conflict reconstruction (Pugh, 2006, pp. 127–9).

In each of the three cases studied above, there have clearly been some serious failures. Yet there is one final factor that also needs to be taken into account, which is probably of greater advantage to Bosnia and Kosovo than to Timor-Leste. Because the collapse of the fragile peace in either state could jeopardise the stability of the Balkans as a whole, with a knock-on effect on wider international relations, both the EU and the US have been keen to prevent this from happening. In particular, as noted above, the EU has been acting strategically in the whole of the former Yugoslavia and Albania by holding out the prospect of future membership in return for compliance with a variety of conditions, including a renunciation of violence. The fact that EU membership is regarded as a worthwhile goal therefore introduces an important contextual factor within each national situation. And it is certainly conceivable that this will eventually tip the balance in favour of a sustainable peace. However, even the successful use of 'soft power' by the EU would provide no guarantees against the resumption of violence, particularly given the increasingly sharp economic disparities between its central and peripheral regions and its weak role in securing minority rights once states have joined. In the case of Timor-Leste, there is little comparable geopolitical interest, although Australia is particularly anxious to prevent the collapse of the state. In these circumstances, the evolution of a sustainable peace might be even more difficult to achieve.

None of these critical comments implies that international governmental regimes should never be established in future. They do, however, suggest that humanitarian intervention should not be considered without a realistic assessment of the probable difficulties that will follow, and that international governmental regimes will have limited long-term success unless they are prepared to address the issues that are conducive to movement towards a positive peace. It must be recognised that in the societies considered above there were profound sources of structural and cultural violence, and this is likely to be the case in all societies in which there has been civil war or mass atrocities. There is no blueprint for successful external involvement in such situations, but if international actors are to contribute positively, rather than negatively, to the establishment of a sustainable peace, they require sensitivity to local traditions and cultural practices, a genuine attempt to foster domestic self-government, and a willingness to accept results that depart from standardised formulae derived from Western political and economic systems. The apparent reluctance of international regimes and their backers to learn these lessons reinforces the critique of current policies and their underlying assumptions. It also highlights the contradiction between acceptance of the need for humanitarian intervention in exceptional circumstances and recognition that the subsequent international presence may fail to achieve its professed goals and be tainted by neo-imperialist tendencies.

# 6

# The Responsibility to Protect

This book has been highly critical of both the theories and practices that have dominated Western interventionist policies. In particular, it has argued that humanitarianism needs to address issues of global inequality and poverty, that neo-liberalism and the liberal peace theory often exacerbate conflict in vulnerable societies, and that international governmental regimes following humanitarian interventions have had very limited success in establishing sustainable peace. This chapter seeks to provide a wider conception of humanitarianism that incorporates these critical observations, and therefore also underpins any justification for military action as a last resort in extreme circumstances.

It is structured as follows. Section 1 focuses on conceptual issues in relation to humanitarianism and humanitarian intervention. After considering some alternatives, it draws on the concept of human security and the framework of 'the responsibility to protect' elaborated in the report of the International Commission on Intervention and State Sovereignty (ICISS, 2001). Section 2 also uses the ICISS report as a basis for a wider discussion about aspects of Just War doctrine, with a particular emphasis on the notions of 'Right Intention' and 'Right Authority'. This leads to a discussion of possible reforms at the UN and, in this context, Section 3 examines the adoption of the terminology of the 'responsibility to protect' and considers the significance of this change. The concluding section argues that, while offering an important conceptual advance, the current interpretation of the new framework remains too narrow and fails to address some central issues.

## Rethinking humanitarian intervention: conceptual issues

In chapter 3 the complex relationships between the humanitarian and political realms were discussed. It was suggested that humanitarian action is rooted in the concern to relieve suffering and offer protection, but inevitably takes place in a world dominated by relations of power and inequality that affect it fundamentally. Furthermore, humanitarian actions have political consequences that need to be considered by those involved in the humanitarian sector. Politics, by contrast, is rooted in the world of power, with differing ideological and theoretical conceptions offering contrasting views of the means to achieve goals, such as equality, freedom, and justice. Yet humanitarian concerns will temper all those forms of politics that acknowledge the need to reduce suffering on a universal basis as an urgent and immediate goal. I believe that certain implications follow from both the overlaps and the differences between the two realms.

In chapter 3 I suggested that the *appeal* of traditional humanitarianism has been related to its apparently apolitical nature—its claim that the relief of human suffering should transcend boundaries of class, ethnicity, sex, religion, ideology and political and economic interests. It follows, I believe, that if an enlarged conception of humanitarianism is to gain wider acceptance, particularly in the advanced capitalist countries, it needs to make a similar appeal. This is obviously a challenging task for, unlike traditional humanitarianism, the enlarged conception introduced in chapter 3 maintains that international humanitarian duties extend beyond the immediate relief of suffering and must address 'gross violations' of the human person arising from acute poverty, starvation, preventable illness, and premature death. I also argued that this meant incorporating an aspect of *development* into humanitarianism. However, such notions confront international structures of power in ways that the traditional conception of humanitarianism does not, making it far more difficult to secure acceptance, particularly by those who benefit from those structures.

Two conclusions follow from this. First, it is necessary to recall that traditional humanitarianism also needed to argue and campaign in order to win support. There was no inevitability about the establishment of the Red Cross or wider acceptance of its principles or the development of international humanitarian law. There was resistance both to humanitarian actions and to the underlying conceptions. Similarly, the fact that an enlarged conception of humanitarianism may be opposed does not mean that it will not secure recognition in future. However, the second conclusion is that it remains necessary to maintain a boundary between humanitarianism and politics, whilst acknowledging its fuzziness, and this has important implications for the way in which the enlarged conception is elaborated.

No conception of humanitarianism can ever be a substitute for politics, and both left-liberals and the left will (and, in my view, must) always regard progress towards such goals as equality, solidarity and human emancipation as key elements in any just solution to world problems. This requires both theoretical work and political action. However, an enlarged notion of humanitarianism requires a different discourse and conceptual framework. It is not designed to achieve the goals of political liberalism, let alone socialism, but to shift the boundaries of humanitarianism without submerging it fully within the world of politics. The first purpose of this section is therefore to consider some concepts that may help to do this. The second aim of this conceptual discussion is to clarify the relationship between humanitarianism and humanitarian intervention. For although this book has argued that there are very exceptional circumstances in which military intervention may be justified for humanitarian purposes, it has not explained how such intervention may be embedded in the wider conception of humanitarianism. This section suggests that the notion of human security and the framework of the 'responsibility to protect' offer this possibility.

*Development and human security.* One possible way of broadening the notion of humanitarianism would be through embracing the concept of the Right to Development. This idea originated in a proposal by a Senegalese jurist, Keba M'baye, in 1972, as a framework for international resource redistribution, with the potential to make development assistance a legal obligation, based on ethical conceptions (Barsh, 1991, p. 322). This eventually led to the 1986 UN Declaration, which set out this Right in ten articles, and some of the most important of these are shown in Box 6.

There were two fundamental problems in securing practical action through this Declaration. First, it was passed as a resolution rather than a treaty and therefore remained non-binding. Secondly, there was a North-South split in the vote on it, with advanced capitalist countries rejecting it 'because they saw it as the imposition of one-sided obligations and an invasion into what should be, according to them, the discretionary/voluntary field of development assistance' (Cornwall and Nyamu-Musembi, 2005, p. 13). Although the Right to Development is still supported by many Southern governments, as well as

Box 6

*1986 UN Declaration on the Right to Development*

*Article 1*

1. The right to development is an inalienable human right by virtue of which every human person and all peoples are entitled to participate in, contribute to, and enjoy economic, social, cultural and political development, in which all human rights and fundamental freedoms can be fully realised.
2. The human right to development also implies the full realization of the right of peoples to self-determination, which includes, subject to the relevant provisions of both International Covenants on Human Rights, the exercise of their inalienable right to full sovereignty over all their natural wealth and resources.

*Article 3*

1. States have the primary responsibility for the creation of national and international conditions favourable to the realization of the right to development.
2. The realization of the right to development requires full respect for the principles of international law concerning friendly relations and co-operation among States in accordance with the Charter of the United Nations.
3. States have the duty to co-operate with each other in ensuring development and eliminating obstacles to development. States should realise their rights and fulfil their duties in such a manner as to promote a new international economic order based on sovereign equality, interdependence, mutual interest and co-operation among all States, as well as to encourage the observance and realization of human rights.

*Article 4*

1. States have the duty to take steps, individually and collectively, to formulate international development policies with a view to facilitating the full realization of the right to development.
2. Sustained action is required to promote more rapid development of developing countries. As a complement to the efforts of developing countries, effective international co-operation is essential in providing

these countries with appropriate means and facilities to foster their comprehensive development.

*Article 10*

Steps should be taken to ensure the full exercise and progressive enhancement of the right to development, including the formulation, adoption and implementation of policy, legislative and other measures at the national and international levels.

Source: Declaration on the Right to Development, Adopted by General Assembly resolution 41/128 of 4 December 1986 Office of the United Nations High Commissioner for Human Rights Geneva, Switzerland, 1996–2002.

development NGOs and other activists, it has generally been disregarded or reinterpreted by the rich countries (Marks, 2003). No doubt this is mainly because, if implemented, it would have threatened the interests of the North in the international political economy, and there are several ways in which the policies of the World Bank, the IMF, the WTO and other international institutions transgress rights specified in the Declaration (Orford, 2001, pp. 145–74). It was therefore convenient to argue that the apparent privileging of economic development over human rights could legitimise repressive states and authoritarian policies.

However, the inclusion of particular statements provided an alibi for refusal to accept the Declaration. Article 5, for example, dealt exclusively with the human rights abuses perpetrated by rich countries, and the statement, in both the Preamble and Article 1, that the self-determination of peoples included the inalienable right to full sovereignty over all their natural wealth and resources could be regarded as incompatible with any form of transnational capitalism. Furthermore, the Right of Development was clearly embedded in the discourse of emancipation and political transformation, as is evident in Articles 1 and 2. Naturally, the left and left-liberals will support such calls for a radical redistribution of power and resources, and the Declaration is generally helpful in providing both a critique of existing structures and policies and an alternative approach in the discourse of rights (Orford, 2001, pp. 175–84). But I would nevertheless suggest that the Right of Development went beyond the parameters of even an enlarged conception of humanitarianism because it departed from notions of protection and the alleviation of suffering in favour of a more explicitly political framework.

185

Another recent concept is that of human development, pioneered by Mahbub ul Haq and the United Nations Development Programme (UNDP) (Ul Haq, 1995). This places the emphasis on human beings, rather than inanimate economic aggregates such as GDP, commodity production, and growth. The argument, stated explicitly in the first *Human Development Report* in 1990, was that economic growth was not always correlated with human development, and this proposition gave rise to the influential Human Development Index, derived from indices on life expectancy, educational attainment and GDP per capita. Since these were all based on a judgement about the necessary ingredients of a reasonable quality of life (and aimed to inspire policies designed to remove impediments to enjoying such a life), human development has a close relationship with humanitarianism. However, as Amartya Sen has pointed out, this notion has a 'powerfully buoyant quality' since it is concerned with progress and augmentation (United Nations, 2003, p. 8). This is not as directly political as the idea of emancipation, but it still implies an upward trajectory towards universal fulfilment. Again, this differs from the typical connotations of humanitarianism, which are of protection or rescue, rather than progress. Certainly, this is a fine distinction, since the elimination, or even reduction, of the desperate poverty that causes massive suffering would simultaneously create circumstances in which greater fulfilment of human potential became possible. Nevertheless, it is a distinction with a difference.

The idea that comes closest to the conception of humanitarianism elaborated in this book is that of 'human security'. This was also developed first within the UN, and was popularised by the 1994 *Human Development Report* published by the UNDP. It is a powerful though imprecise idea, whose essence is to shift the understanding of security away from the traditional focus on the military realm, by focusing on individuals and communities and the multiple threats to security that they face in their own lives. The 1994 report included seven dimensions of human security (and insecurity)—economic, food, health, environment, personal, community and political. At the UN Millennium Summit in 2000 the proposal for an independent commission was launched, and this was subsequently established with Amartya Sen and Sadako Ogata as co-chairs. When it reported in 2003, with the title *Human Security Now*, it urged the need for integrated policies focusing on people's survival, livelihood and dignity. To this end, it concentrated on the following distinct, but interrelated, areas concerned with conflict and poverty: protecting people during violent conflict and in post-conflict situations; defending people who are forced to move; overcoming economic insecurities; guaranteeing the availability and affordability of essential health care; and ensuring the elimination of illiteracy, educational deprivation and schools that promote intolerance:

Human security means protecting fundamental freedoms—freedoms that are the essence of life. It means protecting people from critical ... and pervasive ... threats and situations. It means using processes that build on people's strengths and aspirations. It means creating political, social, environmental, economic, military and cultural systems that together give people the building blocks of survival, livelihood and dignity (United Nations, 2003, p. 4).

And in a personal contribution to the report, Sen argued that human security, unlike human development, paid attention to downside risks. These were the insecurities that threatened human survival and the safety of daily life; or those that imperilled the natural dignity of men and women, or exposed human beings to the uncertainty of disease and pestilence; or those that subjected vulnerable people to abrupt penury; and those caused by downturns that led to the dangers of sudden deprivation (United Nations, 2003, pp. 8–9).

If the classic point of departure for humanitarianism (typified by the Red Cross and Red Crescent tradition) was the relief of suffering, human security reinforces this by proposing that all the major insecurities that affect human beings need to be tackled in an integrated way. Because these include a whole range of problems emanating from poverty, it follows that policies to overcome human insecurity must incorporate an aspect of development that addresses international structural issues. The notion of human security is therefore very helpful in offering a basis for an enlarged conception of humanitarianism. Yet even this has sometimes been interpreted in the terms of political discourse.[1]

The authors of the 2003 Report claimed that human security was 'to protect the vital core of all human lives in ways that enhance human freedoms and human fulfilment' (United Nations, 2003, p. 4) and also insisted that if protection was the first ingredient in a human security policy, it was equally important to include *empowerment* to reinforce the ability of people to act on their own behalf and mobilise for the security of others (United Nations, 2003, p. 11). Similarly, the concept adopted by a Study Group on European Security Capabilities (led by Marlies Glasius and Mary Kaldor) and presented

[1] My concern to focus on the aspects that relate to humanitarianism differs from the criticism of 'conceptual overstretch' which suggests that the term 'human security' should be confined to threats emanating from organised violence, and should preclude those emanating from poverty and inequality (MacFarlane and Khong, 2006, pp. 228–53).

in the so-called Barcelona Report to the EU High Representative for Foreign Policy in September 2004 incorporated seven principles that traversed the ethical, political and military fields.[2] I have no doubts about the importance of such concepts as empowerment, participation, human rights or multilateralism, but I do not believe that they are integral to humanitarianism.[3] However, the concept of human security is very helpful when it concentrates on the notion of *protection*, which has always been central to the humanitarian tradition. This was the way in which another extremely important international commission approached it, and it is to this that I now turn.

*The responsibility to protect.* Aspects of the report of the International Commission on Intervention and State Sovereignty (ICISS) have already been discussed in chapter 3, but it is helpful to recall its origins.[4] As noted in chapter 2, after the crisis over the Kosovo war, Kofi Annan issued a challenge for the 'international community' to forge unity around a new definition of sovereignty, and in a speech to the General Assembly on 20 September 1999, he posed the central issue in stark terms: 'If humanitarian intervention is, indeed,

[2] The Barcelona Report enumerated seven principles: 1. the primacy of human rights; 2. clear political authority; 3. multilateralism; 4. the bottom-up approach; 5. regional focus; 6. use of legal instruments 7. appropriate use of force. It also elaborated several other dimensions, including the capabilities required, and the kind of institutional embedding and resourcing that would be necessary, including issues such as democratic control and relations with NGOs and private corporations (Glasius and Kaldor, 2004, pp. 325–56 in Glasius and Kaldor [2006], which includes further essays that explain and seek to apply the idea). A slight variation of the principles appears in Kaldor, Martin and Selchow (2007). This includes only the first five principles, although the last two are clearly present in the argument as a whole.

[3] Certainly a humanitarian policy may be operated more effectively if some of these approaches are used, as is illustrated by an analogy. Health care may be improved if patients are empowered to participate in their own treatment rather than being passive recipients of whatever doctors prescribe for them. But participation does not *define* the health system. Similarly, humanitarian organizations may be improved if they encourage participation and empowerment, but this is not their essence or definition. The claim of *Human Security Now* that human security is 'to protect the vital core of all human lives in ways that enhance human freedoms and human fulfilment' has also been criticised as too amorphous or too difficult to distinguish from the definition of Human Development in the 1994 UNDP report (Thakur, 2006, p. 83).

[4] The ICISS report has also been criticised from various viewpoints. For a discussion and bibliography, see Macfarlane, Thielking and Weiss (2004), and for a particularly hostile critique, see Chandler (2004).

an unacceptable assault on sovereignty, how should we respond to a Rwanda, to a Srebenica—to gross and systematic violations of human rights that offend every precept of our common humanity?' (quoted in ICISS, 2001, p. vii).

In response, in September 2000 the Canadian government established the ICISS, jointly chaired by Gareth Evans, President of the International Crisis Group and former Australian Foreign Minister, and Mahmoud Sahnoun of Algeria, Special Adviser to the UN Secretary-General and formerly his Special Representative for Somalia and the Great Lakes of Africa. The Commission was exceptional in its composition and expertise, in the differing initial stances of its membership, in the range of consultation that it undertook, and in the extent of the research that it utilised (Thakur, 2006, pp. 247–8). The quality of the report was impressive, as were both its unanimity and the pragmatic way in which this was explained. The Co-Chairs thus made it clear that there were unresolved differences amongst the group on key issues:

> But the text on which we have found consensus does reflect the shared views of all Commissioners as to what is politically achievable in the world as we know it today. We want no more Rwandas, and we believe that the adoption of the proposals in our report is the best way of ensuring that. We share a belief that it is critical to move the international consensus forward, and we know that we cannot begin to achieve that if we cannot find consensus among ourselves. We simply hope that what we have achieved can now be mirrored in the wider international community. (ICISS, 2001, p. viii)

The first significant point concerned terminology. If the words 'humanitarian intervention' are taken at face value, they obviously suggest an intervention that is carried out for humanitarian purposes. However, as noted in chapter 3, such usage remains highly contentious. The ICISS therefore decided *not* to use the term. This was partly because it was anathema to many in the humanitarian sector (ICISS, 2001, 1.40, p. 9), but also because the language of humanitarian intervention (along with that of the 'right to intervene') was seen as unhelpful. First, it focused attention on the claims, rights and prerogatives of the potentially intervening states rather than the urgent needs of potential beneficiaries. Secondly, it did not adequately take into account the need for either prior preventive action or subsequent follow-up assistance. Thirdly (although the Commission was anxious not to overstate this), it tended to trump sovereignty with intervention at the outset of the debate by implicitly de-legitimizing dissent as anti-humanitarian (ICISS, 2001, 2.28, p. 16). But, above all, the ICISS believed that an alternative discourse could simultaneously incorporate different emphases and make it more likely that a new consensus could be established. As it explained:

One of the virtues of expressing the key issue in this debate as "the responsibility to protect" is that it focuses attention where it should be most concentrated, on the human needs of those seeking protection or assistance. The emphasis in the security debate shifts, with this focus, from territorial security, and security through armaments, to security through human development with access to food and employment, and to environmental security. The fundamental components of human security—the security of *people* against threats to life, health, livelihood, personal safety and human dignity—can be put at risk by external aggression, but also by factors within a country, including "security" forces (ICISS, 2001, 2.22, p. 15).[5]

This framework could *in principle* accommodate the full range of humanitarian concerns discussed in earlier chapters. For example, not only did it include a development aspect (as in the quotation above), but it also acknowledged the responsibility of the rich North in fuelling instability and conflict in developing countries. In this respect, it drew attention to the role of monetary policies, the flow of weapons, the debt burden, trade policies and the terms of trade (ICISS, 2001, 1.20, p. 5; 3.8, p. 20). All this was related to the fundamental principle that *prevention* was the single most important dimension of the responsibility to protect and that:

Without a genuine commitment to conflict prevention at all levels—without new energy and momentum being devoted to the task—the world will continue to witness the needless slaughter of our fellow human beings, and the reckless waste of precious resources on conflict rather than social and economic development. The time has come for all of us to take practical responsibility to prevent the needless loss of human life, and to be ready to act in the cause of prevention and not just in the aftermath of disaster (ICISS, 2001, 3.43, p. 27).

This put the emphasis on the whole range of preventive measures—from addressing the root causes of conflict in their political and economic dimensions to direct prevention efforts, including diplomacy, mediation, arbitration and, in some cases, forms of sanctions. In this way, the recommendations of the Commission are similar to a major argument of this book—that the version of intervention propounded by Western leaders and some commentators has been skewed towards *military* action. This has meant both inadequate attention to prevention and a (convenient) disregard for the responsibility of

---

[5] The ICISS was building on the conception of sovereignty as responsibility developed by Francis Deng (1995). In 2007 he was appointed UN Special Adviser on the Prevention of Genocide.

the advanced capitalist countries in fuelling conflicts in developing and transitional countries. Similarly, as noted in the last chapter, discussions in the 1990s often virtually ignored the complexities that would follow any military intervention. However, the ICISS accepted that the responsibility to protect included, as an integral element, the responsibility to rebuild. It insisted on the necessity for an exit strategy as part of pre-intervention planning, a substantial commitment for a considerable period, and policies to promote sustainable development (ICISS, 2001, 5.1–5.21, pp. 39–43). It also stressed that the operating principles underlying the rebuilding task were to eliminate the threats to human life, rather than to achieve any particular political goals, and that the enterprise must not be tainted with any suspicion that it was a form of neo-colonial imperialism (ICISS, 2001, 5.23, p. 43, 5.31, p. 45). Again, this recognised many of the tensions identified in chapter 5.

Yet the most contentious issue of all remains the relationship between sovereignty and intervention, and the ICISS hoped that the notion of the responsibility to protect could also provide a bridge across the apparent dichotomy between these two concepts. Its attempt to do so was based on simultaneous recognition of the crucial importance of *both* state sovereignty *and* human security. This, it argued, meant that sovereignty implied 'a dual responsibility: externally—to respect the sovereignty of other states, and internally, to respect the dignity and basic rights of all the people within the state' (ICISS, 2001, 1.35, p. 8).[6]

The 'responsibility to protect' certainly qualified the principle of state sovereignty. The state was the primary agent in the protection of the safety and lives of citizens and the promotion of their welfare. But if the state would not or could not carry out its protective function, the ICISS argued that the external aspect came into play: national political authorities were responsible both to their own citizens 'and to the international community through the UN' (ICISS, 2001, 2.15, p. 13). There are, I believe, theoretical difficulties in the notion that the state has responsibility to the 'international community'. It is not clear that any existing state has ever genuinely accepted that there is such a community to which it is accountable. The whole notion expresses a valuable aspiration, rather than a current reality. Nor is it self-evident that the idea of a 'responsibility to protect' requires the existence of any such entity. It would,

---

[6] The ICISS used the discourse of both human rights and human security. It did not define 'basic rights', despite using the phrase, implying that it understood this as almost equivalent to the needs defined by the notion of human security.

for example, be possible to ground the concept in a combination of ethical and legal principles without invoking the notion of an 'international community'.[7] But the crucial point is that the ICISS was attempting to consider the situation from the perspective of those seeking or needing support. Its argument was thus that the 'duty to protect communities from mass killing, women from systematic rape and children from starvation' must be discharged internationally only when national authorities were unwilling or unable to carry out their responsibilities or were the perpetrators (ICISS, 2001, 2.29, p. 17).

These conceptual aspects of the ICISS report have been summarised at length because they are closely related to some of the ideas developed in this book. The notion of a responsibility to protect—if genuinely taken in *all* of its aspects—could provide a basis for rethinking humanitarian intervention in the light of experience and theory. It helps to focus attention on the whole range of interactions between rich and poor countries and the responsibilities that the former have in relation to the latter; and it makes it absolutely clear that military intervention should be a last resort, undertaken only in very exceptional and limited circumstances. Unfortunately, as argued below, the subsequent *interpretation* of the doctrine was more restricted than that suggested in the report itself, and this undermined its potential to offer a wider conception of humanitarianism. However, it is first necessary to consider the issue of coercive intervention.

*Just wars*. The ICISS may have been justified in believing that the term 'military intervention for human protection purposes' was more acceptable in some circles than 'humanitarian intervention', but it is the *fact* of military intervention, rather than the discourse used to describe it, that remains so controversial. And the real issues remain the justifications for such decisions to be made and the agency (or agencies) that are entitled to make them.

Chapter 3 argued in favour of a very restricted set of circumstances in which military intervention might be justified, and noted that the ICISS took a very similar position on these issues. However, there is ultimately no objective way of determining the precise point at which the threshold conditions

---

[7] It is probable that this idea was introduced at least in part because of a wish to sanctify the role of the UN as the representative of such a community—and therefore the sole body that could make a legitimate decision to authorise an international intervention without the consent of the target state (see below).

apply, for some human agency needs to make a decision that in *this* case (but not in *that*) the only means of protection is through military action. Like many others, the Commission used the Just War tradition, the origins of which are normally identified with Augustine (354–430) in the early Christian tradition, in its attempt to define the principles that should guide such decisions. Its main innovation was the prudent purging of any reference to the original religious source (Box 7). The following discussion refers extensively to its formulation of these principles.

Principle 1, the 'Just Cause' threshold, has already been discussed in chapter 3, and the issues of 'Right Intention' (2A) and 'Right Authority' (3) will be considered below. It is not possible to discuss all the conditions here, but they certainly provide useful insights into some of the cases discussed earlier in the book

In the interventions of the 1990s there was not always adherence to the 'last resort' criterion (2B). In the 1991 war against Iraq, which subsequently led to the 'safe haven' policy, the US unleashed the war without waiting for compelling evidence that there was no other way of making Saddam Hussein comply with the UN ultimatum to withdraw from Kuwait. Similarly, rather than the Rambouillet conference being an *alternative* to war over Kosovo, it made war more probable by including proposals that were known to be unacceptable to Serbia and which had nothing to do with the humanitarian crisis. Nor did the war over Kosovo comply with other principles. By relying on high level bombing rather than ground forces, the means used were not proportional (2C) or based on incrementalism and gradualism in the use of force (4C). Nor is it clear that they involved total adherence to international humanitarian law (4D),[8] and the war also probably infringed 4E. The principle of 'reasonable prospects' (2D) was not observed in Somalia, where there was an ill-conceived

[8] The Independent International Commission on Kosovo (2000) expressed concerns about the air campaign against strategic targets in Serbia proper, increasing the risk of civilian casualties, the use of cluster bombs, the environmental damage caused by the use of depleted-uranium tipped armour-piercing shells and missiles and by toxic leaks caused by the bombing of industrial and petroleum complexes in several cities, and the attack on Serbian television. It suggested that some practices were vulnerable to the allegation that violations might have occurred but, on the existing evidence, disagreed with the view expressed by Amnesty International, that the NATO action should be referred to the International Criminal Tribunal for the Former Yugoslavia under the Laws of War. However, it argued for a higher threshold of protective standards in any future case of humanitarian intervention, suggesting that a new Protocol to the Geneva Convention should be negotiated (pp. 4–5, pp. 177–84).

### Box 7

*The Responsibility to Protect: principles for military intervention*

#### 1. The just cause threshold

Military intervention for human protection purposes is an exceptional and extraordinary measure. To be warranted, there must be serious and irreparable harm occurring to human beings, or imminently likely to occur, of the following kind:

A. **Large scale loss of life**, actual or apprehended, with genocidal intent or not, which is the product either of deliberate action, or state neglect or inability to act, or a failed state situation; or
B. **Large scale 'ethnic cleansing'**, actual or apprehended, whether carried out by killing, forced expulsion, acts of terror or rape.

#### 2. The precautionary principles

A. **Right Intention**: The primary purpose of the intervention, whatever other motives intervening states may have, must be to halt or avert human suffering. Right intention is better assured with multilateral operations, clearly supported by regional opinion and the victims concerned.
B. **Last resort**: Military intervention can only be justified when every non-military option for the prevention or peaceful resolution of the crisis has been explored, with reasonable grounds for believing lesser measures would not have succeeded.
C. **Proportional means**: The scale, duration and intensity of the planned military intervention should be the minimum necessary to secure the defined human protection objective.
D. **Reasonable prospects**: There must be a reasonable chance of success in halting or averting the suffering which has justified the intervention, with the consequences of action not likely to be worse than the consequences of inaction.

#### 3. Right authority

A. There is no better or more appropriate body than the United Nations Security Council to authorise military intervention for human protection purposes. The task is not to find alternatives to the Security Council as a source of authority, but to make the Security Council work better than it has.
B. Security Council authorization should in all cases be sought prior to any military intervention action being carried out. Those calling for an intervention should formally request such authorization, or have the Council raise the matter on its own initiative, or have the Secretary-General raise it under Article 99 of the UN Charter.

C. The Security Council should deal promptly with any request for authority to intervene where there are allegations of large scale loss of human life or ethnic cleansing. It should in this context seek adequate verification of facts or conditions on the grounds that might support a military intervention.

D. The Permanent Five members of the Security Council should agree not to apply their veto power, in matters where their vital state interests are not involved, to obstruct the passage of resolutions authorizing military intervention for human protection purposes for which there is otherwise majority support.

E. If the Security Council rejects a proposal or fails to deal with it in a reasonable time, alternative options are:

I. consideration of the matter by the General Assembly in Emergency Special Session under the "Uniting for Peace" procedure; and

II. action within area of jurisdiction by regional or sub-regional organizations under Chapter VIII of the Charter, subject to their seeking subsequent authorization from the Security Council.

F. The Security Council should take into account in all its deliberations that, if it fails to discharge its responsibility to protect in conscience shocking situations crying out for action, concerned states may not rule out other means to meet the gravity and urgency of that situation–and that the stature and credibility of the United Nations may suffer thereby.

### 4. Operational principles

A. Clear objectives; clear and unambiguous mandate at all times; and resources to match.

B. Common military approach among involved partners; unity of command; clear and unequivocal communications and chain of command.

C. Acceptance of limitations, incrementalism and gradualism in the application of force, the objective being protection of a population, not defeat of a state.

D. Rules of engagement which fit the operational concept: are precise; reflect the principle of proportionality; and involve total adherence to international humanitarian law.

E. Acceptance that force protection [i.e. protecting the troops of the intervening powers] cannot become the principal objective.

F. Maximum possible coordination with humanitarian organizations.

Source: The Responsibility to Protect, pp. xii–xiii.

military intervention, compounded by failures at the operational level (4B), leading to the debacle that continued to affect the country in the first decade of the twenty-first century. The intervention in Bosnia was marred throughout at the operational level—above all under 4A, with constantly changing mandates. Finally, aspects of the failures in relation to Rwanda were not included in the list at all, for it was not a question of *either* the UN acting *or* others doing so (3F), but of misconceived action before the genocide and a failure of anyone to act when it took place.

*Right intention.* The notion of 'right intention' may suggest that in a war for human protection purposes, this will be the primary motivation of those who authorise and participate in it. However, mixed motives are far more normal even in 'just wars'. In my view, the war against Nazi Germany deserves this designation, but this may seem to imply that the anti-Nazi forces were activated primarily by 'right intention'. In fact, the motivations of the Allied powers were much less pure. For example, the principal objectives of the British government were to prevent Germany from threatening the UK and its Empire, rather than to prevent extermination and enslavement. Nor have even the justified military interventions discussed in this book (for example, the Tanzanian invasion of Uganda in 1979) always been motivated *solely* by human protection purposes. Some authors therefore place much less emphasis on motivation, and take a more utilitarian approach, which instead emphasises the *consequences* for the victims of the violations (Semb, 1992, p. 65, p. 79; Wheeler, 2000, pp. 37–40; Ramsbotham and Woodhouse, 1996, pp. 72–6). However, as many of these authors themselves recognise, narrow utilitarianism seems to set the bar too low. Let us suppose that after the military defeat of Saddam Hussein in 2003, the American-led occupation had not been so disastrous and that a new non-repressive regime had been established in Iraq that was welcomed by the majority of the population. A *purely* utilitarian evaluation might therefore consider the consequences to be beneficial and regard US motivations in launching the war as irrelevant. But most people would not regard it as sufficient to judge the justification *solely* in terms of consequences. In any case, such a judgement could only be retrospective, while the notion of 'right intention' falls within the *precautionary principles*. This means that those who authorise and carry out the action have to demonstrate motivation *in advance*.

This leads to a series of difficulties. For if the sole motive was that of 'right intention' it is highly unlikely that an intervention would be carried out at all, since pure altruism is rarely evident in international relations, particularly when it involves serious risks. On the other hand, if an intervention is to be regarded as genuinely humanitarian it is surely important that the prevention or the ending of mass atrocities is a significant element in the motivation for the action, rather than its possible by-product. But since it is notoriously difficult for others to possess reliable knowledge about particular actors' intentions, this also means that that there must be a general *perception* that 'right intention' is an important element in motivation in any particular case.

Naturally, it is difficult to carry conviction about this in a deeply divided world (Reichberg and Syse, 2002, p. 319). If the US and its closest allies now *claim* that an action is motivated by a concern about atrocities, this assertion will justifiably be viewed with great scepticism in much of the world. This could be reduced if there were a genuine multilateral agreement about a particular case, incorporating countries that are diverse in levels of development, regional location, religious affiliation and political alignments, and also geographically dispersed civil society movements. The greater the diversity amongst those leading a campaign for action, the greater the likelihood that professions of humanitarian motivation will be accepted. I would therefore conclude that, while it is inadequate to judge the intervention purely in terms of consequences, it is unrealistic to suggest that right intention should be the sole motivation. However, for an intervention to be regarded as humanitarian, human protection purposes must be a significant element in the motivations; if they are, this will also increase the likelihood that an intervention will be perceived as legitimate by a broad range of international opinion.

The issue of consistency is closely related to motivation, but is inevitably complex. The justified perception of inconsistency has been a significant factor in eroding the belief that human protection purposes have played any role in military interventions (Miller, 2003, pp. 228–9; Pogge, 2006; Chomsky, 1999, pp. 1–24, pp. 150–7). Some of this scepticism could be diminished by active policies to address some specific issues of injustice by the West—most notably in relation to the Israeli occupation of Palestinian territories. However, there are inevitable limits to the pursuit of consistency. First, there are more powerful advocates of action in some cases of oppression than others. It is unlikely that in 1994 the Western powers would have acquiesced in genocide in Europe, as they did in Rwanda, or that they would subsequently have tolerated a European civil war on the scale of that in the Democratic Republic of Congo. Secondly, there are cases that could not be addressed by military action even in the event of massive violations. For example, Western military intervention in Chechnya could precipitate a world war and, more generally, armed conflict against any powerful state could have immense costs in human life. This means that such interventions would be prohibited on the grounds of proportionality (2C) and the likelihood of success (2D). And because there are very strong pragmatic grounds for maintaining reasonable relations between the major states, it is very common for such violations to be ignored in their inter-state relations—as is currently the case, again, with Chechnya. But this means that military action is far more likely when the risks are low—that is, against weak and isolated states. Some advocates of intervention have been unconcerned about this (Semb, 1992, pp. 62–5) and there has even been an attempt to make a virtue of necessity on ethical grounds (Brown, 2003, pp. 31–50). Yet consistency should surely be a goal, even if it can never be fully achieved. I would accept that it is better to take effective action to halt massive violations in cases where there is a relatively high probability of success than to take no action because of the danger of inconsistency. But the fact that such inconsistency will almost certainly be at the expense of weaker and poorer states reinforces the argument that rich states should be adopting economic and political policies that help developing and transitional countries, rather than policies that reinforce the instabilities.

*Right authority.* The issue of 'right authority' is more complex still. As the whole of Principle 3 suggests, the ICISS was convinced that the UN Security Council constituted legitimate legal and political authority in the international system. This was scarcely surprising, given Annan's role in inspiring the establishment of the Commission and his hopes that a new consensus could be forged in the aftermath of the Kosovo War. 3A–3C may be read as a plea to the US not to act outside the UN, but it was evident that Washington did not consider itself bound by the UN Charter if intent on military action. The ICISS therefore sought to make such unilateralism less likely. 3D–3F implied a belief that the probability of a Russian veto had led the US and its NATO allies to go ahead without Security Council authorization in the case of Kosovo. 3D followed the proposal made by France in the aftermath of that war, while 3E was a rather desperate attempt to provide some way of saving the UN if the Security Council remained deadlocked in future cases. In fact, of course, such an impasse subsequently occurred over the use of force for non-humanitarian reasons in the 2003 Iraq war, and threatened to occur again over Iran. The clash between the US and the UN is therefore very apparent. However, it would be over-simplified to regard this as the only dimension to the clash over 'right authority'. There are also potential conflicts between ethical principles and that authority, between ethics and law, and between rival conceptions of political justice.

The argument that the Security Council has primacy in terms of authority and legality includes a claim about the normative basis of the international order. However, many advocates of military action for human protection purposes have *not* seen UN authorization as essential, although the majority have believed it to be highly desirable. Others are less precise, using formulae such as authorization by the 'international community' (Ramsbotham and Woodhouse, 1996, p. 226), or 'multilateral authority' (Heinze, 2004, p. 472), or simply making it clear through their analysis that they do not regard UN authorization as *necessary* for humanitarian intervention (Wheeler, 2000, pp. 34–52, pp. 285–31).[9] This follows logically from the elevation of ethical arguments over all others.

In principle, the idea of upholding the UN as the source of legality and legitimacy has a strong appeal for left-liberal and left-wing opinion. The fact that there was no UN authorization for the Kosovo war was thus a major reason for the initial controversy about the intervention. Yet the claim that the Security Council is, and must remain, the unique source of legitimate decision-making rests on one or other of the following assumptions: *either* that it will in practice act conscientiously and effectively in cases of military intervention for human protection purposes; *or* that it is more important to uphold the position of the Security Council than to attempt to try to save the victims of atrocities even when the other Just War conditions are fulfilled. Few have wanted to advocate the second position explicitly, so there is a tendency to rely on the first assumption. Yet there are grounds for scepticism about the reliability of decision-making in the Security Council.

With regard to Kosovo, the KLA no doubt deliberately sought to provoke Serb aggression in order to secure international intervention, and the US fought the war for a variety of reasons other than human protection purposes. Had the NATO countries given the same level of support to Rugova, who had advocated peaceful resistance, as they offered the KLA, it is possible that large-scale violence could have been avoided (Seybolt, 2007, pp. 82–5). Nevertheless, certain disquieting facts remain. By late 1998 the majority of the population in Kosovo was suffering from extreme repression and there were

[9] Tesón's analysis, which conflates humanitarian intervention and regime change in an argument based on moral absolutism about individual rights, explicitly denies the necessity for UN agreement. On Kosovo, for example, he argued: 'While I concur that it is preferable to have the Security Council (or anyone else, for that matter) on the side of freedom, I believe NATO had a *stronger* claim to legitimacy in authorising humanitarian intervention ...than the Security Council. This is because NATO is the entity that comes closest to representing the liberal alliance, the community of nations committed to the values of human rights and democracy.' (Tesón, 2005b, p. 388)

good reasons for believing that the Serbian forces would not desist from this without military action. There was also very recent evidence from the Bosnian war that extreme Serbian nationalist forces were prepared to perpetrate atrocities. However, Russia (backed by China) made it clear that it would veto intervention for various reasons, including a fear that this would lead to the further weakening of Serbia and the consolidation of Western power in the Balkans. Because the Security Council was evaded, the question of whether it would ultimately have acted effectively had the violations worsened remains hypothetical. Yet Russia's behaviour up to that point suggests a strong probability that the prevention of Western military action against Yugoslavia would have remained a higher priority than protection of the Kosovar Albanians. China's interests in the Balkans are clearly far more remote than those of Russia, but it too opposed military action over Kosovo, fearing that this would further undermine the non-intervention principle, potentially internationalizing similar disputes within its own territories (Choeden, 2005, pp. 51–4). China has also been prepared to use its veto for purposes that have had no relationship with the issue in question. When Macedonia negotiated a mutual recognition and trade agreement with Taiwan, China took revenge by vetoing the proposed extension of the mandate (in February 1999) of a UN mission designed to prevent the eruption of violent conflict between the Albanian and Macedonian populations (Bellamy, Williams and Griffin, 2004, p. 266). Subsequently, when signing a Treaty of Friendship and Co-operation in July 2001, Russia and China declared their intention to counter—as they put it—any attempts to subvert the fundamental norms of international law with the help of such concepts as 'humanitarian intervention' and 'limited sovereignty' (quoted in Macfarlane, 2005, p. 27). And, of far greater concrete significance, China shielded the Sudanese government from stronger resolutions over Darfur because, in this case, it did have significant interests involved.

It would therefore be over-simplified to assert the supremacy of the Security Council as the 'right authority' for decision-making on the assumption that there will be never be clashes between this principle and the responsibility to protect. A variety of reforms to Security Council decision-making procedures and membership have been suggested (Thakur, 2006, pp. 301–9), and, of course, there have been long-standing demands to democratise the UN by shifting power to the General Assembly. Other ideas include that of the former Canadian Finance Minister, Paul Martin, that the leader of a wider range of states, the so-called L20, should serve as an informal security council on major issues of this kind,[10] and the establishment of an appropriate 'jury' to judge the justification for intervention in each case. Thomas Franck proposed that there could be three arenas for 'international jurying'—legally, in the International Court of Justice, politically, in the Security Council and the General Assembly, and in a court of public opinion (Franck, 2003, pp. 204–31). Others have tried to develop this idea in other ways, for example by establishing a stronger role for global civil society through bringing humanitarian NGOs into the jury (Lu, 2006, p. 151). Such attempts at reform have a variety of objectives: to include a wider range of actors in decision making in humanitarian crises, so as to enhance legitimacy; to reduce the likelihood of selectivity; to make it less probable that a veto would be used, or to weaken its impact in the event of an overwhelming majority in favour of an action. However, these differing aims are barely compatible with one another. Enhancing legitimacy by including more actors, representing a wider variety of interests and perspectives, might also make it more difficult to make decisions in crisis situations. Attempts to weaken the veto could further undermine the incentives for the current Permanent Members to work within the UN. In any case, no changes can be made without the agreement of these states and it is difficult to envisage any radical proposals being accepted. There is also one final difficulty: changing the basis of the decision-making system can never entirely circumvent the fundamental ethical problem. Had a greater number of actors taken the key decisions over Rwanda in April 1994 this would not necessarily have led to effective action to halt the genocide. Whatever the location for the 'right authority', it can still make an immoral decision.

Others have therefore paid less attention to reforming the decisionmaking than to the need for incremental change in the legal and normative position. This is based on the pragmatic consideration that any attempt to institute a fundamental change precipitously could increase dissent, rather than resolve the problems (Stromseth, 2003, pp. 268–9). In this context the history of the concept of the 'responsibility to protect' is very relevant.

A new commitment or new words?

Even during its own consultation process the ICISS experienced great difficulties in convincing many developing countries that the idea of the

[10] The current G20 of finance ministers are from Argentina, Australia, Brazil, Canada, China, France, Germany, India, Indonesia, Italy, Japan, South Korea, Mexico, Russia, Saudi Arabia, South Africa, Turkey, the UK, the US and the EU.

'responsibility to protect' constituted a significant advance (Thakur, 2006, pp. 264–72). The Non-Aligned Movement (with 113 members) had rejected the 'so-called "right of humanitarian intervention"' three times after the Kosovo war and many remained unconvinced that the change of terminology was significant. The hardest line was taken at a Round Table Discussion in Beijing in June 2001, but there was also suspicion in many other parts of Asia and the Asian-Pacific region. In the Middle East very strong views were expressed about the double standards in relation to Israel and Palestine, and in Latin America there was continuing bitterness about memories of US interventions. In Africa, there was a greater appreciation of the fact that the shift in terminology embraced preventive and post-conflict peace-building. There was also less opposition to intervention *per se* than elsewhere, partly because the constitutive act of the African Union in 2000 included a right 'to intervene in a member state....in respect of grave circumstances, namely war crimes, genocide and crimes against humanity' (quoted in Adibe, 2003, p. 84), and also because of the fears of state failures leading to humanitarian crises. However, in all the consultations in developing countries there was unanimous opposition to the idea of unauthorised Western military interventions, and also serious concern with the issues of double standards and inconsistency. However, as one member of the Commission subsequently recalled:

In all consultations, people were prepared to concede that sometimes, outsiders may indeed have to step in with military force to protect innocent victims from perpetrators of mass killings and ethnic cleansing. In every single case, when pressed people preferred the option of 'No more Rwanda' where genocide took place with no intervention, to 'No more Kosovo' where there was intervention outside the framework of UN authorisation (Thakur, 2006, p. 284).

This perhaps indicated that if future actions *were* authorised by the UN, there might be a basis for forging a consensus on the 'responsibility to protect' leading to modification of the norm of non-intervention. In fact, 9/11 occurred three months before the ICISS report was published and the subsequent US-led 'war on terrorism' appeared to make a new agreement much less likely. However, the new discourse suggested in the ICISS report was to prove sufficiently robust to withstand the international crisis over the Iraq war.

One reason for the continued life of the concept was a determined attempt to involve NGOs in its promotion. After initial consultations, the government of Canada invited the World Federalist Movement-Institute for Global Policy (WFM-IGP) to play an active role in reaching out to NGOs and other civil society actors.[11] It sought to create awareness of the ICISS Report and the inter-governmental process; to deepen the debate within civil society organizations about the Report; to determine what relevant civil society activities were already taking place and how civil society organizations might become more deeply involved in this process; and to generate interest in continued involvement among civil society groups (World Federalist Movement-Institute for Global Policy, 2003). Although there was considerable scepticism in this sector, the consultation process led to the definition of three forms of NGO involvement. The first related to an attempt to influence international norms, focusing on the change in terminology, and the idea that the responsibility to protect involved a continuum of appropriate responses from prevention to reaction to rebuilding, with the priority on preventive measures. The second track sought to establish the political will for early and appropriate responses by governments as situations emerged, and for other options, up to and including military intervention, to be considered where these measures failed. Finally, there was the role of advocacy to strengthen the capacity of individual governments and inter-governmental bodies at all levels to keep to the commitments that they had already made. It is difficult to assess the impact made by the NGO sector, but the WFM-IGP took advantage of lobbying at various levels, from the World Social Forum in Porto Alegre, Brazil in January 2003, attended by approximately 5,700 NGOs from all over the world, to more elite gatherings, such as the Wilton Park conference in the UK, bringing together government, UN and NGO representatives (World Federalist Movement-Institute for Global Policy, 2003).

Despite such activity, there was continuing scepticism, both about whether the 'responsibility to protect' was a tool of the powerful countries to erode the

---

[11] WFM's formal history began in 1946 in Luxemburg and in 1947 in Montreux when many national and international peace movements agreed to form a 'coalition' world movement for world federation. It envisages 'a federation of nation-states, each ceding sovereignty to a larger union through common institutions while maintaining a unique society, culture and political structure' based on 'the application of the political philosophy of democratic federalism, developed at national levels in nations throughout the world, to the international level and to global governance'. It 'embraces the belief in the rule of law as the primary basis for achieving and maintaining world peace...based on constitutional democratic principles, including universal suffrage, guaranteed individual and minority rights, independent judiciary, separation of powers and subsidiarity'. Its mission is to bring about a 'just world order through a strengthened United Nations'. The Institute for Global Policy is the research and policy analysis arm of WFM. www.wfm. org (accessed 24 May 2007)

sovereignty of smaller developing countries and about the use of force, particularly on a unilateral basis (Pace, 2007). At the same time, there was 'a consensus around the inevitability of future crises of the magnitude of Rwanda, Cambodia, East Timor, Kosovo, and so many others' and the belief that civil society organizations could play a role in holding governments, regional and sub-regional bodies and international organizations to account regarding their existing commitments to prevent such atrocities (World Federalist Movement-Institute for Global Policy, 2003, pp. 3–5, 25). NGOs were therefore receptive to a revised notion of sovereignty to include protection and an international commitment to a continuum of protective measures that emphasised prevention, with force treated as a last resort. But they were not prepared to advocate a doctrine justifying military intervention, particularly without Security Council or multilateral approval. The emphasis shifted as a result of the crisis in Darfur (Pace, 2007).

The immediate origins of the conflict went back to 2001, when two rebel groups in Darfur began to organise a movement against the Sudanese state. They initiated attacks on government, police and military targets late the next year, which intensified in 2003. When the government failed to crush this rebellion through conventional military forces, it increasingly relied on the Janjaweed, armed Baggara herders, who had put down an uprising in the Nuba Mountains and the region of southern oil fields in the late 1990s, with massive human rights violations (Flint and de Waal, 2006, pp. 60, 101–3). By 2004, the killings and forced movement of peoples had thus led to a major humanitarian crisis and calls for intervention. Subsequently, the situation was to worsen. In January 2005 an International Commission of Inquiry on Darfur reported that the Government and the Janjaweed were responsible for violations that were so widespread and systematic that they might constitute crimes against humanity (Human Rights Council, 2007, para. 58).[12] And by 2007, the UN (seen by many as a relatively conservative source) estimated that, since the outbreak of the violence in 2003, some 200,000 civilians had been killed as a direct result of the conflict or through its impact on access to the essentials of life, with over 2 million internally displaced people, 233,000 refugees in Chad, and many others in communities along the border. In addition, there had been numerous major atrocities, with rape and sexual violence, including gang rape (Human Rights Council, 2007, paras. 38–9).

[12] It also found credible evidence that, while not widespread and systematic, rebel forces were responsible for serious violations of human rights and humanitarian law which may amount to war crimes (ibid.).

It was Darfur, above all, that appears to have shifted opinion about the 'responsibility to protect'. By the spring of 2004, the fact that there had been no effective response to the crisis and the atrocities led many, including NGOs, to invoke this as a basis for a call for further international action there (Pace, 2007).[13] This, and the continuation of activity amongst sympathetic governments, helped to maintain the impetus when Kofi Annan established a High-level Panel on Threats, Challenges and Change, with Gareth Evans, the co-chair of the ICISS, as one of the members. This was an attempt to find a basis for simultaneously moving the international agenda towards US concerns following the war in Iraq while maintaining the UN as the centre of legitimacy and law. When the Panel reported in December 2004, it embraced the concept of the 'responsibility to protect' (United Nations, 2004, paras. 199–202), concluding:

We endorse the emerging norm that there is a collective international responsibility to protect, exercisable by the Security Council authorizing military intervention as a last resort, in the event of genocide and other large-scale killing, ethnic cleansing or serious violations of international humanitarian law which sovereign Governments have proved powerless or unwilling to prevent (United Nations, 2004, para. 203).

This paved the way for a further breakthrough at the high level plenary meeting of the UN World Summit in September 2005. Several African and Latin American governments now supported the notion of a 'responsibility to protect' and Annan himself was a major advocate of developing this as a new

[13] There is no doubt about the gravity of the humanitarian crisis but, as always, there is some selectivity in focusing on this question rather than others. In terms of sheer loss of life the civil war in the Democratic Republic of the Congo (DRC) was far worse, but there was no similar call for action in that country. This could be rationalised with the argument that the UN already had a peacekeeping mission in the DRC, but given the scale of the death and destruction there, this is not very convincing. There is therefore an immediate question of why Darfur has had such a high profile internationally. Since there has been greater public attention on it in the US than elsewhere, there has been some speculation as to why this is so. It is perhaps true that the situation is more readily interpreted than is the case in the DRC as a battle between ruthless oppressors and victims, but it has also been suggested that it has suited an American agenda to represent the former category, in a simplistic way, as Arabs (Mamdani, 2007). There has also been some suspicion that the US was keen to focus on Darfur as a way of diverting attention from Iraq, perhaps also because the main supporters of the Sudanese government have been China and the Arab League. Kofi Annan also feared that the US sometimes sought to highlight the immensity of the problem by using the term 'genocide' in 2004 without intending to play a key role in the resolution of the crisis—thereby further undermining the UN when it failed to act effectively (Prunier, 2005, pp. 140–1).

norm. A significant breakthrough had also occurred in June of that year when the Chinese government's official paper on UN reforms indicated movement on the issue. Subsequently, at the summit itself, all the governments adopted a statement incorporating the responsibility to protect. The construction of this consensus was no doubt facilitated by a renewed emphasis on the host state's primary responsibility and the requirement for Security Council agreement before any action could be undertaken (Bellamy, 2006, cited in Weiss, 2007, pp. 57–8).

After specifying the use of appropriate diplomatic, humanitarian and other peaceful means, the statement continued:

In this context, we are prepared to take collective action, in a timely and decisive manner, through the Security Council, in accordance with the Charter, including Chapter VII, on a case-by-case basis and in cooperation with relevant regional organizations as appropriate, should peaceful means be inadequate and national authorities are manifestly failing to protect their populations from genocide, war crimes, ethnic cleansing and crimes against humanity (United Nations, 2005, para. 139).

This commitment to the use of force as a last resort was coupled with a stress on peaceful means if possible, and also on the need to help states, where necessary and appropriate, to 'build capacity to protect their populations from genocide, war crimes, ethnic cleansing and crimes against humanity and to assisting those which are under stress before crises and conflicts break out' (United Nations, 2005, para. 139). Six weeks later the General Assembly adopted this commitment, and on 28 April 2006 the Security Council reaffirmed it in Resolution 1674, which also emphasised the importance of a range of other measures in preventing conflict, protecting civilians and particularly vulnerable groups during situations of armed conflict, and establishing durable peace following such conflict. In August 2007 the new UN Secretary-General, Ban Ki-moon, proposed the creation of a Special Adviser on the Responsibility to Protect, and following Security Council endorsement, Edward Luck was appointed to this position (part-time) in February 2008.[14] His role was to develop conceptual clarity and consensus for the evolving norm and he was expected to work closely with the Office of the Special Adviser on the Prevention of Genocide.

---

[14] Luck was Director of the Center on International Organization of the School of International and Public Affairs at Columbia University and had been Staff Director of the General Assembly's Open-ended High-level Working Group on the Strengthening of the United Nations System, and Senior Consultant to the Department of Administration and Management of the United Nations during the UN reform process.

Meanwhile an NGO network, 'The Responsibility to Protect—Engaging Civil Society Project', was established to promote the new framework.[15] And as the Security Council edged towards stronger action against Sudan over Darfur during 2006–7, with a Chapter VII resolution for a joint UN-African Union peacekeeping force, it relied upon the 'responsibility to protect' as its basis for authorizing the use of force. This represented a significant normative and conceptual shift, at least in an embryonic form. For it meant that the UN was now acknowledging that there was a legitimate international responsibility to prevent massive violations within a state and that it was no longer necessary to justify this by claiming that the atrocities represented a threat to international peace and security. Yet, even apart from the fundamental question about the way in which governments would translate this into reality, there were very significant limitations in the way in which the doctrine was now being interpreted.

One weakness, noted by the executive director of the organization leading the NGO campaign, was that the UN Outcome Document, following the World Summit, did not include the 'responsibility to rebuild' following an intervention authorised to prevent mass atrocities (Pace, 2007). It did establish a Peacebuilding Commission, but this was not coupled with a specific responsibility located in the Security Council, and the Commission's authority was weaker than that envisaged by the High Level Panel, which had originally recommended its creation (Thakur, 2006, pp. 309–10). There were also major lacunae in institutional capacities at both national and international levels for operationalizing the framework recommended by the ICISS. However, my major concern is at the *conceptual* level.

This book has emphasised the extent to which a narrow understanding of humanitarianism, coupled with neo-liberal economic policies and the promotion of a crude form of democratization, have contributed to crises and con-

---

[15] Its goals included: increasing awareness of the ICISS Report and other relevant documents on preventing conflicts and protecting civilians; encouraging discussion of the concepts put forth in these documents through individual outreach to governments and civil society organizations, and at relevant meetings and conferences worldwide; contributing to the success of the inter-governmental process to promote and operationalise the concept of the Responsibility to Protect; and contributing to the development of NGO monitoring mechanisms to ensure earlier and more effective international responses to emerging crises. An impressive number of NGOs from across the globe signed up to the project, which is still organised by the WFM-IGP, with support from the Canadian and British governments and the MacArthur Foundation. (www.responsibilitytoprotect.org)

flicts in developing and transitional countries. The concept of human security, as embraced in the ICISS report, was therefore potentially of great importance. Interpreted radically, the notion of a responsibility to protect by providing human security suggests a duty to eradicate the conditions that create insecurity. Since so many of these emanate from extreme poverty, which numerous governments do not have the independent capacity to overcome, it follows that poverty reduction is also an *international* duty. Furthermore, if the current policies of advanced capitalist countries contribute to instability and violent conflict in developing and transitional countries, it also follows that changes are required in international political economy so as to enhance human security. As argued earlier, the ICISS appeared to recognise this. However, in the formulations adopted by the World Summit, and subsequently by the General Assembly and Security Council, these elements effectively disappeared. All the emphasis was upon prevention of the most extreme forms of violent abuse: that is, those that could in principle warrant military intervention. And to the extent that non-military forms of protection were envisaged—including the possibility of long-term policies of prevention—these were circumscribed by focusing on protection only against such crimes.

Certainly, it is right to confine consideration of the possibility of military intervention to such cases, and this must also mean that non-military options to prevent such crimes need to be implemented. But this is quite different from *excluding* a consideration of wider human security issues. For, as this book has argued, humanitarianism demands consideration of such problems and they are, in any case, invariably involved in the crises and conflicts that may lead to extreme violations. The suggestion that they are irrelevant both diverts attention from the consequences of Northern-dominated policies and means that fundamental causes of conflict are not addressed. It is true that the NGO campaign called for both long-term and immediate measures in situations of conflict, but the emphasis was on identifying potential conflicts and seeking ways of early engagement that might prevent their eruption. For example, in June 2007 William Pace, the leading figure in the current NGO project, argued that some of those involved in the Responsibility to Protect campaign had 'chosen to define it too broadly, encompassing all human security problems, such as poverty, climate change and HIV/AIDS' (Pace, 2007). He urged civil society groups to focus instead on genocide, war crimes, crimes against humanity, and ethnic cleansing, emphasizing non-military measures as well as force. This subsequently became the sole focus of the NGO campaign (R2PCS, 2008a). Such work is certainly necessary, but it is too narrow and fails to acknowledge the extent to which each crisis is multi-dimensional, with broader human security issues integrally involved, and with the international already embedded in the local. The Darfur conflict exemplifies these interactions.

The first crucial point, as in several other crises considered in this book, was the mobilization of issues of identity in a situation of economic and political marginalization. Darfur, which is approximately the size of France, had been independent for several hundred years until 1916, when the British absorbed it into Sudan. While the region contains several distinct peoples, Darfurians have also retained a distinct collective memory that could be reawakened by a sense of discrimination by Khartoum. One element in this is certainly economic, for Darfur is significantly poorer than the central region, and has generally been excluded from social services provided by the state. The region has much higher than average poverty rates and much lower Human Development Index ratings than other areas of the country, with high disease rates, inadequate health services, high rates of child malnutrition, low numbers of families with adequate food supplies, and a general lack of access to justice (Human Rights Council, 2007, paras. 54 and 69). Secondly, there is an important environmental aspect, related to climate change, in the growing instability within Darfur itself. In fact, in 2007 a study by the UN Environmental Programme concluded that the true genesis of the Darfur conflict was attributable to the fact that in the last forty years the desert in northern Sudan had advanced southwards by sixty miles and rainfall had dropped by between 16% and 30% (UNEP, 2007). This had led to significant movements of people, and intensified conflicts between nomadic tribes and the more settled groups. These environmental changes are, of course, related to the impact of the major economies on climate change. Thirdly, there has been a brutally oppressive regime exploiting a situation in which there is a highly complex array of political forces. In the prolonged civil war between the North and South of Sudan, which ended in the fragile settlement reached in 2005, Darfur, as an Islamic region, had fought for the North, but it was then omitted from the North-South negotiations and peace deal. There were some Arabs who treated Darfurians as 'the other', although the population is mixed and neither Arab nor non-Arab groups have been uniform in their political sympathies (Prunier, 2005, pp. 76–80; International Crisis Group, 2007, pp. 13–16). The Northern-dominated Government of Sudan used such forces when it failed to crush the rebellion in other ways. But other tensions within Darfur were exploited by the government, and these erupted after the failure of the Darfur Peace Agreement of May 2006, leading to a proliferation of rebel groups.

Fourthly, internal differentiation within Sudan is related to the wider international interactions in international political economy discussed in chapter 3. These factors have been exacerbated by the importance of Sudan's oil, and the existence of oilfields in Southern Darfur has probably reinforced Khartoum's brutality there. Divide and rule tactics and massive population displacement help to ensure that local interests do not threaten the Sudanese government's control over the resource (Middleton and O'Keefe, 2006, pp. 549–52). Finally, the crisis in Darfur is also embedded in wider international conflicts which themselves have a multi-dimensional nature (International Crisis Group, 2007, pp. 16–18). In addition to regional disputes, involving several neighbouring states, China has been a major actor. Its general support for the non-intervention norm, and its increasing role in Africa, would have made it reluctant to exert pressure on Khartoum in any case. But this reluctance has been reinforced by its extensive oil interests in Sudan, which have been built up since 1996. Beijing has a 40% share in the Sudanese government's Greater Nile Petroleum Operating Corporation and Chinese involvement has transformed oil into Sudan's principal export, which also supplies 10% of China's own oil requirements (Alden, 2007, p. 12).

All these complexities have made it very difficult to contain the violence and overcome the humanitarian crisis in Darfur. And despite some indications in 2007 that an attempt to forge agreement with China on the Security Council was partially successful, leading to graduated pressure on the Government of Sudan and an agreement on a UN/African Union peace-keeping force (UNAMID), the situation deteriorated again the following year. Thus a UN report in April 2008 argued that the prospect of negotiating a political solution to the crisis had become ever more remote as both the Sudanese Government and the rebels appeared determined to pursue a military solution. Ban Ki-moon reported a lack of progress on all fronts, highlighting government restrictions on UNAMID movement, attacks on food convoys and general violence hindering the provision of humanitarian aid, and high rates of sexual and gender-based violence in and around camps for internally displaced persons (UN News Service, 2008). Clearly, international forces had failed to carry out their responsibility to protect in the more narrowly defined sense of taking effective action in situations of genocide, war crimes, ethnic cleansing and crimes against humanity. The deployment of UNAMID was proceeding at a snail's pace, only reaching 10,600 personnel (including 1,400 civilians), and richer states had done little to provide helicopter, transport and other logistical support to back up the under-funded African Union forces. But it is simplistic to suggest that there could be a military solution to this multi-dimensional crisis. In the long term the establishment of a sustainable peace will probably require the involvement of groups, including women, who have generally been excluded from the negotiations (International Crisis Group, 2007, pp. 21–6), and it will also need to address the fundamental problems of human security.

If acknowledgement of international responsibilities needs to be applied in a broad sense in specific crises, such as that in Darfur, this is equally evident when the human security situation is considered globally. This was demonstrated by the dramatic increase in world food prices—estimated at an average of 83% over the three years up to 2008, following a fall of around 75% in inflation-adjusted terms over the previous thirty years. This was caused by a range of factors, including poor harvests (partly due to climate change), rising oil prices, the growth in demand by China and India, the substitution of bio-fuel production for food crops, speculation on commodities, and the ongoing impact of EU and US export subsidies. The result was food riots in at least a dozen countries, the possibility of a further 100 million people being pushed into poverty and, according to the UN Secretary-General at the UN Trade and Development Conference in Accra, the cancelling out of progress towards meeting the UN's Millennium Development Goal of halving world poverty by 2015 (Topping, 2008). Once again, this showed the impact of the policies of the North on the South, and the inter-connections between different humanitarian crises and the various dimensions of human security. All this reinforces the lesson that a wider development agenda must *underpin* the 'responsibility to protect', even if the terminology itself is invoked only in relation to 'genocide, war crimes, ethnic cleansing and crimes against humanity'.

## Conclusion

A major theme of this book has been to highlight the fundamental contradictions between professions of humanitarian ideals and the actual impact of existing international policies on many developing and transitional countries. This is still more striking because those who possess the greatest international power often play a key role in creating or exacerbating crises and conflicts. Hence the need for a wider conception of humanitarianism that incorporates an international duty in relation to development, and the reduction of global inequality and poverty.

This chapter has argued that the concept of 'human security' and the framework of the 'responsibility to protect' could, in principle, provide the necessary links between this wider conception and military intervention, guided by Just War principles, as an exceptional response to atrocities on a mass scale. If humanitarian principles were also being applied internationally so as to provide human security—above all by dramatically reducing world poverty and inequality—this would reinforce both the ethical case for the use of military power in such circumstances and its international legitimacy. Yet while the 'responsibility to protect' *could* provide a new framework that might help resolve the contradictions, this does not mean that it *will* be used in that way. As this chapter has noted, the international responsibility now appears to be interpreted more narrowly than in the ICISS report, and there has been no significant shift in the policies of those who wield the greatest international power. If this continues, many on the left, and many governments, will regard 'the responsibility to protect' as a new slogan to justify military intervention against weaker and poorer states.

# Afterword

# Facing the Future: Humanitarianism and Politics

In the immediate aftermath of the Cold War there was optimism that the new era heralded the prospect of international peace and co-operation. Although the left deplored the claim that the disintegration of the Soviet bloc signified the failure of socialism, many shared the belief that it would now be possible for the UN to fulfil the potential that had been blocked by the East-West division. There was also much support for the ideas of enhanced international human rights protection, cosmopolitan democracy and the obsolescence of the nation-state. Coupled with this was a tendency to believe that, while it was tragic that atrocities were occurring within states, it was at least positive that there now seemed to be a new willingness to regard them as matters of international concern. In this context, during the early 1990s many on the left called for robust military intervention for humanitarian reasons, while conservatives and realists often clung to more traditionally defined notions of national interest. All this has changed and humanitarian intervention is now widely viewed as a form of imperialism.

Scepticism about 'the new military humanism' is certainly justified. Even when arguments about human rights have not been distorted so as to make a case for forcible regime change, the results of interventions have been very mixed. There is also a need for caution about assuming that non-military humanitarian action is always beneficial. As David Kennedy argues in *The Dark Sides of Virtue* (2004), many were over-optimistic in the 1990s, with a naïve assumption that international action in the name of humanitarianism was bound to be positive because it was pure and untainted by politics. Instead many humanitarian organizations found that they were subordinate actors in a Western project to promote neo-liberalism and liberal-democracy. And sometimes international NGOs have even played a role in perpetuating the conflicts and humanitarian crises that they sought to ameliorate. Yet shedding illusions should not lead to an undifferentiated opposition to all the earlier ideas, but to a critical approach. This book has attempted to provide this by looking at the issues both conceptually and in the light of historical experience.

It has sought to demonstrate the *complexity* of the issues involved and the need to avoid mono-dimensional approaches. For example, it has shown that it is simplistic to treat humanitarian intervention solely as an ethical issue, for this may preclude adequate consideration of both the fundamental causes of atrocities and the consequences that may follow from intervention. But it is also mistaken to ignore the ethical dimension so as to preserve the impunity of the sovereign state. I have therefore argued both that the notion of a 'responsibility to protect' is positive and that, as currently interpreted and applied, it fails to address the multiple ways in which advanced capitalist countries contribute to humanitarian crises elsewhere. Similarly, the book has highlighted the inter-connectedness of phenomena that are often treated as discrete. Atrocities in a particular country may thus be related to processes of transformation precipitated by international economic policies, the effects of climate change and the impact of an external attempt to institute a particular form of peace settlement. If so, it follows that attempts both to prevent humanitarian crises and to rebuild societies in their aftermath also require a multi-dimensional approach. I have therefore sought to indicate weaknesses in both the theories and the practices of recent interventions, based on different conceptions and frameworks of analysis.

It is, of course, one thing to elaborate alternative concepts and quite another to establish their influence over the international agenda. Much of the argument about development issues has been elaborated over many years by social movements, left-liberal and left-wing forces and radical NGOs. In this context, however, the establishment of the NGO network to campaign for the Responsibility to Protect (R2P) had the potential to be very positive. In principle, this could have linked advocacy for preventive action to avert mass atrocities to the existing agendas of development and human security. This might have brought together an effective coalition of NGOs to promote these connected ideas, feeding them into political arguments and movements. A new initiative in

September 2007 to build a global civil society coalition by organizing a series of consultative roundtables worldwide, supported by Oxfam International, Human Rights Watch, the International Crisis Group and Refugees International, therefore appeared very encouraging. The idea was to build a global coalition with representation from both Northern and Southern NGOs with three major aims: to increase understanding of R2P and how it applied to conflicts in each region; to explore how to strengthen regional and international mechanisms to support R2P; and to forge partnerships with those interested in joining a core group in building an NGO coalition. To this end a series of conferences was held in 2008, with the first four in Bangkok, Ottawa, Buenos Aires and Johannesburg (R2PCS, 2008b).

Unfortunately, in my view, much of the potential in this initiative was lost with the decision to follow the priorities set by governments and the UN, by focusing solely on action to prevent mass atrocities, rather than also emphasizing the wider agenda. Although there was certainly a stress on non-military approaches, this restrictive interpretation made it more likely that those concerned with wider human security issues would lose interest, and that the Responsibility to Protect would become associated with a Western concept of humanitarian intervention.

The current situation in the inter-state system remains daunting. At present relations between the United States and both China and Russia are very strained and competitive. Nor, despite commitments on debt relief, has the 'global North' adopted the kind of economic policies that might help to stabilise the 'global South' and reduce the likelihood of violent conflicts and humanitarian crises. The predominant international theme is therefore the drive for power, markets and resources rather than the provision of human security. Even with unity on a more holistic interpretation of the Responsibility to Protect, radical NGOs and social movements would therefore find it difficult to shift the opinions of political and economic elites and governments.

There are, however, some grounds for cautious optimism. The first is the enormous amount that has been learnt since the end of the Cold War. It is now possible to understand, as perhaps it was not in 1989, that the establishment of sustainable peace is a highly complex task. Many of those involved in the fields of humanitarian work, development, and peace-building have a sophisticated understanding of what needs to be done in vulnerable societies. Their problem is to induce decision-makers to listen to what they are saying. But this leads to a second reason to believe in a more positive future. The

Bush-Blair era was not a conducive climate in which to promote complex ideas about humanitarian policies. Both men preferred to see (or at least to represent) international politics as a clash between good and evil in a world without history. However, this period is now coming to an end and, in this respect at least, the scale of the failure in Iraq may be salutary. Those who are less contaminated by this defeat may perhaps be more willing to learn that military supremacy can play only a very limited role in stabilizing societies or securing a sustainable peace. If so, this will provide more openings for those who hold that current international priorities contribute to conflicts, state collapse and humanitarian crises and that effective peace-building and state-building are multi-level and long-term activities.

Nevertheless, it will be a difficult task to change the agenda, and there is no major state or international organization that may be counted on to promote alternative policies. In principle, the EU is perhaps in the best position to do so. Having surmounted centuries of conflict amongst its own members, and with an effective recent use of a carrot and stick policy of enlargement as a way of pacifying its 'near abroad', it has considerable relevant experience. It is a major actor in the provision of humanitarian and development assistance and, at least on paper, it has a multi-dimensional approach to crisis and conflict management. However, there are also major weaknesses in the EU. Internal divisions have made it reluctant to develop an approach that is sufficiently independent of the US, and its theoretical commitments to overcoming the root causes of conflict are more convincing in theory than in practice. Moreover, the EU has mainly followed neo-liberal practices in its international economic policy, even though its rhetoric differs from that of the US. Other regional bodies in poorer regions, including the Economic Community of West African States and the African Union, may play a constructive role and may be expected to emphasise the importance of human security and development issues, but they are clearly less well resourced than the EU and can therefore offer less assistance to others. Nor do African states always take a more principled stance on the Responsibility to Protect than those elsewhere.

Finally, the UN retains a crucial role. Certainly, the Security Council continues to exhibit numerous problems in relation to legitimacy and effectiveness, and the organization as a whole faces almost intractable difficulties in co-ordinating policies between departments and reconciling incompatible viewpoints amongst its members. The Secretary-General also has the constant difficulty of steering the UN between marginalization by the US or subordination to it. Nevertheless, the UN remains an indispensable source of influence in promoting a balanced view of humanitarianism, by arguing for new approaches to global issues. Directly or indirectly, it has promoted the concepts of human development, human security and the responsibility to protect, and it remains the only truly international organization.

Nor should the *potential* practical importance of ideas be ignored. Despite the subsequent distortions, some of the new theories about cosmopolitanism and the limitations of state sovereignty at the end of the Cold War were very positive. However, as the ICISS noted, the terms 'humanitarian intervention' and the 'right of intervention' loaded the dice in favour of those who sought military intervention. Those who opposed the use of force in particular cases were put onto the defensive, with suggestions that they regarded state sovereignty or existing international law as more important than the lives of those who were being abused. In principle, this position could be reversed by acceptance of an enlarged conception of international humanitarianism, drawing on human security and the Responsibility to Protect. If so, it would follow that the use of military power could only ever be conceived as a remote possibility in the most extreme and exceptional circumstances. The whole focus of discussions about humanitarian intervention would thus have been transformed. This leads to one final point.

This book has argued that humanitarianism and politics converge, but remain distinct realms. This has implications for both the present and future. There is currently intense suffering across much of the world, as a result of poverty, gross inequality, and violent conflict. The fundamental question is: what role might the two realms of humanitarianism and politics play in transforming this situation? In my view humanitarianism, in the enlarged sense suggested here, can play an important part. The hope is that eventually the notion that all human beings should be assured a necessary minimum of protection will be accepted in the same way as conventional humanitarianism secured increasing support during the nineteenth and twentieth centuries. However, it is also clear that this will not come about without shifts in international structures and policies, which will depend upon *political* change, brought about through argument, pressure, and the mobilization of power.

Yet political action would continue to be necessary even with the achievement of human security. Humanitarianism can play a key role in seeking to alleviate human suffering, but left-liberalism and socialism have always sought something beyond this, for they have also offered the prospect of human freedom and emancipation. Socialism, in particular, has been a *transformative* doctrine committed to the belief that it is possible to establish societies, both nationally and internationally, that are based on the principles of equality, co-operation and solidarity. The attainment of basic human security requirements would not diminish the need for political struggles by those inspired by such a vision: it would provide new opportunities to show that another world is possible.

# Bibliography

Adam, Hussein M. (2004) 'Somalia: International versus Local Attempts at Peace-building' in Ali and Matthews.

Adelman, H. and Suhrke, A. (eds) (1999) *The Rwanda Crisis from Uganda to Zaire: The Path of a Genocide*, Edison, New Jersey: Transaction Publishers.

Adibe, Clement E. (2003) 'Do Regional Organizations Matter? Comparing the Conflict Management Mechanisms in West Africa and the Great Lakes Region' in Boulden.

African Rights (1993) *Somalia and Operation Restore Hope: A Preliminary Assessment*, London: African Rights.

Alden, Chris (2007) *China in Africa*, London and New York: Zed Books.

Ali, Taisier M. and Robert O. Matthews (eds) (2004) *Durable Peace: Challenges for Peacebuilding in Africa*, Toronto: University of Toronto Press, 2004.

Ali, Taisier M. and Robert O. Matthews and Jan Spears (2004) 'Failures in Peace-building: Sudan (1972–1983) and Angola (1991–1998)' in Ali and Matthews.

Alqaq, R. (2006) 'UN Peace Operations and the Management of World Order', PhD thesis, London: School of Oriental and African Studies.

Anderson, Mary B. (1999) *Do No Harm: How Aid Can Support Peace—or War*, Boulder, CO: Lynne Rienner.

Annan, Kofi (1999) *The Question of Intervention*, New York: United Nations.

Ashdown, Paddy (2002) 'What I Learned in Bosnia', *New York Times*, 28 October.

——— (2007) *Swords and Ploughshares: Bringing Peace to the 21st Century*, London: Weidenfeld and Nicolson.

Atack, Iain (2002) 'Ethical Objections to Humanitarian Intervention', *Security Dialogue*, 33 (3), pp. 279–92.

Azar, Edward (1990) *The Management of Protracted Social Conflict: Theory and Cases*, Aldershot: Dartmouth.

Bain, William (2006) 'In Praise of Folly: International Administration and the Corruption of Humanity', *International Affairs* 82 (3), pp. 525–38.

Barnett, Michael (2002) *Eyewitness to a Genocide: the United Nations and Rwanda*, Ithaca, NY: Cornell University Press.

Barsh, R.L. (1991) 'The Right to Development as a Human Right: Results of the Global Consultation', *Human Rights Quarterly* 13 (August), pp. 322–38.

Bartholomew, Amy (2006) *Empire's Law: The American Imperial Project and the 'War to Remake the World'*, London: Pluto.

———— and Jennifer Breakspear (2004) 'Hunan Rights as Swords of Empire' in *Socialist Register*, London: Merlin.

Bellamy, Alex J., Paul Williams and Stuart Griffin (2004) *Understanding Peacekeeping*, Cambridge: Polity.

Bieber, Florian (2006) *Post-War Bosnia: Ethnicity, Inequality and Public Sector Governance*, Basingstoke: Palgrave Macmillan.

Blair, Tony (1999) 'Doctrine of the International Community', Speech at the Economic Club, Chicago. http://www.pm.gov.uk/output/page1297.asp (Accessed 2 July 2007).

Bolton, John and John Eriksson (2004) *Lessons from Rwanda—Lessons for Today, Assessment of the Impact and Influence of Joint Evaluation of Emergency Assistance to Rwanda*, Copenhagen: Ministry of Foreign Affairs.

Boulden, Jane (2003) *Dealing with Conflict in Africa: The United Nations and Regional Organizations*, Basingstoke: Palgrave.

Bowring, Bill (1995) 'The "droit et devoir d'ingérence": A Timely New Remedy for Africa?' *African Journal of International and Comparative Law* 7 (3), pp. 493–510.

Brauman, Rony (1997) 'Is Humanitarianism a Form of Political Commitment?' *Les Temps Modernes*, numéro special 50me anniversaire (English version), www.peace-center.sciences-po.fr/pdf/rb-**humanitarianism**-politics-english-97.pdf

Brown, Chris (2003) 'Selective Humanitarianism: in Defense of Inconsistency' in Chatterjee and Scheid.

———— with Kirstin Ainley (2005) *Understanding International Relations* (3rd edition), Basingstoke: Palgrave Macmillan.

Brown, Michael E., Sean Lynn-Jones and Steve Miller (eds) (1996) *Debating the Democratic Peace*, Cambridge: MIT Press.

Buckley, Mary (2001) 'Russian Perceptions' in Buckley and Cummings.

———— and Sally N. Cummings (2001) *Kosovo: Perceptions of War and its Aftermath*, London and New York: Continuum.

Bull, Hedley (1971) 'Order vs. Justice in International Society', *Political Studies*, 19 (3), pp. 269–83.

Bush, George W. (2002) 'Introduction' in United States (2002).

Byers, Michael and Simon Chesterman (2003) 'Changing the Rules about Rules: Unilateral Humanitarian Intervention and the Future of International Law' in Holzgrefe and Keohane.

Camilleri, Joseph A. and Jim Falk (1992) *The End of Sovereignty? The Politics of a Shrinking and Fragmenting World*, Aldershot: Edward Elgar.

Caplan, Richard (2005) *International Governance of War-Torn Territories*, Oxford University Press.

CAVR (2005) Part 5, 'Resistance: Structure and Strategy', *Chega! Final Report of the Commission for Reception, Truth and Reconciliation in East Timor* http://www.etan.org/news/2006/cavr.htm

Chandler, David (1999) *Bosnia: Faking Democracy after Dayton*, London: Pluto.

———— (2002) *From Kosovo to Kabul: Human Rights and International Intervention*, London: Pluto.

———— (2004) 'The Responsibility to Protect? Imposing the Liberal Peace', *International Peacekeeping*, 11 (1), pp. 59–81.

———— (2006) *Empire in Denial: The Politics of State-Building*, London: Pluto.

Chatterjee, Deen K. and Don E. Scheid (eds) (2003) *Ethics and Foreign Intervention*, Cambridge University Press.

Chesterman, Simon (2001, paperback edition 2002) *Just War or Just Peace? Humanitarian Intervention*, Oxford University Press.

———— (2004) *You, the People: The United Nations, Transitional Administration and State-Building*, Oxford University Press.

Choedon, Yeshi (2005) 'China's Stand on UN Peacekeeping Operations: Changing Priorities in Foreign Policy' *China Report*, 41 (1), pp. 39–58.

Chomsky, Noam (1999) *The New Military Humanism: Lessons from Kosovo*, London: Pluto.

Chopra, Jarat (2000) 'WIIS Scholar Witnesses Timorese Transition Process: Interview with Jarat Chopra', Spring. www.watsoninstitute.org/pubs_news/chopraint-erview.pdf

Chua, Amy (2003) *World on Fire: How Exporting Free-Market Democracy Breeds Ethnic Hatred and Global Instability*, London: William Heinemann.

Cilliers, Jakkie (2001) 'Still ... France Versus the Rest in Africa?' *African Security Review*, 10 (3) http://www.iss.co.za/ASR/10No3/Cilliers2.html

Collier, Paul (2000) 'Doing Well out of War: an Economic Perspective' in M. Berdal and D.M. Malone (eds) *Greed and Grievance: Economic Agendas in Civil Wars*, Boulder, CO: IDRC/Lynne Rienner.

———— (2007) *The Bottom Billion: Why the Poorest Countries are Failing and What Can Be Done About It*, Oxford and New York: Oxford University Press.

Collier, P., L. Elliot, H. Hegre, A. Hoeffler, M. Reynal-Querol and N. Sambanis (2003) *Breaking the Conflict Trap*, Washington. DC: World Bank and Oxford: Oxford University Press.

Cornwall, A. and C. Nyamu-Musembi (2005) 'Why Rights, Why Now? Reflections on the Rise of Rights in International Development Discourse' *Institute of Development Studies Bulletin*, 36, pp. 9–18.

Cramer, Christopher (2006) *Civil War is not a Stupid Thing: Accounting for Violence in Developing Countries*, London: Hurst.

Dallaire, Romeo (2003) *Shake Hands with the Devil: The Failure of Humanity in Rwanda*, Toronto: Random House Canada.

De Waal, A. (1994) 'Dangerous Precedents? Famine Relief in Somalia, 1991–93' in J. Macrae and A. Zwi (eds) *1994: War and Hunger: Rethinking International Responses to Complex Emergencies*, London: Zed Books.

Dee, M. (2001) '"Coalitions of the Willing" and Humanitarian Intervention: Australia's Involvement with INTERFET', *International Peacekeeping*, 8 (3), pp. 1–20.

Deng, Francis M. (1995) 'Frontiers of Sovereignty', *Leiden Journal of International Law*, 8 (2), pp. 249–86.

Dodd, Mark (2000) 'UN staff battle over E Timor's independence policy', *Sydney Morning Herald Monday*, 13 March.

Douzinas, Costas (2007) *Human Rights and Empire: The Political Philosophy of Cosmopolitanism*, Abingdon and New York: Routledge-Cavendish.

Doyle, Michael (1983) 'Kant, Liberal Legacies and Foreign Affairs' Parts I & II, *Philosophy and Public Affairs* 12 (3). pp. 205–35 and (4). pp. 323–53.

Duffield, Mark (1997) 'Post-modern Conflict, Aid Policy and Humanitarian Conditionality', Research Report for ODA/ESCOR.

—— (2001) *Global Governance and the New Wars—The Merging of Development and Security*, London and New York, Zed Books.

Evans, Gareth (2008) 'Facing up to our responsibilities' guardian.co.uk/commentisfree, 12 May. http://commentisfree.guardian.co.uk/garethevans/2008/05/facing uptoourresponsbilities.html

Evans, Malcolm D. (ed.) (2003) *International Law*, Oxford University Press.

Farer, Tom J. (2003) 'Humanitarian Intervention before and after 9/11: Legality and Legitimacy' in Holzgrefe and Keohane.

Farmer, Paul (1997) 'On Suffering and Structural Violence: A View from Below' in Arthur Kleinman, Veena Das and Margaret Lock (eds) *Social Suffering*, Berkeley, Los Angeles and London: University of California Press.

Fawn, Rick (2008) 'The Kosovo—and Montenegro—Effect', *International Affairs* 84 (2), pp. 269–94.

Findlay, Trevor (2002) *The Use of Force in UN Peace Operations*, Oxford: Sipri/Oxford University Press.

Flint, Julie and Alex de Waal (2006) *Darfur: A Short History of a Long War*, London: Zed Books.

Forsyth, David P. (2006) *Human Rights in International Relations*, 2nd edition, Cambridge University Press.

Franck, Thomas M (2003) 'Interpretation and Change in the Law of Humanitarian Intervention' in Holzgrefe and Keohane.

Freeman, Christopher P. (2006) 'Liberal Trusteeship: The Convergence of Interest and Ideology in International Administration' in Knudsen and Laustsen.

Friesecke, Uwe (2004) 'Can We Learn the Lessons From the Genocide in Rwanda?' *Executive Intelligence Review*, 7 May.

Galtung, Johan (1969) 'Violence, peace and peace research', *Journal of Peace Research*, 6 (3), pp. 167–91.

—— (1985) 'Twenty Five Years of Peace Research: Ten Challenges and Responses', *Journal of Peace Research*, 22 (2), pp. 414–31.

—— (1990) 'Cultural Violence', *Journal of Peace Research*, 27 (3), pp. 291–305.

Glasius, Marlies and Mary Kaldor (2004) 'A Human Security Doctrine for Europe, The Barcelona Report of the Study Group on Europe's Security Capabilities' in Glasius and Kaldor (2006).

——— (2006) *A Human Security Doctrine for Europe: Project, Principles, Practicalities*, London and New York: Routledge.

Global Humanitarian Assistance (2006) Global Assistance, Lake Oswego, Oregon www.globalassistance.org

Gott, Richard (2005) *Cuba, A New History*, New Haven, CT: Yale Nota Bene, Yale University Press.

Gray, Christine D. (2000) *International Law and the Use of Force*, Oxford University Press.

Graybill, Lyn (2002) '"Responsible...by Omission": The United States and Genocide in Rwanda' *Seton Hall Journal of Diplomacy and International Relations*, Winter/Spring, pp. 86–103.

Hanlon, Joseph (2006a) '200 Wars and the Humanitarian Response' in Yanacopulos and Hanlon.

——— (2006b) 'External Roots of Internal War' in Yanacopulos and Hanlon.

Harvey, David (2005) *A Brief History of Neoliberalism*, Oxford University Press.

Heinze, Eric A (2004) 'Humanitarian Intervention: Morality and International Law on Intolerable Violations of Human Rights', *International Journal of Human Rights*, 8 (4), pp. 471–90.

Held, David (1993) 'Democracy: From City-states to a Cosmopolitan Order?' in Held, David (ed.) *Prospects for Democracy, North, South, East, West*, Cambridge: Polity.

Helsinki Citizens' Assembly (1993) *Conflicts in Europe: Towards a New Political Approach*, Pamphlet 7, Helsinki Citizens' Assembly, London and Prague.

Holbrooke, Richard (1998) *To End a War*, New York: Random House.

Holzgrefe, J.L. (2003) 'The Humanitarian Intervention Debate' in Hozgrefe and Keohane.

——— and Robert O. Keohane (eds) (2003) *Humanitarian Intervention: Ethical, Legal and Political Dilemmas*, Cambridge University Press.

Human Rights Council (2007) *Report of the High-Level Mission on the Situation of Human Rights in Darfur*, A/HRC/4/80, 7 March, Human Rights Council, United Nations. http://www.ohchr.org/english/bodies/hrcouncil/docs/4session/A-HRC-4-80.doc

Human Rights Watch (1999) *Leave None to Tell the Story: Genocide in Rwanda*, New York and Paris: Human Rights Watch and the International Federation of Human Rights.

——— (2000) 'Civilian Deaths in the Nato Air Campaign', New York: Human Rights Watch.

——— (2004) 'Failure to Protect: Anti-Minority Violence in Kosovo, March 2004' hrw.org/reports/2004/kosovo0704/1.htm (accessed 30 April 2007).

Ignatieff, Michael (2003) *Empire Lite—Nation-Building in Bosnia, Kosovo and Afghanistan*, London: Vintage.

IKS (Kosovar Stability Initiative) (2007) *Reconstruction National Integrity System Survey Kosovo 2007*, Prishtina: IKS.

Inazumi, Mitsue (2005) *Universal Jurisdiction in Modern International Law: Expansion of National Jurisdiction for Prosecuting Serious Crimes under International Law*, Antwerp: Intersentia.

Independent International Commission on Kosovo (2000) *The Kosovo Report*, Oxford University Press.

International Commission (2005) *International Commission on the Balkans: The Balkans in Europe's Future*. www.balkan-commission.org/activities/Report.pdf

International Commission on Intervention and State Sovereignty (ICISS) (2001) *The Responsibility to Protect. Report of the International Commission on Intervention and State Sovereignty*. Ottawa: International Development Research Centre for ICISS (also available on www.iciss.ca).

International Crisis Group (2007) *Darfur: Revitalising the Peace Process*, Africa Report, No. 125, 30 April, Nairobi/Brussels: International Crisis Group. www.crisisgroup.org/home/index.cfm?id=4769 - 32k -

——— (2008a) *Kosovo's First Month*, Europe Briefing No. 47, 18 March, Pristina/Belgrade/Brussels: International Crisis Group. www.crisisgroup.org/home/index.cfm?id=5335 - 29k

——— (2008b) *Timor-Leste's Displacement Crisis*, Asia Report No. 148, 31 March, Dili/Brussels: International Crisis Group. www.crisisgroup.org/home/index.cfm?id=5355 - 31k

Jones, Bruce D. (1995) '"Intervention without Borders": Humanitarian Intervention in Rwanda, 1990–94', *Millennium: Journal of International Studies*, 24 (2) pp. 225–48.

——— (2001) *Peacemaking in Rwanda: The Dynamics of Failure*, Boulder: Lynne Rienner.

Judah, Tim (2000) *Kosovo: War and Revenge*, New Haven, CT: Yale University Press.

Juhasz, Antonia (2004) 'Ambitions of Empire: The Bush Administration Economic Plan for Iraq (and Beyond)', *Left Turn Magazine* 12, Feb./March, pp. 27–32.

Kaldor, Mary (1999) *New and Old Wars: Organized Violence in a Global Era*, Cambridge: Polity Press.

——— (2001) 'Decade of Humanitarian Intervention: The Role of Global Civil Society' in H. Anheier, M. Glasius and M. Kaldor (eds) *Global Civil Society Yearbook*, Oxford University Press.

Kaldor, Mary and Jan Faber (1999) 'What is Humanitarian Intervention?' (Unpublished paper).

Kaldor, Mary and Radhar Kumar (1993) 'New Forms of Conflict' in Helsinki Citizens Assembly.

Kaldor, Mary, Marty Martin and Sabine Selchow (2007) 'Human Security: A New Strategic Narrative for Europe', *International Affairs*, 83 (2), pp. 273–88.

Kamola, Isaac A. (2007) 'The Global Coffee Economy and the Production of Genocide in Rwanda', *Third World Quarterly*, 28 (3), pp. 571–92.

Kampfner, John (2003) *Blair's Wars*, London: Free Press.

Kennedy, David (2004) *The Dark Sides of Virtue: Reassessing International Humanitarianism*, Princeton and Oxford: Princeton University Press.

Keohane, Robert O (2003) 'Political Authority After Intervention: Gradations in Sovereignty' in Holzgrefe and Keohane.

Kerr, Rachel and Eirin Mobekk (2007) *Peace and Justice: Seeking Accountability After War*, Cambridge: Polity Press.

King, Ian and Whit Mason (2006) *Peace at any Price: How the World Failed Kosovo*, London: Hurst.

Knudsen, Tonny Brems (2006) 'From UNMIK to Self-Determination: The Puzzles of Kosovo's Future Status' in Knudsen and Laustsen.

Knudsen, Tonny Brems and Carsten Bagge Laustsen (eds) (2006) *Kosovo between War and Peace: Nationalism, Peacebuilding and International Trusteeship*, London and New York: Routledge.

——— (2006) 'The Future of International Trusteeship: Conclusive Reflections' in Knudsen and Laustsen.

Krasner, Stephen (2002) 'Troubled Societies, Outlaw States and Gradations of Sovereignty', Stanford University Paper.

Kreilkamp, J.S. (2003) 'UN Postconflict Reconstruction', *New York University Journal of International Law and Politics* 35 (3), pp. 619–70.

Kristensen, Rasmus Abildgaard (2006) 'Administering Membership of International Society: the Role and Function of UNMIK' in Knudsen and Laustsen.

Kumar, Radhar (1997) *Divide and Fall? Bosnia in the Annals of Partition*, London and New York: Verso.

Kuper, Leo (1982) *Genocide—Its Political Use in the Twentieth Century*, New Haven and London: Yale University Press.

Kurasawa, Fuyaki (2006) 'The Uses and Abuses of Humanitarian Intervention in the Wake of Empire' in Bartholomew.

Lacey, Marc (2005) 'Tallying Darfur terror: guesswork with a cause', *International Herald Tribune*, 11 May.

Lu, Catherine (2006) *Just and Unjust Interventions in World Politics—Public and Private*, Basingstoke: Palgrave Macmillan.

MacFarlane, S. Neil (2005) 'International Politics, Local Conflicts and Intervention' in Natalie Mychajlyszyn and Timothy M. Shaw (eds), *Twisting Arms and Flexing Muscles: Humanitarian Intervention and Peacebuilding in Perspective*, Aldershot: Ashgate.

——— and Yuen Foong Khong (2006) *Human Security and the UN: A Critical History*, Bloomington: Indiana University Press.

Macfarlane, S. Neil, Caroline J. Thielking and Thomas G. Weiss (2004) 'The Responsibility to Protect: is Anyone Interested in Humanitarian Intervention?' *Third World Quarterly*, 25 (5), pp. 977–92.

Mamdani, Mahmood (2002) *When Victims Become Killers: Colonialism, Nativism and the Genocide in Rwanda*, Princeton University Press.

——— (2007) 'The Politics of Naming: Genocide, Civil War, Insurgency', *London Review of Books*, 8 March.

MfDR (Managing for Development Resources) (2005) *Paris Declaration on Aid Effectiveness: Ownership, Harmonisation, Alignment, Results and Mutual Accountability* http://www.mfdr.org/sourcebook/2-1Paris.pdf

Marks, Stephen (2003) 'Obstacles to the Right to Development', Boston, Mass: Harvard School of Public Health, pp. 1–20. www.hsph.harvard.edu/fxbcenter/FXBC_WP17-Marks.pdf

Martin, Ian (2001) *Self-Determination in East Timor: The United Nations, the Ballot and International Intervention*, Boulder, CO and London: Lynne Rienner.

Meehan, Elizabeth (1993) *Citizenship and the European Community*, London: Sage.

Melvern, Linda and Paul Williams (2004) 'Britannia Waived the Rules: The Major Government and the 1994 Rwandan Genocide', *African Affairs*, 2004, 103, pp. 1–22.

Miall, Hugh, Oliver Ramsbotham and Tom Woodhouse (2005; originally 1999) *Contemporary Conflict Resolution: The Prevention, Management and Transformation of Deadly Conflicts*, Cambridge: Polity.

Miliband, Ralph (1980) 'Military Intervention and Socialist Internationalism' *The Socialist Register 1980*, London: Merlin.

Mill, John Stuart (1963) *Essays on Politics and Culture*. Edited, and with an introduction by Gertrude Himmelfarb, New York: Anchor Books, Doubleday and Co.

Miller, Richard W. (2003) 'Respectable Oppressors, Hypocritical Liberators: Morality, Intervention and Reality' in Chatterjee and Sheid.

Minn, Pierre (2007) 'Toward an Anthropology of Humanitarianism', *Journal of Humanitarian Assistance*, August, pp. 1–17. http://jha.ac/2007/08/06/toward-an-anthropology-of-humanitarianism/

Moorhead, Caroline (1998) *Dunant's Dream: War, Switzerland and the History of the Red Cross*, London: HarperCollins.

Nafziger, E.W. and J. Auvinen (2002) 'Economic Development, Inequality, War and State Violence', *World Development*, 30 (2), pp. 153–63.

Nardin, T. and Melissa S. Williams (eds) (2006) *Humanitarian Intervention*, New York: New York University Press.

Neher, Clark D (2003) 'Southeast Asia' in Edward A. Kolodziej (ed.) *A Force Profonde—The Power, Politics, and Promise of Human Rights*, Penn: University of Pennsylvania Press.

Netherlands Institute for War Documentation (2002) 'Srebrenica: a "safe area". Reconstruction, background, consequences and analysis of the fall of a safe area', Summary for the press, April. http://www.srebrenica.nl/en/perssamenvatting.htm (accessed 11 June 2007).

Newbury, Catherine (1988) *The Cohesion of Oppression. Citizenship and Ethnicity in Rwanda 1860–1960*, New York: Columbia University Press.

Newman, Michael (1996) *Democracy, Sovereignty and the European Union*, London: Hurst.

——— (2002) *Ralph Miliband and the Politics of the New Left*, London: Merlin.

——— (2005) *Socialism: A Very Short Introduction*, Oxford University Press.

Norad (Norwegian Agency for Development Cooperation) (2007) *Review of Development Cooperation in Timor Leste*, Final Report 7/2007, October, Oslo. www.norad.no/default.asp?V_ITEM_ID=10603 - 28k

Ohaegbulam, F. Ugboaja (2004) *US Policy in Post-Colonial Africa: Four Case Studies in Conflict Resolution*, New York: Peter Lang Publishing.

Ohlsson, Leif (2000) *Livelihood Conflicts—Linking Poverty and Environment as Causes of Conflict*, Stockholm: Environmental Policy Unit. http://www.staff.ncl.ac.uk/david.harvey/AEF806/OhlssonLivelihoods.pdf.

Ohmai, Kenichi (1995) *The End of the Nation State: The Rise of Regional Economies*, New York and London: Free Press.

Ombudsperson Institution in Kosovo (2002) Second Annual Report 2001–2002, 10 July. www.ombudspersonkosovo.org

Oppenheim, L.F.L. (1996) *International Law*, Robert Jennings and Arthur Watts (eds) 9th edition, London: Longmans.

Orford, Anne (2001) 'Globalization and the Right to Development' in Philip Alston (ed.) *People's Rights*, Oxford University Press.

——— (2003) *Reading Humanitarian Intervention: Human Rights and the Use of Force in International Law*, Cambridge University Press.

Pace, William R. (2007) 'The Critical Role of CSOs in the Evolution of R2P', Speech and Written Presentation, Oxfam International conference, *The African Union and the Responsibility to Protect: From Non-Interference to Non-Indifference* 8 June. www.responsibilitytoprotect.org

Paris, Roland (2004) *At War's End—Building Peace after Civil Conflict*, Cambridge University Press.

Percival, Valerie and Thomas Home-Dixon (1995) 'Environmental Scarcity and Violent Conflict: The Case of Rwanda', Occasional Paper, Project on Environment, Population and Security, Washington, DC: American Association for the Advancement of Science and the University of Toronto, Parts 1 and 2.

Petritsch, Wolfgang (2001) 'What Message I Got across to the SDS', 9 November http://www.ohr.int/ohr-dept/presso/pressi

Pilger, John (2000a) 'Britain is Recolonising Sierra Leone in an Attempt to get its Hands on the Country's Diamonds', *New Statesman*, 18 September.

——— (2000b) 'Australia ignores the plight of the East Timorese, but keeps a watchful eye on their oil and gas', *New Statesman*, 11 December.

Pogge, Thomas W. (2002) *World Poverty and Human Rights*, Cambridge: Polity.

——— (2006) 'Moralising Humanitarian Intervention: why Jurying Fails and how Law can Work' in Nardin and Williams.

Prunier, Gérard (1998) *The Rwanda Crisis: History of a Genocide*, London: Hurst.

——— (2005) *Darfur—The Ambiguous Genocide*, London: Hurst.

Pugh, Michael (2006) 'Crime and Capitalism in Kosovo's Transformation' in Knudsen and Laustsen.

Ramsbotham, Oliver and Tom Woodhouse (1996) *Humanitarian Intervention in Contemporary Conflict*, Cambridge: Polity.

Rawls, John (1999) *The Law of Peoples*, Cambridge, Mass: Harvard University Press.

Reichberg, Gregory and Henrik Syse (2002) 'Humanitarian Intervention: A Case of Offensive Force', *Security Dialogue*, 33 (3), pp. 309–22.

Reimann, Kim D. (2005) 'Up to No Good? Recent Critics and Critiques of NGOs' in Richmond and Carey.

Reisman, W. Michael (1984) 'Coercion and Self-Determination: Construing Charter Art 2 (4)' *American Journal of International Law*, 78 (3), pp. 642–5.

———— (2000) 'Unilateral Action and the Transformation of the World Constitutive Process: The Special Problem of Humanitarian Intervention', *European Journal of International Law* 11 (1), pp. 3–18.

R2PCS Responsibility to Protect-Engaging Civil Society (2007) 'About the Project' www.responsibilitytoprotect.org (accessed 24 May, 2007)

———— (2008a) Prospects for an International Coalition on the Responsibility to Protect, Civil Society Consultation Final Report, 7 March, Ottawa. www.responsibilitytoprotect.org

———— (2008b) Building an International Coalition on R2P www.responsibilitytoprotect.org

Richmond, Oliver P. and Henry F. Carey (eds) (2005) *Subcontracting Peace: the Challenges of NGO Peacebuilding*, Aldershot: Ashgate.

Rieff, David (2002) *A Bed for the Night: Humanitarianism in Crisis*, London: Vintage.

Roberts, Adam (2000) *The So-Called Right of Humanitarian Intervention* Trinity Papers, No. 13 Melbourne, Trinity College.

Robinson, Darryl (1999) 'Defining "Crimes Against Humanity" at the Rome Conference', *The American Journal of International Law*, 93 (1), pp. 43–57.

Rodley, Nigel S. (1992) 'Collective Intervention to Protect Human Rights and Civilian Populations: the Legal Framework' in Nigel S. Rodley (ed.) *To Loose the Bands of Wickedness: International Intervention in Defence of Human Rights*, London: Brassey's.

Rummel, R.J. (1995) 'Democracy, Power, Genocide and Mass Murder', *Journal of Conflict Resolution*, 39 (1), pp. 3–26.

———— (1997) *Power Kills: Democracy as a Method of Non-Violence*, New Brunswick, New Jersey: Transaction.

Sands, Philippe (2006) *Lawless World: Making and Breaking Global Rules*, London: Penguin.

Schabas, William A. (2005) 'Genocide, Freedom From' in R.K.M. Smith and C. van den Anker (eds) *The Essentials of Human Rights*, London: Hodder Arnold.

Schell, Jonathan (2005) *The Unconquerable World—Why Peaceful Protest is Stronger than War*, London: Penguin Books.

Schwarz, A. (1994) *A Nation in Waiting: Indonesia in the 1990s*, Sydney: Allen and Unwin.

Scorgie, Lindsay (2004) 'Rwanda's Arusha Accords: A Missed Opportunity', *Undercurrent*, 1 (1), pp. 66–76. http://www.undercurrentjournal.ca/200411%20-%20 scorgie.pdf

Sellström, Tor and Lennart Wohlgemuth (1996) *The International Response to Conflict and Genocide: Lessons From the Rwandan Experience*, Study 1: *Historical Perspective: Some Explanatory Factors*, Copenhagen: Joint Evaluation of Emergency Assistance to Rwanda, Foreign Ministry of Denmark.

Semb, Anne Julie (1992) *The Normative Foundation of the Principle of Non-Intervention*, PRIO Report No. 1, Oslo: International Peace Research Institute (PRIO).

Seybolt, Taylor B. (2007) *Humanitarian Military Intervention: The Conditions for Success and Failure*, Oxford University Press and SIPRI.

Shue, Henry (1980) (2nd edition 1996) *Basic Rights: Subsistence, Affluence and US Foreign Policy*, Princeton University Press.

Slim, Hugo (1995) 'The Continuing Metamorphosis of the Humanitarian Practitioner: Some New Colours for an Endangered Chameleon', *Disasters*, 19 (2), pp. 110–26.

——— (1997) 'International Humanitarianism's Engagement with Civil War in the 1990s: A Glance at Evolving Practice and Theory', A Briefing Paper for ActionAid UK, also in *Journal of Humanitarian Assistance*, pp. 1–16. http://www.jha.ac/articles/a033.htm

Sørensen, Birgitte Refslund (2006) 'Violence and Humanitarian Assistance: Reflections on an Intricate Relationship', *Journal of Humanitarian Assistance*, September, pp. 1–24. www.jha.ac/articles/a194.pdf

Spyridaki, Evangelia (2008) 'International Liberalism or International Structural Violence? The Case of Pre-genocide Rwanda', MA dissertation, London: London Metropolitan University.

Smillie, I. (1995) *The Alms Bazaar: Altruism Under Fire—Non Profit Organizations and International Development*, London: Intermediate Technology Publications.

——— and Larry Minnear (2004) *The Charity of Nations: Humanitarian Action in a Calculating World*, Bloomfield CT: Kumarian Press.

Stewart, Frances (2000) 'Crisis Prevention: Tackling Horizontal Inequalities', *Oxford Development Studies*, 28 (3), pp. 245–62.

Stoddard, Abby, Adele Harmer and Katherine Haver (2006) *Providing Aid in Insecure Environments: Trends in Policy and Operations*, London: Overseas Development Institute, HPG Report 23.

Stromseth, J. (2003) 'Rethinking Humanitarian Intervention: the Case for Incremental Change' in Holzgrefe and Keohane.

Terry, Fiona (2002) *Condemned to Repeat? The Paradox of Humanitarian Action*, Ithaca, NY and London: Cornell University Press.

Tesón, Fernando (1988) *Humanitarian Intervention: An Inquiry into Law and Morality*, Dobbs Ferry, NY: Transnational.

——— (2005a) 'Ending Tyranny in Iraq', *Ethics and International Affairs* 2005, 19 (2), pp. 1–20.

—— (2005b) *Humanitarian Intervention: An Inquiry into Law and Morality*, 3rd edition, Ardsley, NY: Transnational.

Thakur, Ramesh (2006) *The United Nations, Peace and Security*, Cambridge University Press.

Thompson, Janna (1992) *Justice and World Order: A Philosophical Inquiry*, London: Routledge.

Tisdall, Simon (2008) 'Lies, damned lies and mortality figures', *The Guardian*, 28 April.

Topping, Alexandra (2008) 'Food crisis threatens security, says UN chief', *The Guardian*, 21 April.

Ul Haq, Mahbub (1995) *Reflections on Human Development*, New York and Oxford: Oxford University Press.

United Nations (2001) 'No Exit without Strategy, Security Council Decision-Making and the Closure or Transition of United Nations Peace-Keeping Operations, Report of the Secretary General'. Document S/2001/394, 20 April. pbpu.**un**lb. org/pbpu/library/No%20exit%20without%20strategy%20(20–04–2001).pdf

—— (2003) Commission on Human Security, *Human Security Now*, New York: United Nations Publications. http://www.humansecurity-chs.org/finalreport/

—— (2004) High Level Panel on Threats, Challenges and Change, *A More Secure World: Our Shared Responsibility* New York: UN.

—— (2005) Resolution adopted by the General Assembly, 60th Session, *World Summit Outcome*, A/Res/60/1, 24 October, New York: UN. unpan1.un.org/intradoc/groups/public/documents/UN/UNPAN021752.pdf

—— (2006a) *Beyond Scarcity: Power, Poverty and the Global Water Crisis, Human Development Report 2006*, New York: UNDP. http://hdr.undp.org/hdr2006/report.cfm

—— (2006b) UNDP Country Fact Sheets, Timor-Leste 2006. hdr.**undp**.org/hdr**2006**/statistics/countries/**country_fact_sheets**/cty_fs_TMP.html

—— (2006c) Recent Timor-Leste Violence: Reminder Democracy "Still Fragile", Department of Public Information Report on 5432nd Meeting of Security Council, Document SC/8712, 5 May 2006. www.un.org/News/Press/docs/2006/sc8712. doc.htm

—— (2007a) Somalia: Key Socio-Economic Indicators, UNDP. http://www. so.undp.org/page.asp?id=6999

—— (2007b) Report of the Secretary-General on United Nations Interim Administration in Kosovo [UNMIK], S/2007/134 9 March. www.un.org/Docs/sc/sgrep07.htm

UN News Service (2008) 'Hopes for political solution in Darfur wilt under military action'—says SG Ban in new UN Report, 16 April. United%20Nations%20-%20 African%20Union%20Mission%20in%20Darfur%20(UNAMID).webarchive

UNEP (2007) 'Environmental Degradation Triggering Tensions and Conflict in Sudan', Press Release, Geneva/Nairobi, 22 June http://www.unep.org/Documents. Multilingual/Default.Print.asp?DocumentID=512&ArticleID=5621&l=en

Unicef (2007) UNICEF Humanitarian Action Report 2007 Timor-Leste. www.uni-cef.org/har07/index_37386.htm

UNIS (UN Information Service) (2001) 'East Timorese Leader Commends UN-TAET'S "Timorization" Policy in Day-Long Security Council Debate on Territory', 29 January 2001, UNIS/SC/1307 UNSC%20debate%20on%20E.Timor,%20Jan%202001.webarchive

UNMIT (2006) *Timor Leste—UNMIT (United Nations Integrated Mission in Timor-Leste)—Background*, Department of Peacekeeping Operations, UN. http://www/un.org/Depts/dpko/missions/unmit/background.html

UNOSEK (2007a) The Comprehensive Proposal for Kosovo Status Settlement: Report of the Special Envoy of the Secretary-General on Kosovo's future status, March. www.unosek.org/unosek/en/**statusproposal**.html

——— (2007b) 'Vienna High-level meeting concludes 14 months of talks on the future status process for Kosovo', Press Release, UNOSEK/PR/19, 10 March.

United States (2002) The National Security Strategy of the United States. http://www.whitehouse.gov/nsc/nss.html

——— (2006) The National Security Strategy of the United States. http://www.whitehouse.gov/nsc/nss/2006/

Uvin, Peter (1998) *Aiding Violence: The Development Enterprise in Rwanda*, Bloomfield, CT: Kumarian.

Vieira de Mello, Sergio (2000) 'How Not to Run a Country: Lessons for the UN from Kosovo and East Timor', Unpublished Manuscript.

Walker, R.B.J. and Saul Mendlovitz (eds) (1990) *Contending Sovereignties: Redefining Political Community*, Boulder, CO: Lynne Rienner.

Wallis, Andrew (2006) *Silent Accomplice: The Untold Story of France's Role in the Rwandan Genocide*, London: Tauris.

Walzer, Michael (1977) *Just and Unjust Wars: A Moral Argument with Historical Illustrations*, New York: Basic Books.

——— (1980) 'The Moral Standing of States: A Response to Four Critics', *Philosophy and Public Affairs*, 9 (3), pp. 209–29.

——— (2000) *Just and Unjust Wars: A Moral Argument with Historical Illustrations*, 3rd Edition, New York City: Basic Books.

——— (2004) (paperback 2005) *Arguing about War*, New Haven, CT: Yale University Press.

Weiss, Thomas G. (2007) *Humanitarian Intervention: Ideas in Action*, Cambridge: Polity.

Welch, C.E. (1981) 'The OAU and Human Rights: Towards a New Definition', *Journal of Modern African Studies*, 19 (3).

Welsh, Jennifer (2004) *Humanitarian Intervention and International Relations*, Oxford University Press.

Wheeler, Nicholas J. (2000) *Saving Strangers: Humanitarian Intervention in International Society*, Oxford University Press.

——— (2004) 'The Humanitarian Responsibilities of Sovereignty: Explaining the Development of a New Norm of Military Intervention for Humanitarian Purposes in International Society' in Welsh.

Willetts, Peter (ed.) (1996) *'The Conscience of the World': The Influence of Non-Governmental Organisations in the UN System*, London: Hurst.

Williams, Paul (2004) 'Peace Operations and the International Financial Institutions: Insights from Rwanda and Sierra Leone', *International Peacekeeping*, 11 (1), pp. 103–23.

Woodward, Susan L. (1995) *Balkan Tragedy: Chaos and Dissolution after the Cold War*, Washington DC: Brookings Institution.

World Bank (2002) *Globalization, Growth and Poverty: Building an Inclusive World Economy*, New York: The World Bank and Oxford University Press, 2002.

World Federalist Movement-Institute for Global Policy (2003) *Civil Society Perspectives on the Responsibility to Protect, Final Report*, New York. NGOConsult_Report_Final.pdf www.responsibilitytoprotect.org/

Yanacopulos, Helen and Joseph Hanlon (2006) *Civil War, Civil Peace*, Oxford: James Currey/Columbus: Ohio University Press/Open University.

Young, Iris Marion (2003) 'Violence against Power: Critical Thoughts on Humanitarian Intervention' in Chatterjee and Sheid.

Zaum, Dominik (2007) *The Sovereignty Paradox: The Norms and Politics of International Statebuilding*, Oxford University Press.

# About the Author

Michael Newman is Professor of Politics and Jean Mounnet Professor of European Studies at London Metropolitan University, where he leads the degree in Peace and Conflict Studies. His books include *Socialism—A Very Short Introduction* (Oxford University Press, 2005), *Ralph Miliband and the Politics of the New Left* (Merlin Press, 2002) and *Democracy, Sovereignty and the European Union* (Hurst, 1996).

# About This Book

If a state is carrying out or sanctioning atrocities on a mass scale within its borders, is there an international right, or even duty, to intervene in support of the victims? Or does this notion undermine state sovereignty at the expense of weaker states? These are key questions in the debate on humanitarian intervention, which has become increasingly polarised in the twenty-first century. Many now view this as little more than a rationale for US imperialism, while others uphold it as a crusade for liberal-democracy and individual rights.

This book seeks to establish an alternative position. It provides a critique of current international policies by examining their impact on developing and transitional countries, and it argues that military interventions have had limited success in building sustainable peace. But it endorses the notion of a 'responsibility to protect', suggesting that a more progressive future would be possible if this were interpreted radically and combined with an enlarged conception of 'humanitarianism' that addressed issues of global inequality and poverty.

This work will have particular resonance for those who have opposed recent Anglo-American policy, but have simultaneously believed that 'something must be done' to save those threatened with genocide or other atrocities. Drawing on a range of disciplines and offering a distinct approach, it is aimed at all those who wish to understand a complex issue of contemporary importance. It will be particularly useful for students of international relations, contemporary history, peace and conflict studies, international law, politics, and development studies, and those working in NGOs in the humanitarian and development areas.

# Index

Adam, Hussain M., 115
Adelman, H., 133
Adibe, Clement E., 202
adjustment, structural, 130
administration, 167–9
Afghanistan, 22, 23, 141, 162
Africa:116, 202; West 50 *see also
individual countries*
African Development Bank, 130
African Rights, 57
African Union, 122, 202, 207, 210, 216
agriculture, 130, 172
Ahtisaari, President Martti, 160–1
aid/assistance: 3–5 *passim*, 10, 30, 52,
53, 56, 63, 64, 73, 82, 98, 100–10
*passim*, 112, 115, 125, 129–31, 134,
135, 153, 173, 174, 179, 183, 210,
216; Marshall 153, 179; Paris
Declaration on Effectiveness 109
Aidid, Gen. Mohamed Farah, 53, 55
Ainley, Kirstin, 46
Albania, 66,180
Albanians, Kosovar, 66–8 *passim,* 155,
157–9, 161–3 *passim*, 178, 200
Albright, Madeleine, 68, 80
Alden, Chris, 210
Algeria, 20
Ali, Taisier M., 125, 126
Alkatiri, Mari, 170, 173–5 *passim*
Amato, Giuliano, 151n

Amin, Idi, 23, 33–5 *passim*
Amnesty International, 32, 34
Anderson, Mary, 103
Angola: 43, 124–6; Bicesse accord,
125; economy, 125; elections, 125,
126; MPLA/UNITA 124–6; and
US, 124–5
Annan, Kofi 1, 67, 78, 79, 152, 170,
174, 188–9, 198, 205
anthropology, 119
apartheid, 15, 16, 29, 51
Arabs, 116, 209
Arendt, Hannah, 24
Aristide, Jean-Bertrand, 50n
arms: embargo, 51, 53, 60, 63, 125;
supplies, 190
Ashdown, Paddy, 149–52 *passim*
Asia: 34, 44, 116, 202; -Pacific, 202
Atack, Iain, 24
Augustine, 193
Australia, 164, 165, 171, 174, 175, 189
Austria, 61

Bain, William, 143–4
Balkans, International Commission on,
159–60, 162
Ban Ki-moon, 206, 210
Bangladesh, 21, 30, 36
Barcelona Report, 187–8
Barnett, Michael, 54, 129, 136

Barre, Mohammed Siad, 53, 115
Barsh, R.L., 183
Bartholomew, Amy, 83
Belarus, 68
Belgium, 28, 29, 52, 126–7
Bellamy, Alex J., 43, 78, 122, 163, 164, 171, 200, 206
Bieber, Florian, 63, 146, 149, 150, 152–4 *passim*
Blair, Tony, 80, 216
Bosnia-Herzegovina: 1, 2, 5, 46, 49, 59–65, 72, 74–5, 77, 78, 114, 141–3, 145–55, 178, 195, 200; Brcko District, 148–9; Constitution, 146, 150; Dayton Accords, 62, 65, 77, 146, 152, 178; economy, 148, 150, 153; elections, 146–50 *passim*, 153–4, 178; High Representative, 146–55 *passim*, 178; International Police Force, 147; NATO in, 62, 64; Peace Implementation Council, 146–8 *passim*; referendum, 62, 151; Srebrenica massacre, 63–5 *passim*; Tuzla, 74–5
Boulden, Jane, 30
Boutros-Ghali, Boutros, 43, 53, 54, 56, 64
Brauman, Rony, 101, 106
Breakspear, Jennifer, 83
Bremer, Paul, 141
Britain/UK: 14, 33–4, 47, 48, 50–2 *passim*, 61, 63, 64, 67, 78–81 *passim*, 99, 132, 158, 164; House of Lords, 47; Westminster Foundation for Democracy, 46; Wilton Park Conference, 203
Brown, Chris, 46, 198
Brown, Michael E., 123
Bruguière, Jean-Louis, 136n
Buckley, Mary, 65
Bull, Hedley, 26
Burma/Myanmar, 3
Burundi, 28–9, 36, 117, 127, 132, 135

Bush, George, 124, 125
Bush, George W. 2, 48, 52–4 *passim*, 81–2, 216
Byers, Michael, 80

Cambodia: 14, 22–4 *passim*, 31–3, 36, 43, 122; and China, 32, 33, 37; Paris peace conference, 43; Pol Pot regime, 14, 23, 31–2, 37
Camilleri, Joseph A. 41
Canada, 79, 132, 189, 202
capitalism 22, 40, 117–21, 185
Caplan, Richard, 142, 146–51 *passim*, 154, 156–8, 165–9 *passim*, 171, 178–9
Carrington, Lord, 61
Carter, Jimmy, 50n
Castro, Fidel and Raúl, 21
CAVR, 163, 169, 170
Central America, 43, 49, 87 *see also individual countries*
Chandler, David, 83, 143, 153
Chechnya, 197, 198
Chesterman, Simon, 10, 25–6, 30, 43, 53–5 *passim*, 67, 78, 80, 84, 87, 142, 147, 149, 153, 156, 158, 166, 167, 169, 177
Chile, 33, 47
China: 28, 31–3 *passim*, 37, 48, 52, 63, 82, 99, 206, 211, 215; Beijing Round Table, 202; and Bosnia, 200; and Burundi, 29; and Cambodia, 32, 33, 37; and intervention, 51, 66–8 *passim*, 77, 81, 88, 200; and Kosovo, 155, 200; and Soviet Union, 32, 33; and Sudan 200, 210; and Vietnam, 22, 30, 32
Choedon, Yeshi, 200
Chomsky, Noam, 83, 197
Chopra, Jarat, 167–8, 171
Chua, Amy, 113, 114, 116–18, 127
citizenship, 40, 41
civil service, 149, 150

civil society, 40, 45, 49, 75, 77, 105, 123, 124n, 131, 137, 177, 201, 203, 204, 207, 208, 215
clan system, 115, 126
class factors, 22–4, 40–2 *passim*
climate change, 113, 208, 209
Clinton, Bill, 48, 53, 55, 56, 82, 122, 125, 147
co-existence, peaceful, 26–7, 38
coffee, 129, 130
Collier, Paul, 111n, 113n
colonialism: 29, 126, 127, 172; post-, 142
communism, 22, 39, 40, 43, 60
conflict: 5, 6, 10, 43, 71–7, 103, 104, 106, 108–21, 123, 139, 173–5, 181, 190–1, 204, 206, 208–11, 214–17 *passim*; social, 71–4, 77, 120
Congo: 43; DRC, 197, 205n
consequences, of intervention, 27, 36, 102–3, 111, 137–80 *passim*, 196, 214
consistency, 27, 197–8, 202
Cook, Robin, 80–1
Cornwall, A., 183
Cramer, Christopher, 119–21
crimes: against humanity, 11, 16–17, 28, 31, 47, 202, 204, 206, 208, 210, 211; war, 46, 47, 146, 202, 206, 208, 210, 211
Croatia/Croatians, 60, 61, 64, 114, 117, 146, 153
Cuba: 21, 34, 124; Bay of Pigs, 21; and US, 21–2
culture: 20, 165–6, 180; violence, 98, 176, 177, 180
Czechoslovakia, 11

Dallaire, Gen., 135–6
Darfur: 200, 204–5, 207, 209–11; economy, 209; International Commission of Inquiry on, 204;

peace agreement, 209; and UN, 205, 207, UNAMID, 210
de Waal, Alex, 204
debt, 109, 112–14 *passim*, 129, 190, 215
decolonization 10, 15, 140, 171
Dee, M., 163, 164
demilitarization, 142, 146
democracy/democratization: 2, 5, 18, 39–46 *passim*, 49, 75, 97, 117, 123, 125, 149, 207–8; Inter-American—Charter, 45; National Endowment for, 45–6; Westminster Foundation for, 46
devaluation, 130
development: 106–10 *passim*, 112, 118–21, 153, 179, 182–91 *passim*, 211, 214, 217; Human—Index, 186, 209; right to, 183–5 *passim*; UN Declaration 183–5 *passim*
diamonds, 78, 126
displaced/displacement: 16, 31, 68, 72, 101, 130, 146–8, 150, 151, 156, 164, 175, 204, 209, 210; Guiding Principles on, 16
Dodd, Mark, 171
donors, 105, 130–2 *passim*, 134, 136
Douzinas, Costas, 98n
Doyle, Michael, 123
drought, 129–30
Duffield, Mark, 96, 98, 103, 118–19
Dunant, Henry, 15, 95, 105

East Timor: 5, 50, 141–5 *passim*, 163–76, 178, 180; CNRT, 169; Constitution, 169, 170; economy, 171–2; elections, 169–71 *passim*, 175; F-FDTL, 174; FATILINTIL, 170; FRETILIN, 169–70, 175; INTERFET, 164; National Consultative Council, 169; PNTL, 174; referendum, 50, 164;

UNMISET, 171, 174; UNMIT, 174; UNTAET, 164–71, 174
economic factors, 3–5 *passim*, 10, 21, 23, 40–1, 112–21, 137,179, 215, 216 *see also under individual countries*
ECO-MOG, 50
ECOWAS, 50, 78, 122, 216
Egypt, 42
Eichmann, Adolf, 14
El-Bushra, J., 177
elections, 44, 45, 123, 124n, 179 *see also under individual countries*
El Salvador, 49
emancipation, 6, 18, 19, 185, 186
emergencies, 105, 107–8
equality, 6, 9, 10, 27, 140, 183
ethical factors, 2, 50, 56–7, 69–73, 77, 94, 198, 212, 214
Ethiopia, 99, 101, 105, 115, 139
ethnic cleansing, 13, 46, 52–8 *passim*, 84, 90n, 91, 194, 202, 206, 208, 210, 211
ethnicity, 111, 116–18, 124n, 126–37, 145–76 *passim*
Europe: 44; Council of 151; Convention on Human Rights, 12, 88; East 13, 23, 34, 43, 60, 74; Nuclear Disarmament, 74; OSCE, 44–5, 66, 67, 75, 146; Social Charter, 12; Study Group on Security Capabilities 187–8
European Union: 44, 45, 59, 61, 62, 75, 122, 130, 143, 180, 216; and Bosnia, 150–2, 154, 155, 180; and Kosovo, 160–3, 180; Lomé Convention, 45; and Serbia, 160, 163, 180; Security Study Group 187–8; Stabilization and Association Agreements, 151–2, 163; Treaty of Amsterdam, 45
EULEX 161n
Evans, Gareth, 189, 205
exit strategy, 179, 191
extradition, 47

Faber, Jan, 69n
Falk, Jim, 41
famine, 53, 88, 101
Farer, Tom J., 84, 85
Farmer, Paul, 108
Findlay, Trevor, 42, 43, 54, 55, 57, 64
Flint, Julie, 204
Forsyth, David P., 17, 46
France: 29, 33, 48, 51, 42, 57n, 61, 63, 64, 81, 128n, 132, 134, 198; Opération Turquoise, 57n
Franck, Thomas, 201
Freeman, Christopher P., 141, 166

G8, 111n
Galtung, Johan, 176, 177
Gandhi, Mahatma, 25
Geldof, Bob, 101
Geneva Conventions: (1864), 15; (1949), 15–17 *passim*, 63, 89–90; (1977) Protocols, 15
genocide: 4, 13–14, 16, 28–32 *passim*, 36, 37, 46, 47, 50, 57–9, 71, 83, 84, 88, 94, 131, 136–7, 197, 202, 206, 208, 210, 211; Convention, 13–14, 17, 58, 89
Germany: 7, 13, 23–4, 61, 99–100, 132, 142, 149, 196; Nazis, 11, 13, 23, 99–100, 196
Glasius, Marlies, 79, 187
Global Humanitarian Assistance, 105
Goradze, 64
Gorbachev, Mikhail, 43, 124
Gott, Richard, 21
governance: good, 44, 82; international, 98, 118–19, 141–81 *passim*
Gowan, Peter, 59, 68
Gray, Christine D., 87
Griffin, Stuart, 43, 78, 122, 163, 164, 171, 200
Guatamala, 11, 49
Gusmao, Xanana, 169, 170, 173–5 *passim*

Habyarimana, Juvénal, 128, 130–6
*passim*
Haekkerup, Hans, 156
Hague Convention (1907) 16
Haiti, 50n
Hammarskjöld, Dag, 42
Hanlon, Joseph, 100, 103, 113
Harmer, Adele, 105
Harvey, David, 112, 113, 141
Haver, Katherine, 105
Heinze, Eric, 88–93 *passim*, 199
Held, David, 41
Helsinki: Accord, 13;
   Citizens'Assembly, 74–5; Process, 45
Hitler, Adolf, 25
HIV/AIDS, 208
Holbrooke, Richard, 148
Holzgrefe, J.L., 3
Horn of Africa, 115
Horowitz, D.L., 116
Horta, José Ramos, 174, 175
human rights: 1, 2, 5, 12, 17, 39–42,
   46–9, 70, 71, 77, 79, 84–93, 112,
   133, 134, 150, 213; European
   Convention on, 12, 88; European
   Court of, 146; UN Commission/
   Commissioner on 29, 31, 33, 34, 46;
   Council, 204, 209; Universal
   Declaration, 12, 44, 46, 84; viola-
   tions, 1, 3, 7, 22, 28, 31, 33–5, 48–52
   *passim*, 55, 69–71, 87–93 *passim*,
   136, 140, 158, 185, 189, 197–8, 204,
   207; World Conference (Vienna), 46
Human Rights Watch, 57, 69, 134, 159,
   204, 215
humanitarianism, 2–6 *passim*, 79–84,
   93–110, 181–3 *passim*, 186, 187,
   207–8, 211, 213–17
Hussain, Saddam, 2, 51, 52, 78, 85, 86,
   193
Hutus, 28, 58, 101, 126–8, 131, 133–6
*passim*

ICRC, 15–16, 53, 56, 61, 63, 95, 96,
   99–101, 105
ideology, 31, 38, 40, 87, 99, 170, 182
Ignatieff, Michael, 100, 144
IKS, 159
IMF, 60, 114, 115, 130, 146, 159, 164,
   171, 185
imperialism: 2, 9–10, 22, 27, 34, 36, 57,
   78, 79, 83, 140–5, 156, 176, 180,
   191, 213; anti-2–3
Inazumi, Mitsue, 14
India, 21, 30–1, 36, 63, 68, 77, 211
Indonesia, 50, 163–5 *passim*, 169, 170
inequality, 6, 10, 98, 106, 108, 113,
   124n, 140, 153, 181, 211, 212, 217
inhumanity, 111–37
International Commission on Intervention and State Sovereignty (ICISS),
   1–4 *passim*, 50, 79, 90–1, 93, 181,
   188–96, 198, 201–3 *passim*, 207,
   208, 212, 217
International Commission of Jurists,
   30, 32, 34
International Court of Justice, 86–7,
   201
International Criminal Court: 46–8,
   82n, 90; Coalition for, 46
International Criminal Tribunal
   (Tokyo), 16
International Crisis Group, 161, 173,
   175, 189, 209–11 *passim*, 215
International Military Tribunal
   (Nuremberg), 16
intervention, humanitarian:1–7 *passim*,
   26–37, 49–111 *passim*, 139–40,
   180–201 *passim*, 206, 213, 214, 217;
   coercive/military, 2–7 passim, 10,
   23, 24, 38, 42, 73, 80, 84–6, 92–4
   *passim,* 109–10, 138, 140, 181, 183,
   191–202 *passim*, 204, 206, 208, 212,
   217; duty/right of, 27, 51, 52, 59, 69,
   189, 202, 217; guiding principles, 81,
   193–201; justification for, 5, 7, 17,

20–1, 25–6, 28–32 *passim*, 70–1, 78,
  80–93 *passim*, 110, 138, 140, 143,
  181, 183, 192–201, 204; unilateral,
  29–36 *passim*, 85, 198, 204
Iran, 51, 198
Iraq: economy, 141; war against (1991),
  1, 2, 51, 52, 55, 77, 78, 193; (2003),
  2, 83, 85, 196, 198, 202, 205, 216
Islamic Courts Union, 139
Islamophobia, 92
Israel, 14, 42, 49, 116, 197, 202
Italy, 99
Izetbegovic, Alija 62

Japan, 11, 99, 142, 164
Jews, 99–100
Johnson, Lyndon 8n
Jones, Bruce D., 127, 132, 134
Judah, Tim, 67
judicial system, 147, 165–6
Juhasz, Antonia, 141
jurisdiction, universal, 14, 47–8, 89
'jurying, international' 200–1
justice, 6, 27, 103, 198

Kagame, Paul, 136n
Kaldor, Mary, 51, 55, 57, 61, 69n,
  74–7, 79, 114, 118, 187
Kambanda, Jean, 47
Kampfner, John, 78
Kant, Immanuel, 123
Karadzic, Radovan, 62
Kennedy, David, 107, 213–14
Kenya, 53
Keohane, Robert O., 85
Kerr, Rachel, 166
Keynesianism, 22, 40, 179
King, Ian, 156, 162
kinship, 116
Knudsen, Tonny Brems, 141, 159, 163
Korea, North, 29
Kosovo: 1, 5, 38, 50, 59, 60, 65–71,
  78–80 *passim*, 83, 114, 141–5

*passim*, 155–63, 178, 193, 198–200
*passim*; economy, 158–9; elections,
  157, 161, 162; and independence,
  155–6, 161–3, 178; Independent
  International Commission on 66–9,
  114, 193n; International Civilian
  Representative, 161, 162; KFOR,
  156, 157, 159, 161, 162; Liberation
  Army, 66–8 *passim*, 155–7, 199;
  Mitrovica, 156, 162; NATO
  bombings, 1, 38, 50, 59, 67–71
  *passim*, 78, 155, 193n, 198, 199;
  Protection Corps, 157; Racak
  massacre, 68; Rambouillet Confer-
  ence, 155, 158, 193; referendum,
  155, 157; Special Representative of
  UN Secretary-General, 156, 158;
  UNMIK, 156–62 *passim*
Kouchner, Bernard, 51, 100, 156
Krasner, Stephen, 85
Kreilkamp, J.S., 144
Kristensen, Rasmus Abildgaard, 159,
  163
Kumar, Radhar, 75, 146
Kuper, Leo, 28–30, 32–4 *passim*, 36
Kurasawa, Fuyaki, 2
Kurds, 49, 51, 52, 78
Kuwait, 51, 193

L20, 200–1
Lajcak, Miroslav, 151
language, 168, 175
Latin America, 116, 119, 202
law, international: 3, 10–17 *passim*,
  25–6, 38, 84–5, 87, 89, 104, 184,
  200, 217; humanitarian, 14–17, 28,
  68, 77, 94, 95, 166, 182, 193
League of Nations, 142
Lebanon: 72; Sabra and Chatila
  massacre, 14
Leprette, Jacques, 33
liberalism/left-wing, 2, 5, 18, 20–2
  *passim*, 27, 39–44, 48–9, 51, 55, 57,

59, 65, 69–77 *passim*, 79, 85–6, 95,
106, 110–23 *passim*, 137, 141, 143,
154, 158, 171, 177, 179, 181, 183,
185, 207, 213, 214, 217
Liberia, 50
Lu, Catherine, 20, 42, 201
Luck, Edward, 206
Lynn-Jones, Sean, 123

Macedonia, 200
Macfarlane, S. Neil, 200
Major, John, 52
Malaysia, 116, 174
malnutrition, 107, 130, 209
Mamdani, Mahmood, 128
Mandela, Nelson, 49
marginalization, 98, 209
markets, 40, 96, 103, 112, 113, 117–18,
120
Marks, Stephen, 185
Martin, Ian, 164
Martin, Paul, 200–1
Marxism, 22, 23, 31, 39–40, 83, 170
Mason, Whit, 156, 162
Matlary, J.H., 81, 84, 85
Matthews, Robert O., 125, 126
M'baye, Keba, 183
mediation, 4, 25, 35, 125, 132, 190
Meehan, Elizabeth, 41
Mendlovitz, Saul, 41
Meredith, M., 28, 34
MfDR, 109
Miall, Hugh, 177
Middle East, 34, 92, 113, 116, 202
Middleton, N., 210
migration, 156, 209
Miliband, Ralph, 22–4
Mill, John Stuart, 18–19, 23
Miller, Richard W., 197
Miller, Steve, 123
Milosevic, Slobodan, 60, 65–8 *passim*,
153, 156
Minear, Larry, 105, 108

Minn, Pierre, 94
minorities, 28, 29, 116–18 *passim*, 147,
148, 150, 156, 159, 160, 163, 178,
180
Mobekk, Eirin, 166
Moorhead, Caroline, 99, 100
motivation, 4, 78, 194, 196–7
Mozambique, 170
MSF, 51, 97, 100, 102
Murray, L., 56
Museveni, Yoweri, 128

Namibia, 43, 122
nationalism, ethnic, 60–2 *passim*, 66,
77, 114, 147–9, 178, 179
NATO: 45, 65, 75, 122, 143; and
Bosnia, 62, 64, 154; and Kosovo, 1,
38, 50, 59, 67–71 *passim*, 78, 155,
193n, 198, 199
Neher, Clark D., 31
Netherlands, 71, 81, 132
neutrality, 51, 73, 96, 97, 99–100, 140
Newbury, Catherine, 127
Newman, M. 9, 22, 40
New Zealand, 174
NGOs: 46, 49, 56, 57, 73, 83, 97,
101–2, 105, 107, 119, 129, 131, 137,
179, 185, 201–4 *passim*, 207, 208,
214, 215; international, 45–6, 65,
96–8 *passim*, 103, 105, 131, 214
Nicaragua, 18, 49, 87
Nigeria: 100, 105; Biafra, 100–1
no fly zones, 52, 78
Non-Aligned Movement, 202
non-intervention, 1, 3, 4, 8–11, 17–38
*passim*, 41–2, 49–50, 52, 55, 71, 200,
202, 210
Norad, 163, 165, 168, 170, 172, 173
Northern Ireland: 72; Good Friday
Agreement, 49
Numeiry, President, 35
Nyamu-Musembi, C., 183
Nyerere, Julius, 34, 35

OAS, 45
OAU, 10, 29, 34, 35, 122, 132
Obasanjo, Olusegun, 35
Obote, Milton, 34
ODIHR, 45
OECD countries, 122
Ogata, Sadako, 186
Ohaegbulam, F. Ugboaja, 124, 125
Ohmai, Kenichi, 41
oil, 126, 171, 210
O'Keefe, P., 210
Ombudsperson, 157, 158
Open Society Institute, 46
Operation Provide Relief, 54
Operation Restore Hope, 54
Oppenheim, L.F.L., 21n
Orford, Anne, 113, 114, 131, 139, 143, 147, 148, 150, 164, 171, 172, 185
OSCE *see* Europe
Oslo Accords, 49
Oxfam International, 215

Pace, William R., 204, 205, 207, 208
Pakistan: 21, 30–1; Awami League, 30; East, 21, 30–1, 36; elections, 30
Palestine, 49, 197, 202
Paris, Roland, 43, 46, 123–6, 134, 147–9 *passim*, 179
Partnership for Peace programme, 45
peace: 8, 121–37 *passim*, 154, 176–7, 180; negative, 176, 177; positive, 123, 176–7, 180; sustainable, 6, 152, 176, 177, 180, 181, 215, 216
peace-building/making: 5–6, 43, 56, 97, 111, 122–4, 132–7, 146–8 *passim*, 151, 152, 154, 177, 179, 202, 215, 216; Commission, 207
peace-keeping, 2, 39, 42, 43, 50, 57, 61, 63, 77, 111, 121–2, 135, 141, 154, 155, 178, 207, 210
Perez de Cuéllar, Javier, 55
Petritsch, Wolfgang, 150
Pilger, John, 78, 171

Pinochet, Gen., 47
pluralism, 40, 45
Pogge, Thomas W., 106, 107, 197
police, 147, 148, 151, 152, 156, 166, 174, 177
politics, 2, 5, 29, 32–4, 39–42, 90, 95–104, 124–37, 142–75 *passim*, 182, 183, 209, 215–18
Portugal/Portuguese, 124, 125, 163, 165, 170, 174
poverty: 6, 107–8, 113, 130, 139, 154, 158–9, 181, 186, 209, 217; reduction 208, 211, 212
prevention, 1, 4, 14, 123, 189, 190, 196, 203, 204, 207, 208, 214, 215
prices, commodity/food, 112, 129, 211
privatization, 96, 118, 130, 141, 150, 158, 159
protection: 1–3 *passim*, 6, 7, 12, 15, 97, 134, 158, 163, 182, 187–97, 204, 208, 213, 217; responsibility to protect, 4, 6, 42, 79, 188–208 *passim*, 211, 212, 214–17 *passim*, NGO network on, 207, 214, 15, Principles, 193–201, Special Adviser, 206
protectionism, 112
Prunier, Gérard, 209
Pugh, Michael, 158, 159, 179

Ramsbotham, Oliver, 61, 63, 64, 71–4, 115, 177, 196, 199
Rawls, John, 85–6, 106–8 *passim*
Reagan, Ronald: 40, 112; doctrine, 86–7
*Realpolitik*, 26, 28–9, 31, 33, 36, 37, 41
reconstruction, 97, 179, 191, 203, 207, 214
Red Cross, 15, 51, 95, 99, 182
referenda *see under individual countries*
refugees: 30, 53, 72, 101–2, 127–8, 135, 139, 146, 148, 150, 151, 204; Convention on Status of, 16; UNHCR, 53, 61, 75

Refugees International, 215
regime change, 3, 5, 20–3 *passim*, 50n, 80, 84–7, 90, 92, 93, 109, 138, 141, 142, 213
Reichberg, Gregory, 197
Reimann, Kim D., 97
Reinado, Alfredo, 175–6
Reisman, Michael, 84–5
religion, 111
Rhodesia, 29, 35
Rieff, David, 97
right authority, 194–5, 198–201
right intention, 194, 196–8
rights:12–13, 41, 91, 134 *see also* human rights; civil/political, 12–13, 40, 46, 92; to development,184–5; economic/cultural/social, 12–13, 46
rioting, 159, 160, 211
risks, 187, 198
Roberts, Adam, 78
Robinson, Darryl, 16
Roma, 99, 159
Rubin, James, 68, 80
Rugova, Ibrahim, 157, 199
Rummel, R.J., 123
Russia, 48, 59, 82, 161, 198; and Bosnia, 63, 64, 200; and intervention, 52, 63, 81, 200; and Kosovo, 65–8 *passim*, 155; and US, 65, 78, 215
Rwanda, 4, 5, 14, 28, 46, 47, 50, 57–9, 71, 72, 78, 94, 101–2, 116, 117n, 126–37, 195–7 *passim*, 201; Arusha peace process, 132–7 *passim*; CDR, 133, 134; economy, 129–30, 136; elections, 127; Interahamwe, 133; International Criminal Tribunal for, 46, 47, 90–1; MRND, 128, 131; referendum, 127; RPF, 128, 130–3 *passim*, 136; and UN 57–8, UNAMIR, 135–6

'safe havens', 1, 49, 51, 52, 55, 63–5 *passim*, 193

Sahnoun, Mahmoud, 53, 57n, 189
sanctions, economic, 3–4, 10, 21, 23, 33, 91, 125, 190
Sands, Philippe, 47, 48
Savimbi, Jonas, 124–6 *passim*
Schabas, William A., 14
Schell, Jonathan, 24
Scorgie, Lindsay, 132, 133
secession, 68, 151, 154, 162
security, human, 6, 79, 91, 134, 173–5 *passim*, 177, 179, 181, 186–92 *passim*, 208–9, 211, 214, 215, 217, 218; UN Commission on, 186–7
self-defence, 8, 29, 30, 35–6, 63, 87
self-determination, 15, 18, 23, 144, 184, 185
self-government, 140, 143, 154, 157, 158, 180
Sellström. Tor, 128–30 *passim*, 133, 134
Semb, Anne Julie, 20, 26, 27, 33, 88, 196, 198
Sen, Amartya, 186, 187
Serbia/Serbians: 2, 38, 60, 62, 66–8 *passim*, 155, 161, 193; Bosnian, 62, 64, 146, 149–51, 153, 156, 178, 200; Kosovar, 156, 157, 160–3 *passim*, 199–200
Seybolt, Taylor B., 54, 55, 199
Shue, Henry, 88
Shwarz, A., 163
Sierra Leone, 50, 78–9
Slim, Hugo, 96–8 *passim*, 104
Slovenia/Slovenians, 60, 61, 114, 117
Smillie, I., 100, 105, 108
Smith, Ian, 35
socialism, 22, 23, 39–41, 60, 121, 183, 213, 217–18
Solferino, battle of, 15, 95, 105
Somalia: 1, 29, 49, 53–7, 72, 77, 122, 139, 193, 195; economy, 115; Somaliland/Puntland, 139n; UNITAF, 54–5; UNOSOM, 53, 55, 56n

Sorensen, Birgitte Refslund, 95, 97, 98, 108

Soros, George, 46

Souare, I.K., 50

South Africa, 33, 35, 49, 51, 124

sovereignty, state: 1–2, 4, 7–28 *passim*, 30–1, 36, 38–42, 46, 47, 51, 52, 66, 76, 77, 78, 85, 87, 140, 161, 185, 188–9, 191, 204, 217 *see also* ICISS; conditional, 85, 92, 200

Soviet Union: 13, 28, 31–3 *passim*, 36, 38, 39, 60, 67, 86–7, 99, 112, 113; and Afghanistan, 22–3; and Angola, 124, 125; Brezhnev doctrine, 11n; and intervention, 10, 11, 23; KGB, 11; and US, 29, 38; and Vietnam, 32–3

Spears, Jan, 125, 126

Sri Lanka, 72

state-building, 56, 97, 101, 147, 151, 152, 154, 165, 179, 216

Stewart, Frances, 113

Stoddard, Abby, 105

Stromseth, J. 81, 201

Sudan: 118, 200, 204–5, 207, 209–11; Janjaweed, 204

Suhrke, A., 133

Sweden, 20

Switzerland, 132

Syse, Henrik, 197

Taiwan, 200

Tanzania, 29, 33–6 *passim*, 101, 132, 134, 196

Taylor, Charles, 47n

terminology, 3–4, 94, 143, 189–90, 202, 203

terrorism: 75; 9/11, 2, 81, 141, 202; war on 2, 48, 81–3, 141, 202

Terry, Fiona, 94, 97, 100–3 *passim*, 106

Tesón, Fernando, 85, 199n

Thaçi. Hashim, 157n, 161

Thailand, 32

Thakur, Ramesh, 122, 189, 200, 202, 207

Thatcher, Margaret, 40, 112

Thompson, E.P., 74

Thompson, Janna, 20

Tito, Josip, 114

Topping, Alexandra, 211

torture: 16, 102; Convention on, 89

trade, 10, 109, 190, 200

trade unionism, 40

trusteeship: 76, 142–5 *passim*; UN Council, 143

Tutsis, 28, 58, 116, 126–8, 131–4 *passim*

Twa, 126n

Uganda, 23, 24, 33–6, 128, 132, 196

Ul Haq, Mahbub, 186

UN: 1, 4, 8, 12, 13, 15, 30, 33, 34, 36, 42–4, 50–68 *passim*, 70, 75, 76, 79–81 *passim*, 96, 105–7 *passim*, 122, 132, 135, 136, 139, 143, 152, 179, 181, 186, 193, 198–201, 204–7 *passim*, 210, 213, 216–17; and Bosnia, 59, 63, 64, 146; Charter, 8, 9, 11, 25, 29, 42, 53, 54, 71, 72, 84, 184, 198; and Darfur, 205, 207, UNAMID, 210; and East Timor, 163–71, 174, 176; General Assembly, 10, 13, 34, 44, 195, 200, 201, 208; High Commission for Human Rights, 46; High-Level Panel on Threats, etc., 205, 207; and Iraq, 51n, 52, 55; and Kosovo, 1, 67, 156–7, 160, 161, UNOSEK, 160–1; Millennium Summit, 186; reform, 181, 200–1, 206; Relief Committee, 30; and Rwanda, 57–8, UNAMIR, 135–6; Secretary-General, 30, 34, 53, 54, 211, 216; Security Council, 8, 9, 11, 28–30 *passim*, 33, 35, 43, 48,

51–6, 60–8 *passim*, 80, 81, 85, 87,
135, 155n, 161, 164, 165, 169–71
*passim*, 174, 194–5, 198–201, 205–8
*passim*, 210, 216; and Somalia, 53–6,
UNITAF, 54–5, UNOSOM, 53, 55,
56n; Sub-Committee on Prevention
of Discrimination etc., 29, 31–3;
World Summit (2005), 4, 142–3,
205–8 *passim*; and Yugoslavia, 60–1,
UNPROFOR, 61, 63, 64, 74
UNCTAD, 211
UNDP, 44, 186
UNEF, 42
unemployment, 113, 150, 154, 158–60
*passim*, 165, 172n
UNEP, 209
UNHCR, 53, 61, 75
UNICEF, 61, 175
UNIS, 170
United States: 1, 2, 5, 8, 10, 11, 13, 14,
18, 28, 29, 31, 33, 38, 65, 67, 80–8
*passim*, 117, 122–6 *passim*, 132, 134,
135, 164, 165, 179, 180, 196–9
*passim*, 202, 205, 215; and Angola,
124–5; Bosnia, 59, 62, 64, 78, 146,
147; CIA, 11; and Cuba, 21–2; and
Guatemala, 11; Helms-Burton Act
(1996), 21; and ICC, 48; and Iraq, 1,
2, 51n, 52, 83; and Kosovo, 65, 67,
78, 80, 155, 157, 161; National
Security Strategy, 81–3; National
Endowment for Democracy, 45–6;
and Nicaragua, 18, 87; and Rwanda,
28; and Somalia, 53–7 *passim*, 122,
139; and Soviet Union, 29, 38; and
UN, 81, 122, 146,198
Uvin, Peter, 131, 134, 135

values, 20, 73–7
Vance, Cyrus, 61
Vieiro de Mello, Sergio, 164, 167, 169
Vietnam. 8, 19, 22, 23, 31–3 *passim*, 36

Vincent, John, 26–7

wages, 130, 153
Walker, R.B.J., 41
Wallis, Andrew, 133
war: Boer, 99; China-Vietnam, 22, 32;
civil, 47, 96, 108, 119–21, 125–6,
128–9, 135–6, 180, 197, 209,
Somali, 53, 115, Nigerian, 100, 105,
Sudan, 118; Cold, 1, 4–5, 7–38,
40–2 *passim*, 46, 59, 92, 112, 115,
121–3 *passim*, post- 24, 27, 38–79,
121, 122, 141, 179, 213, 215;
Indo-Pakistan, 30; Iraq (1991), 1, 2,
51, 52, 55, 77, 78, 193, (2003), 2, 83,
85, 196, 198, 202, 205, 216;
Iran-Iraq, 51; Italy-Ethiopia, 99; just,
19–20, 25, 70, 138, 181, 192–6. 212;
Korean, 8; 'new', 75, 77, 97, 110–12
*passim*, 118–19; Ogaden, 115; Suez,
42; on terrorism, 2, 48, 81–3, 141,
202; Uganda-Tanzania, 34–5;
Vietnam, 8, 19, 31; Vietnam-
Cambodia 32–3; World War II, 23,
142, 196, post-, 8–11, 142
Walzer, Michael, 19–21
Weiss, Thomas G., 105, 206
Welch, C.E., 34
Westphalia, treaty of, 18
Wheeler, Nicholas J., 30, 32, 34–6,
51–4 *passim*, 56, 64, 66, 67, 69–71
*passim*, 88, 196, 198
Willetts, Peter, 46
Williams, Paul, 43, 78, 122, 163, 164,
171, 200
Wohlgemuth, Lennart, 128–30 *passim*,
133, 134
women, 177, 211
Woodhouse, Tom, 61, 63, 64, 71–4,
115, 177, 196, 199
Woodward, Susan L., 62, 114
World Bank, 113, 115, 130, 134, 136,
171, 185

World Federalist Movement-Institute
for Global Policy, 202–4 *passim*
World Social Forum, 203

Yeltsin, Boris, 65
Young, Iris Marion, 24
young people, 172, 173
Yugoslavia: 38, 39, 59–69, 78, 114–15,
117, 145–63, 180, 200; economy,

114–15; International Criminal
Tribunal for, 46, 47, 62n, 90

Zaire, 101, 102,132
Zambia, 107
Zaum, Dominik, 143, 147, 150, 158,
162, 166
Zimbabwe, 63, 116

# ABOUT THE AUTHOR

*Wall Street Journal* bestselling author Melinda Leigh is a fully recovered banker. A lifelong lover of books, she started writing as a way to preserve her sanity when her youngest child entered first grade. During the next few years, she joined Romance Writers of America, learned a few things about writing a novel, and decided the process was way more fun than analyzing financial statements. Melinda's debut novel, *She Can Run*, was nominated for Best First Novel by the International Thriller Writers. She's also earned three Daphne du Maurier Award nominations and a Golden Leaf Award. Her other novels include *She Can Tell*, *She Can Scream*, *She Can Hide*, *She Can Kill*, *Midnight Exposure*, *Midnight Sacrifice*, *Midnight Betrayal*, *Midnight Obsession*, *Hour of Need*, *Minutes to Kill*, and *Seconds to Live*. She holds a second-degree black belt in Kenpo karate; teaches women's self-defense; and lives in a messy house with her husband, two teenagers, a couple of dogs, and two rescue cats.

**Center Point Large Print**
600 Brooks Road / PO Box 1
Thorndike, ME 04986-0001 USA

**(207) 568-3717**

**US & Canada:**
**1 800 929-9108**
www.centerpointlargeprint.com